IDEAL AGING™

Also by Joyce Shaffer, PhD

***Secrets inside Bones, Brains & Beauty*™**

IDEAL AGING™

7 Steps to Keep Your Brain Fit

Joyce Shaffer, PhD

**Learn how to train more and better brain cells ...
because you simply want more out of life.**

**Ideal Press
Bones, Brains & Beauty™, LLC
Bellevue WA**

Ideal Aging™
7 Steps to Keep Your Brain Fit

Copyright © by Joyce Shaffer, PhD

All rights reserved. No part of this book may be used or reproduced by any means, graphic, electronic, or mechanical, including photocopying, recording, taping or by any information storage retrieval system without the written permission of the publisher except in the case of brief quotations embodied in critical articles and reviews.

For the most up-to-date information on *Ideal Aging*™, please call or visit our Web site; *Ideal Aging*™ books, services and products may be ordered through booksellers or by contacting:

Bones, Brains & Beauty™, LLC
PO Box 765
Bellevue WA 98009-0765
877-226-9396

ISBN-10: 0-9770411-1-5

Printed in the United States of America

Notice to Readers

Every effort has been made to ensure that the information contained herein is complete and accurate. However, neither the publisher nor the author are engaged in rendering professional advice or services to the individual reader. The ideas, procedures, and suggestions contained herein are not intended as a substitute for consulting with your physician or other healthcare provider and obtaining medical supervision as to any activity, procedure, or suggestion that might affect your health. Accordingly, individual readers must assume responsibility for their own actions, safety, and health, and neither the author nor the publisher shall be liable or responsible for any loss, injury, or damage allegedly arising from any information or suggestion in this publication. By reading and using this workbook the reader confirms agreement with this policy. We wish you the very best of vigorous longevity in your Ideal Aging™.

CONTENTS

Acknowledgments..ix
Foreword..xi
Preface..xiii

Part A. Introduction
   Art Linkletter says the most inspiring things – about Ideal Aging™ 1
   7 Steps to Enhance Your Dance of Life 9

Part B. Five Dances to Live For 29

   1. Brain Boost—If it's not around, why am I? 31
       Smarter This Year 33
       Create Conditioned Responses 55
       Connect 67
       Chill 85
       Sleep 91

   2. Happy Habit— For the Health That Is "Contagious" 105
       Laughter 107
       Enduring Happiness 113
       New Linking and Looping 127

   3. Energy Elevator—The vigorous longevity you earn for yourself. 131
       Exercise Right 135
       Eat Smart Deliciously 157

   4. Sexual Saunter—The brain workout that's delicious at any age. 197

   5. World Works—Pass it on for the health of it! 205
       Flow 209
       Participate 217
       Be Rich 225
       Forgive 233
       Untwist Twisted Places 239
       Set Strategic Goals 257
       Celebrate Randomly 267

Part C. The Last Summary 271

Part D. References and Other Resources 275

ACKNOWLEDGMENTS

We don't get where we are without a team. Mine's extraordinary.

"I started out as a child," to quote Bill Cosby. If it were not for my brother, Charles Shaffer, I might still be on the farm of my birth, milking cows and waxing poetic about the magnificent beauty in the Allegheny Mountains. Chuck helped me onto the first rung of the ladder of my many career changes.

In recent years those shifts have been accelerated. Robert G Allen and Mark Victor Hansen formed an Inner Circle of individuals determined to foster enlightened prosperity for the Earth and all her people into perpetuity. Bob, Mark and many members of this group have put a steady wind beneath my wings. Without their help and influence I never would have written my first book on osteoporosis … let alone this first in a long series of books focusing on Ideal Aging™. Pat Burns, Tad Lignell, Michelle Burns, Mary Comtois, Carol Caldwell, Dr. Linne Bourget, Teresa Luquette, Brad Wozny, Greg Poulos, Jann Roney, Jose Espana, Karen Logan Lasoff, Heshie Segal, Tamara Reber, Michelle Rabin, JC Ige, Jim Scott and many others from this group have helped broaden my perspectives. Our "Tree Angel," Cindy Katz has been a steady ray of sunlight on the forest of my growth of more complex brain architecture in the realm of business. Susan Curington adds wisdom. Jennifer Wilkov set a terrific model for publishing. Rob and Lori Basnett's support of my work has been a source of joy. Their daughter, Hannah's, project for writing the biggest book ever on World Peace, is an inspiration for all of us. Linda Bardes adds depth. Alberto and Selena Hoyos bring exuberance to the development of dances that reflect the chapters within. Hope Prins personifies her name as she instills hope in all who know her. Laura and Steve Andrews (my adopted children) love sharing the science about healthy outcomes of having hope. Then along came the editorial comments of John and Peggy McGee. After Peggy's astute suggestions and corrections, this book is a smoother read.

For Diane Sumter I have so much gratitude; her continued work with me on the exercises in all my publications, including the DVD we are producing for osteoporosis, inspires more informed productions for everyone. Diane Cook, a dear friend since we were classmates in Thomas Jefferson University, asks those pointed questions from a nursing perspective that help me clarify critical points. Other classmates from those years continue to support me and inspire me in ways that add joy to my writings.

Janice Katz, MD, is a Pediatrician who came into my life as a writing partner. She adds a unique poetry to tough topics in medicine. To also have the world-renown cardiologist, John Rumberger, PhD, MD, on my team is lovely.

Bruce Brown of SCORE is such a delight. Not only is he a terrific example of Ideal Aging™ in his eighth decade, he also has a keen sense of business, the knack for putting me in front of crowds and the wisdom to refer me to the right person to help me finesse the next hurdle. One such referral was to Darlene Robbins of the Small Business Association to whom I am very grateful for much valuable and straightforward guidance.

Ellen Blizinsky shares my glee in this project, sprinkles invaluable critiques ("YOU need to …") among the compliments and effectively encourages me in my growth. Wes and Joyce Veatch have been pillars in my life since 1980. Their thirst for knowledge and wise use of it continues to inspire me. If it hadn't been for their wise counsel of all these years, it couldn't have occurred to me to attempt to interview stellar examples of Ideal Aging™. This book is better as a result of their influence.

Joycebelle Edelbrock has been the guiding light in all of my recent publications. Her courses in Infopreneuring through the Enlightened Wealth Institute got me started, kept me going and keep advancing me through higher levels of achievement.

William Quinby, Art Director of Seattle Metropolitan, brought more than a touch of class to the cover design. Added to that, he made the interior more readable and so much more appealing! Then Tim McCarthy of Sir Speedy Whittier got this to press with finesse.

The other men-behind-the-scenes includes my husband; without Rich's love and support this book couldn't have come to press so quickly. With son, Matthew's, learned questions more data got integrated. Always and forever I will be grateful to my son, Jay, for his unflagging courage, determination to succeed, commitment to being Smarter This Year and encouragement that all others enjoy the same.

The truth of the matter is that no one has a perfect memory. And this book couldn't hold the whole list of people whose impact reverberates throughout its pages if I could remember them all perfectly. But every cell in my body kneels in gratitude to those mentioned as well as all others who have facilitated the creation and refinement of this collection of information for the sole goal of enriching and empowering the Ideal Aging™ of all whose lives it touches … in the hope that more folks will achieve vigorous longevity with each effort they make at any age.

Thanks to all.

Dr. Joyce

FOREWORD

It is with great pleasure and pride that I write this introduction to Dr. Joyce Shaffer's insightful and inspiring book *Ideal Aging*™. Dr. Joyce leads us, through science, example, and wonderful prose, to realize that the brain is an organ capable of maintaining its function and in fact developing and growing in power throughout our entire life.

The brain is a wondrous and strange organ. It controls all our bodily functions. Involuntary actions such as breathing and digesting food are done without our cognition. These are actions in which we are not necessarily in charge. Voluntary actions, such as raising a glass to your mouth or walking across the street are under our own control. With these actions we are in charge. The brain also remembers, integrates, and processes information beyond anything that a mere computer could do.

Thus the brain is not a static organ, yet it can become stale from disuse! The involuntary actions controlled by our brain continue almost unabated as we age; we continue to breath until the end, we continue to digest food until the end. However, the voluntary actions may become erratic and the processing of information may change as we age.

Is it possible to facilitate and maintain the cognitive functions so that they do not decay with time ... perhaps even improve? In medical science the 'programmed' death of some tissue cells, in various parts of the body, is called apoptosis. We have accepted as gospel that, as we age, there may be some apoptosis of our cognitive function. But is that really true?

As I was growing up, there were many things that I simply could not comprehend, despite mentors trying to explain them thoroughly to me. I later realized this was my own form of dyslexia, but at the time I thought of myself as just 'dense' (a 1960's phraseology for being dumb). Part of my New Year's Resolution, each year, was "I will not be dense". I think it worked, but it is was and is a struggle that requires, as Dr. Joyce describes in Ideal Aging™, continual work to get *Smarter This Year* (and NOT denser, I might add!).

Like atrophy of your muscles from disuse, the brain's cognitive ability can also atrophy from lack of stimulation. Aerobic physical activity can maintain and build our muscles. The brain must also have a form of aerobic conditioning to avoid apoptosis and build better brain architecture for improved cognitive functioning. The continuance, in fact, the celebration of that process is the core message of Ideal Aging™.

I know you will enjoy this wonderful manuscript, I most certainly did.

John A. Rumberger, PhD, MD, FACC
The Princeton Longevity Center
Princeton, New Jersey

PREFACE

It was one of those Seattle mornings when it wasn't raining but the air was just wet enough to leave its delicate traces as it brushed my cheek. We were staying aerobic around the downtown park when it came to me. The realization that "ideal" hasn't been defined yet. Not for health. Not for intelligence. Not for wealth. Not for social intelligence. Not for peaceful coexistence. Not for Ideal Aging™. Not.

My research for Secrets inside Bones, Brains & Beauty® focused on osteoporosis. It was wonderful to discover in the writing of that book how much your efforts to enhance your bone health could influence your brain as well. Also, there was a noticeable and growing trend in science to redefine optimal in physical, mental, social, sexual, emotional and all other realms of health. That was both fun and fascinating to follow.

In 1998 human neurogenesis was proven by post-mortem examination of the brains of individuals between the ages of 55 and 70. That was a myth-busting finding! It has been exhilarating to ride the tidal wave of research on brain matters since then. New data has blown in with hurricane force.

Neurogenesis is the creation of new brain cells or neurons. It's one form of "neuroplasticity." The other form is the care, training and feeding of new and existing neurons such that the functioning and the very structure of your brain changes … for better or for worse. Exciting new neuroscience studies the evolving definition of what optimal brain health is. This includes research aimed at "slowing, arresting, or reversing functional decline in adults." Neuroplasticity includes the lifelong ability of your brain to develop in positive ways, to change and to rewire circuits in ways that had been thought to be impossible.

The growing focus on positive outcomes as your brain ages could potentially be beneficial to all adults. I believe the time has come to replace the old cliché "use it or lose it." It would be more accurate, empowering and motivating to say of your brain cells: "birth them and train them." That's why this book had to be written as a complement to the book on osteoporosis. Neuroplasticity may be one of the best surprise gifts in the dances of life.

Maybe Ideal Aging™ will be an evolving concept. But that highlights the huge and unique benefits of this book. First, its strongest theme is scientific grounding. "Science or silence" has always been my requirement on topics as important as these. This book brings the language of amazing new neuroscience findings to life for fun and for the health of it.

The second huge benefit here is the impact of this new science on all other topics in this book. Increasing numbers of researchers now want to understand what optimal health is. Decades of research on the medical model that focused on pathology and curing disease has saved many lives! The timing for research to define the ideal is NOW—because instant access to global information via the internet and increasing translation of these reports has created a learning revolution. It brought us valuable research on centenarians who have remained vigorous throughout their lives in ways quite uncommon in our home culture. Research that identifies what has resulted in exceptional human longevity with hardiness, resilience and robust health is a much needed complement to pathology.

What a gift to be alive in the age of technology when the information revolution yields more scientific data that are also more positive and hopeful! That's the third distinctly different value this book brings to you. It is a joy to share everything possible about this positive side of science for the health of it!

The fourth unique value is teaching you how to put this new science to work for Ideal Aging™ while enjoying the process. Knowledge is power. But that is really only true when the knowledge is used. How many books have you read, learned a lot from and then returned to the library without making a change in yourself? This book will teach you how you can use this new scientific data to create changes that can be permanent.

Evolving scientific information sets the stage for you, an informed dancer, to work with your healthcare provider in writing your unique, flowing choreography for your dances of life. You have been influencing the architecture of your brain all along! How, if at all, will you change that influence? What you do from this day forward could be good for your mental, emotional, social, physical, sexual, financial and intellectual Ideal Aging™.

It is an honor to bring you these unique perspectives of such huge value. It's been a humbling experience to learn so much about how we create our very existence. In all of these areas the strongest theme in these dances will be scientific grounding. Laced within that will be the clinical perspective. Sometimes what is heard behind the curtain of privacy can be of value to others as long as privacy is maintained. Sometimes observations in passing are also valuable.

I don't make these stories up. I'm not that smart. I just record what I think will add value. I'll point out what is clinical as it enters the stage and conceal all identifying data to protect those who had the wisdom to afford themselves the gift of psychotherapy. I'll also keep quiet about the source of some of the stories observed in the community in order to protect the innocent and the zesty. Their experiences might save you the trouble of learning a few things the slow way or the hard way.

Then there's the focus on helping you define your Ideal Aging™ and evolve in that. And you will want to know my qualifications to bring this information to you.

I was born on a farm, number seven of seven. We knew the kind of poverty where even the patches on our clothes were threadbare. But they were warm.

It never occurred to me back then that I would live with the Peace Corps in Borneo and travel around the globe. Nor had it entered my wildest imagination that I would make a second trip around the world. During the entire year 2000 I was one of 247 bicyclists with the Odyssey 2000 bicycle trek that went into and out of 45 countries on 6 continents averaging 80 miles of pedaling a day. Half of that time we lived in our tent. A free copy of an article I published on that longest bicycle ride I've ever done is available at the base of the page at **StressPower.com**.

Before and between those out-of-country experiences the focus was on the other kind of education—academic, credential-harvesting stuff. Being a registered nurse afforded me the freedom to live in places like Anchorage, Seattle and Baltimore. As a psychologist and nurse, I've served as the expert witness on psychiatric and medical matters for court systems since 1982.

I think you get my gist. My life has not been quiet.

There's something lovely about being your own choreographer in the many dances of life. It's far more efficient and fulfilling to turn the energy of stress into jet fuel for growth than it is to fumble when the cup of stress runneth over. Initially I became an expert in handling stress in self defense and to be helpful to others. Now, I appreciate having the expertise to teach Stress Power™.

Warning: Occasionally you will have the great pleasure of immediate success. You'll enjoy one-trial learning on those rare occasions when it occurs. You'll try something once and it'll be yours for life. Does happen.

But most of the time, you'll need to practice, practice, practice and improve, improve, improve AND reward, reward, reward until it becomes natural as well as new. Each thought or style or behavior will be automatic only after you work hard enough to know it well. Sometimes that takes a lot of practice. That's OK! Because part of the fun is the rewards you earn for each little baby step toward your Ideal Aging™. These are some of the things you will need.

Knowledge.

Action.

Balance.

Choice.

Reinforcement. Refinement. Reward.

Evolution and achievement.

Novelty.

Randomly celebrate life, friends, passions, strengths, growth and Ideal Aging™. This book is about these things…and more. Above all, enjoy working with your healthcare provider in developing the choreography of your dance of life for your Ideal Aging™! It's never too early and never too late to take effective action for the health of it. Here's looking at a smart and delicious choreography for your dances of life to keep your brain fit…because you simply want more out of life.

PART A. INTRODUCTION

Art Linkletter—Says the most inspiring things …about Ideal Aging™

Since I was given up for adoption at birth, the first thing I'm grateful for is that I was not a casualty of abortion. I had to work for everything I got which was another great advantage. I learned at the age of 6 if I wanted something I had to work for it. I learned to like to work. And I like to take chances. I started with nothing so I had nothing to lose.

Mr. Linkletter, what would say was the highlight of your life?

The highlight was discovering what I could do and what I loved to do and I spent my life doing it. That is talking to people, selling, persuading, motivating, cajoling, preaching, teaching and that I was a leader. My life changed when a station offered me a part-time job in radio. I heard a program called *A Man in the Street*—they took a microphone out on the street and stopped people. Anything could happen. My quick wit, humor and ability to talk made me an absolutely perfect prospect to have my own Man in the Street show which I promptly did.

And what are your dreams now for your future?

My, oh well, scientifically, technically my future's about four years. But you never know.

No, you could live to be 120.

I hope for the best. I wouldn't want to be 120 and not be active. I was talking to Billy Graham one time and I said, "Billy, I'm not sure I want to go to Heaven." He said, "What?" I said "Because I don't know what I'd do up there. Nobody has ever come back with a report and the Bible only says you'll have a glorious time but I want to have something to do." I said: "I hate to tell you this Billy but if you went to Hell there'd be all kinds of things to do. There's air conditioning to figure out, ointments for burns, things like that to discover."

But, Mr. Linkletter, you spend your life being totally dedicated to a positive perspective so I think maybe in Heaven you could add to it some way.

Well, I don't know. I think we have to take an awful lot on faith when we're heading to a place that nobody's ever come back from. I'm striving to be something here and now.

If you had every resource you needed—spiritual guidance, social support, time, energy, money— how would you improve the world, if at all?

That is some question! …try to be involved in something where people learn to be tolerant of differences. So that there isn't a constant battle to prove that you are better, bigger, smarter, going to a better Heaven and getting rewards that other people aren't getting. And if they aren't, they're not as good as you. Not that everybody's equal. That's wrong too. But to promote the idea that you have to do the best you can with what you've got. Every human being is unique. I would be a teacher, preacher, writer and travel around and join good causes. It's what I am doing.

Tell me how you define Ideal Aging™.

Ideal Aging™ is adapting to change, welcoming change. Change involves worries and learning some new skills or approaches or convictions under which you can work. And yet change is what makes everything better. I travel probably 200,000 miles a year. I am fortunate enough, being famous, to be guests of kings and presidents and be on the inside of places where most people can't get. And I take advantage of them. I've always put my hand up. I'm a volunteer. I'm an alpha. I'm always looking for the next hill that's a little higher with a better view—something waiting to be learned I never knew. That's a poem isn't it?

One of the lovely ones. I wonder if some people say you're really lucky when in fact you're saying it had a lot to do with working with what you have.

Yes. And taking the blows of life which are going to happen to everyone but nevertheless you have to rise from that and go on. One of my biggest changes occurred in 1939. I was only about 24 years of age. I was already the radio director of the San Francisco World's Fair, planning the opening of that huge extravaganza. The president of the fair fired me.

I went home at 11:00 in the morning to tell my wife that we had a whole new plan for life. I'll never work for anybody again. I never have until this day. I started my own business writing, producing, MC-ing and inside of three months I discovered to my tremendous surprise I was making more money than the president of the fair.

I've gone steadily up with that idea in mind—always selling my own ideas, never auditioning to be on somebody else's program. It changed my whole life. I got my own ideas, I sold my own ideas, I did my own ideas, I never had an agent, and I never had a manager.

If there was anything in your business or your life that you could do differently to make your success even greater, what would that be?

I can't imagine anything. I've just had such a great time. I never really considered that I worked a day in my life. I never made quite as much money as I might've made if I'd had an agent and was more greedy through an agent. I would accept programs and ideas and challenges where the pay wasn't as good but I felt I needed that experience. I needed that ability which would enable me to do it. And that's why I kept growing.

Mr. Linkletter, who was your mentor?

Oh, I had many mentors, starting with the principal of the Virginia High School. I won a $100.00 prize from the Rotary Club for being the outstanding junior high school student. After I got it, I was so giddy with fame and fortune that I cut school and went down to San Diego to a movie. I was picked up by a truant officer and brought back to the office of the principal who, two hours before, had been applauding me for being an outstanding example. He said "Art, I can understand how you feel like kicking up your heels like a young colt but you have, as a leader, a responsibility as a role model. You've got to remember that people are going to be looking at you. You don't want to do anything which will make them disappointed or give them wrong ideas of something they might try." That was a huge thing.

He told me one other thing. I used to MC the school programs. I was funny on stage and made jokes about people. He took me aside. He said, "Art, you're a funny kid. You do quite well but I have a little suggestion to make. When you're in public and you're up on stage, never get a laugh at somebody else's expense. The other day," he said, "You kidded a fat girl in the front row. It mortified her. Don't ever mortify anybody. Nor is it necessary for you to ever be cheapening yourself with what we call a quick dirty laugh where everybody laughs at the shock of it. You know you can shock people but afterwards they say, 'boy he's a vulgar person'." Even though I've been on huge roasts in Hollywood with all the stars in town where they were just tearing each other to pieces with bad language and bad stories, I never did it. Finally, I stopped going to them. I said I'm not even going to sit on a platform and be part of this business where the foulest language and the dirty innuendos are being thrown around as funny.

What a gift that man gave you twice. I truly appreciate several things you said on that one topic…a core focus of Ideal Aging™. The role of positives in our lives is so much more empowering than any of the negatives.

Yes! I've had some wonderful mentors. After I launched my own programs and writing, I had a call from Henry Kaiser who at the time was building liberty ships in Richmond for the war. He said "Art. I've heard you on radio and you have a very persuasive tone and you talk to the people in their own language. I have a great need for women to come over here to our four shipyards and learn to weld because the draft has taken away all the skilled people who are not old and we're having a problem. We can teach women to be welders." So I went over, became his assistant. Now I had a man to watch who had become a tremendous success in his handling of huge projects, dams, automobiles and everything else that Kaiser aluminum did. He had an empire all over the world. I became his right hand as a young guy.

He always called me Art and I used to call him Henry until one day I was up at his house at Lake Tahoe. It was the weekend and I noticed that everybody was calling him Mr. Kaiser including his wife. So when everybody left I said to him, "You know I'm kind of embarrassed. I'm a young sprout and I'm calling you Henry." He says, "Art, when they call me 'Mister' it's not be glorifying. It's just kind of a title like major, or captain, or something. If you want to, you can call me Henry because we're just friends." I never called him Henry again.

I saw him inspire the shipyard workers to do the tough job they were doing. His enthusiasm! I learned it is very important in aging or anywhere—that attitude is one of the most changeable, improvable and actually learnable things that a person can develop. As a psychiatrist once said, by changing the inner aspect of your mind you can change the entire outer aspect of your life. That's really what an attitude does. You can be enthusiastic, happy, helpful, understanding, tolerant, loving, kind and all these things to the best of your ability. He was just great at that. He put his big arms out over his big tummy and talked to 4,000 workers. He'd say, "To begin with I want you to know I love you. I love every one of you here for what you're doing. Our boys are dying overseas and we're sending them on these ships that you're making ….that'll give us the kind of freedom we want to keep."

I was a friend of his until he died. I helped him build a big Kaiser village in Hawaii.

I think you also helped him build the Kaiser Hospitals?

Oh yes. I was on his board of directors of the first Kaiser Hospitals. I've been on boards of probably 10 or 15 huge international corporations. I learn something new each place I go. I think it's very important to have mentors and to promote them and to cultivate them. In fact I'm doing the same thing with young people. I'm a member of Horatio Alger—one of the least known but one of the biggest promoters of the development of youth in the United States.

The Horatio Alger Society was started by Dr. Norman Vincent Peale who was also one of my mentors. Dr. Peale got me through my troubles when my daughter committed suicide 35 years ago from the use of LSD at a party. He told me that one of the most difficult things a minister has to do is to talk about loss of a young child to a good Christian family. But he said, "Art, in your case I can understand that the Lord has delivered you a very tragic and very strong message. He is telling you that you have something you should be getting ready to do. This country is about to go into a drug abuse epidemic reaching young people. Here in America, where the kids have more of anything than anybody has ever had in the history of the world, they are wanting more. They want to have something that'll take them out of this world to give them a different consciousness which is first alcohol, the biggest drug, and then marijuana which is the gateway to every other kind of drug. The American people are grieving with your loss because you've been part of America for the last 30 years interviewing 27,000 children and doing all the things you've done with families. So, you should be out telling parents what they may not believe from anyone else. If a cop tells them or a doctor tells them or a teacher tells them they're more inclined to say. 'Well that's their job to do that.' But it isn't your calling. It's your position of authority, understanding and acceptance by these people that will help save children's lives."

I became an expert on drug abuse. I lectured at the United Nations, introduced by George Bush, Senior. I was in Tibet and I was in all these places where drugs come from. So you see how one thing leads to another. I let it lead me. I don't even know it's there until it runs across my doorstep. Some of it hits you over the head pretty strenuously like that.

What important life lessons do you appreciate now that you didn't when you were 20 or even 40?

Probably forgiveness and human foibles.

Is there anything that is unforgivable?

I can't stand anybody taking advantage of defenseless people whether they're old or young.

Spirituality is very important to you.

Yes. When I told my father I was going out and started hitchhiking and riding freight trains to see the world, he said, "Well, the Lord will take care of you and I'll be praying for you." So I was brought up in that idea but I think you have to do your part. Henry Kaiser used to tell me a funny story. He was talking about the importance of working and contributing. He said a farmer got a lot, a terrible piece of ground out in the desert. Very cheap, no money but there was no water and there was nothing. He dug canals and he finally got a beautiful farm built. He invited the whole congregation of the church out. The minister said in his remarks this demonstrates that the Lord has certainly been good to our brother. So he stepped up to the microphone and he said, "Very true! But you should've seen this place when the Lord had it by Himself."

Mr. Linkletter, what steps do you take to keep your aging ideal?

The first thing I guard jealously is my physical and mental health. Here I am almost 95 and this is the first year I haven't skied since my wife gave away my ski clothes when I was off lecturing. I said, "Why?" She says, "I want to be a wife not a nurse."

She skied with me so we both stopped skiing this year. But I have had a regimen of physical conditioning ever since my first acquaintance with the YMCA in San Diego where I became an expert acrobat. I became a basketball star. I'm in the Hall of Fame in the San Diego State University. I become a top flight swimmer, semi-coast, backstroke, tried out for the Olympics. I have been one of the top national players as I got older 25, 28, 30, 40, 45 years of age in four-wall handball. I played in big national tournaments. It's one of the hardest driving sports for speed and ambidexterity as well as moving, using your left and right hand, shooting into a box from the ceiling and side walls and back walls. And to this day I watch my health. I weigh now exactly what I weighed when I got out of college in a nation where almost everybody is getting fat.

I have been a proponent of lifelong learning. I can go into a book store and spend a whole day just wandering around looking at all these marvelous things that are in that world of the infinite. I've written 23 books. The last one is called *How to Make the Rest of Your Life the Best of Your Life.* It's a good book. I wrote it with Mark Victor Hansen of *Chicken Soup for the Soul.*

In that book you address some of the myths of aging.

The reason why there have been so many myths is that most of the published reports about aging have been the reports of doctors and psychiatrists and other heath people on their clients and on hospital cases and records like that. They haven't gotten out into the community to find the 60 to 70 percent of the older people who are just doing fine.

Who are skiing like you?

Yeah!

Who are staying sexually active?

Yes, that's right. As I say in my lectures, they've finally convinced everybody that if you're over 65 or 70 you're either sick or senile or sexless. I said I can tell you I'm almost 95; as far as sex is concerned I can still talk about it for hours. But when my wife says, "Let's run upstairs and make a little whoopee," I say pick one of those.

You also have an interest in solar energy.

Oh yes, yes. They asked me to be spokesman for the company because they needed somebody to talk at conventions. When I found out what it was, I immediately became an investor. I'm now chairman of the board. I'm an alpha. I don't get into things to lead them but whenever I get into anything, in two to three years I'm the president. That's because I volunteer and I deliver.

That's part of how you keep your brain really active, isn't it, with lifetime learning?

You bet.

Mr. Linkletter, you've said so many beautiful and inspiring things today. Is there anything else you would like to tell my readers about Ideal Aging™?

I'm interested in young people. I speak at colleges and high schools. I raise money for Christian schools all over the country because I think there should be faith and character and ethics as part of our education and you can't get that in most public schools.

I think that everyone has something good to offer to his family, to his church, to his community, to his country and beyond. I'm on the president's volunteering commission. We are promoting volunteerism for which this country is most famous even above our money, power and richness. We are the greatest volunteering country in the history of humankind. There are 73 million people in this country who volunteer for something without pay

In other words helping and growing and working and meeting a challenge in your own neighborhood, in your own mind, in your own group of people. For many, many people volunteering could very well be volunteering to spend more time with your children.

I had a little boy on my program one time. I said, "What two things would you take if you could go to Heaven tomorrow?" He said "I'd take my mother and father." I said, "Gee, isn't that sweet! Why did you pick them?" He said, "Because I think they'd have more time for me up there."

Ooh, ooh! Ooh that was painful! And the family is changed in my lifetime.

There have been divorces, there are working women. Ten percent were working when I was young. Now it's more entrepreneurs who are devoting more time and energy and effort to business careers and professional life than they can possibly spend with their families. Two or three famous people have told me that one of their great disappointments was that they had to make choices to become famous, rich, powerful. That took them away from the family or they couldn't have made it. They took that choice and they're sorry they did. One of them was Lucille Ball.

You have given so much information, so much wisdom…

Well I look forward to your book. It's a great title and we need it.

Taken from an inspirational telephone interview with Mr. Art Linkletter on January 22, 2007

7 STEPS TO ENHANCE YOUR DANCE OF LIFE

"'Older and wiser' is not just a hopeful cliché but can be the reality."
Lawrence C Katz, PhD and Manning Rubin in
Keep Your Brain Alive

It's exhilarating to bring you news about how to improve your brain! Do you know anyone who does not want maximum brain power? If you knew what to do to birth more new brain cells, would you do it? If you knew the things that could help your new and old brain cells live a more fulfilling life in greater service to you, would you do that, too?

Human neurogenesis has been ours all along. Even after legions of rats gave their lives so that we could study how to influence it, we had to rest in the armchairs of theory in the hallowed halls of science. We just didn't have the tools to study it in live humans.

In 1998 Fred Gage examined the brains of people between 55 and 70 years old at autopsy. His finding of new brain cells in these cases was a real myth buster. Until then, we were taught that the human brain only declines with "normal" aging. Since then research continues to show that the brain is highly "plastic"—meaning it easily continues to grow and change as you direct it to. If that news fills you with giggling anticipation of evolving brilliance, wait until you learn how much that laughter contributes to Ideal Aging™! Then you will laugh.

The latest technological advances have markedly increased what we know about what enhances and what suppresses neurogenesis. Both will be presented here so you can increase this and decrease that with a strategic plan for maximum potential return on your investment of time and effort. Since the chemistry of stress has been associated with loss of brain mass, learning how to convert adversity into Stress Power™ will be one key.

Scientists have measured positive changes in human brain architecture with more than one form of active stimulation. Nurture can have at least as much influence as nature in many ways. It's deliciously empowering to realize how you can make yourself Smarter This Year and expect that to change the architecture of your brain.

What a gift it is to be alive in a time when so many stellar scientists are expanding our knowledge about what enhances neuroplasticity—the capacity of the brain to change and grow. To have them provide us this information in ways that can guide us to Ideal Aging™ in spite of our genes, environment and histories is another bonus. That's especially true when the estimated cost of stress-related illnesses in the country may be more than $200 billion per year. If *Social Intelligence* author Daniel Goleman is right that we might view the immune system as a de facto ethical system, perhaps we could also see it as an economic guideline.

How will you choose to balance the positives with the negatives? Will you join the tide of informed dancers who add positives to your life for the health of it? Will you take Goleman's theory of Social Intelligence so seriously that you will maximize your time hanging out with positive people because each of you can enhance the other's health, even alter the other's brain architecture?

While the neuroscience behind the concepts gives us added hope, some concepts are not new. In the 4th century Epictetus advised that "We are not disturbed by things, but by the view we take of things." In the early 1920s Emil Coué gave the world his now famous phrase: "Every day in every way I am getting better and better." After studying models of success in business, Napoleon Hill in *Think and Grow Rich* recommended repeating this phrase a million times combined with strong emotions and FAITH that it expressed truth. There are too many other such perspectives in print before and after these to mention here.

The important things are understanding growth and stress, increasing your awareness of how you react to, changing what you can while flexing with the rest, continually developing your personal smorgasbord of ideal options AND capitalizing on the benefits of intentionally keeping the balance in the positive no matter what. Perhaps the development of those options is the most important part.

The focus of this book is bringing the old and the new scientific data into the most simple, delicious and easy system possible. Ninety-five percent of the people I know seem to be operating at a frenetic pace. My preference is to make changes that fit easily into a life that is already full. I make every effort to do so in ways that overlap with what is already in your life without adding excessively to your To-Do List.

Incidentally, it is expected that you will empower yourself by picking and choosing from these techniques in your own unique, wise way. Celebrate being your own best expert on matters of self. Confer with your healthcare provider on all matters of health and safety. Come up with some new time savers on your own. I couldn't have dreamed up some of these examples myself…like seeing a 40-something year young woman doing a quad stretch with one hand while holding the nozzle in place with the other hand to fill her SUV's gas tank. Never would've come up with that one.

One goal is to teach you how to make your life easier and healthier with maximum brain, emotional, social and career performance while making minimum impact on your calendar. Whenever possible, that may require you to make an initial investment of time. For example, time and practice are essential to build new conditioned responses or habits. You have many of those already. Adding new habits judiciously will be worth every moment it takes to Change Your Brain, Change Your Habits (which are conditioned responses with a shorter label).

Try something now. For a moment, close you eyes and imagine being offered a slice of fresh lemon which you put in your mouth. Did you feel your mouth watering? That's a conditioned response you didn't have until after you experienced the taste of a lemon.

Pavlov's dogs learned to salivate well. To the sound of a bell, even!

Here's another example. Imagine yourself walking out on stage in front of 1,000 people. Without much awareness, your heart probably races at the thought of delivering a speech in public. Did you know that some people fear public speaking more than they fear death? However, after spending enough time to develop a conditioned relaxation response, you can nip that fear in the bud within seconds of being called on stage.

Another goal of this book is to show you how to make as many healthy conditioned responses as possible. Then you simply create new habits of turning your stress energy into improved performance. It can become your habit to turn off the fight-or-flight response whenever it's not needed to save your flank from the lion's jaws. It's my clinical experience that this style of requiring minimum time for maximum benefit helps people gladly learn how to make small changes for larger long term gains.

In the extraordinary book *The END of Stress as We Know It,* Dr. Bruce McEwen presents a hopeful model for understanding stress in new ways. He explains the value of stress as well as the power you have to influence how it effects for your health. That's worth exploring.

Homeostasis is crucial to normal body functioning. It refers to the body's efforts to keep all things constant – or nearly so. Early homeostatic responses aim to prevent problems before they occur. For example the so-called normal body temperature of 98.6 degrees Fahrenheit needs to remain relatively constant. You will sleep better at night when your temperature drops about a degree cooler. That healthy drop in body temperature has a lower limit. Going too far below 98.6 Fahrenheit is dangerous. That's why you shiver to prevent hypothermia until you don more clothing or increase your environmental temperature. When your temperature rises too much, sweating is your body's natural way of lowering it. Letting your body temperature go either too high or too low can cause brain damage … or be lethal.

Oxygen also must be kept within a pretty narrow range. If less than the ideal amount of oxygen reaches your brain even briefly, you could suffer brain damage or death. In contrast, many years ago some premature infants were exposed to too much oxygen in incubators resulting in these babies going blind.

Although the term "allostasis" may have been used in science for decades, it hasn't yet become common vocabulary. But here's how it compares to homeostasis.

Maintenance of body functions and life depends on keeping such thing as your acid-base balance, oxygen saturation and body temperature within a tight range – this is homeostasis. However, allostasis reflects the fact that some bodily functions can tolerate wider ranges of variability. Allostasis links the brain (perception), endocrine system (alarm) and immune (internal defense) system in a communication so well orchestrated that it keeps the body stable while all of these systems change dramatically to prepare for one of two extreme responses – either fight or flight. This is part of the genius of the fight-or-flight or stress response, which McEwen calls allostasis with urgency.

To use the language of Robert Sapolsky in *Why Zebras Don't Get Ulcers*, when you are a zebra forced to race across the savannah to avoid being someone else's lunch, greater variability of some body systems is essential! You'll need more energy in the form of glucose for the sprint and more from fat stores for endurance running. So your blood sugar may go above the "normal" range with no observable damage because you run it off. Increased oxygen requirements are met by breathing more rapidly and deeply while increasing your heart rate to get the oxygen distributed where needed. The inflammation that results causes an increase in stress hormones such as cortisol. In case of injury, infection is fought by an elevated white blood cell count. A lion sinking its teeth into your flank calls for heightened pain tolerance if you're to keep running–so endorphins flow.

The lovely choreography of fight-or-flight, now referred to as "allostasis with urgency," is obviously much more complex than that. But you get the picture. Allostasis is your flexible, dynamic friend in daily life. It orchestrates survival when you need it most. To bring that example to real time, reconsider the title of the book by Sapolsky—Why Zebras Don't Get Ulcers.

Humans do.

Remember the other morning when you were racing to catch the bus just as you caught sight of it rounding the corner without you? No problem. Another bus will be by in 15 minutes. Alas! The next one never comes. Thirty minutes later than you needed to leave for the office a bus stops but it has standing room only. That means two things: you are already half an hour late for your first appointment AND you have no place to sit and review the data critical to that meeting.

This is not a zebra affair. No lion lurks. And an aerobic lurch which might have worked off your angst-induced stress chemistry is probably impossible on a standing-room only bus. This book is unique in its broad scientific approach to old and new dances of life.

Of course it helps to remember that standing will strengthen your bones, dynamic balance and muscles! But wouldn't you really rather see a little chivalry?

Think about your Ideal Aging™. Master the art of turning the energy of distress into Stress Power for growth. Avoid stress overdose.

"Allostatic load" is McEwen's term for this. That's when the dynamic, flexible balance of fight-or-flight does damage by working wrongly or excessively.

Applied to the example above, most of us will never have to deal with a wild animal biting into our flesh to have us for lunch. We ratchet up all systems as if we were. We perceive more threat than exists around the office. Or we take an accurate measure of things which are odious without an equally accurate appreciation of our many options. In either case, we don't use up the chemistry of stress in ways known to put our complex stress chemistry back into the dance of health. We tend to leave problems fidgeting back stage while we lose our footing in the juices that are meant to help us get out of harm's way. Then we put our dance further out of rhythm by harmful lifestyle choices: We've become an overfed nation of sitters who sleep poorly while worrying that external forces or genetics will harm us more than we are already harming ourselves.

Can you see how that provides the ultimate model of hope? Hang in there. This is brilliant. Aging and stress happen. Decay is optional. That's where your power is. Most of the stress reaction is under your control.

> "The very existence of healthy, vigorous centenarians, whose lives were spent long before the advent of modern medicine, proves that the potential duration of human existence exceeds the biblical three score and ten, and that longevity can be achieved without medical care."
> René Dubos in the Introduction of
> *Anatomy of an Illness by Norman Cousins*

Genetics offers about 50% of the script. And the environment will at times drop a heavy curtain. Tragedy is. Allostasis is your internal, dynamic, flexible way of stepping over and around such hurdles with the grace and skill of Baryshnikov.

Allostatic load does not need to create long term disharmony as a result of uninformed choices you have been making. Instead of stress OD, you can build your unique smorgasbord of options to lessen that load.

That's particularly important based on research showing that the lack of perceived control is one of the most distressing circumstances. Instead of falling off stage with a sense of being a powerless victim, you can learn to go from misery to mellow in microseconds, to provide yourself with multiple choices and to empower yourself with judicious use of Positive Reinforcement. You can celebrate your power to create your own glee. You can learn how others have done that and empower yourself even more.

That's the mission of this book. In sync with the science of neurogenesis, neuroplasticity, and using stress (instead of being used up by it), this book provides you with 7 simple steps to vigorous longevity and maximum brain power by learning how to dance to the rhythms of Brain Boost, Happy Habit, Energy Elevator, Sexual Saunter and Global Growth for the health of it.

This is not a quick fix. Nor is it one-size-fits-all. Make change in a gradual way. Add to your menu of choices so you can create new healthy habits based on science. Come to appreciate which ones work for you uniquely in given situations. AND reinforce your progress at the same time that you keep your antennae up for new learning from here to eternity.

Remember the famous quote of Emil Coué: "Every day in every way, I am getting better and better." It works best if you repeat it many times daily while believing that you are getting better and better every day in every way.

Your Ideal Aging™ could include vim, vigor and vitality…whatever those mean to you. Jeanne Calment was a fine model. In her eighties she sold her estate to her attorney for a small monthly sum on a contract that he would inherit it at her death. He died. His family maintained the payments. As the oldest documented human, she lived to be 122 years young. That suggests she died financially secure. When her physician wanted to remove her cataracts so she could see, she reportedly answered, "I'm old. I'm supposed to be blind." You might want to remember that statement when worldview is discussed in subsequent chapters. A quote attributed to her was: "I only have one wrinkle and I'm sitting on it." This feisty, funny female can teach us a lot.

There is the potential for power and health in these techniques. They're designed to turn negative emotions and energy generally associated with stress into jet fuel for Ideal Aging™. These skills can teach you how to recover and excel even with unavoidable stress.

New research focused on health complements the recovery from negative effects of stress. There is wisdom in Goleman's Social Intelligence theory based on new social neuroscience findings. He is clear, cogent and convincing on the profound impact of social decisions. Thanks to the efforts of Martin EP Seligman who condensed the research of decades in helping pioneer the field of positive psychology, we can learn how to develop enduring authentic happiness.

Bruce McEwen integrated decades of science in concluding that almost all of us can balance the positive and negative effects of stress to remain in good health. He uses the term "allostasis" to refer to "the resilience, the power, the seeming intelligence of our bodies' responses to an ever-changing world."

Marian Diamond, Fred Gage, Lawrence Katz, George Vaillant and many other brain research scientists have found reasons to hope for healthy and vigorous longevity as well as ways of living for optimal performance and quality of life.

In reviewing the scientific evidence of the impact of negative and positive emotions on health, Daniel Goleman suggests that these biological imperatives for health might be a guideline for ethical action. A unique value of this book is learning the multitude of benefits that come with mastery of the many Rhythms of Stress Power.

Begin by learning more about yourself. Looking at recent stressful events you have experienced will help you compare yourself to known statistics.

A standard measure in the industry is The Schedule of Recent Experience (SRE). Thomas Holmes at the University of Washington designed it as a research tool. It has proven useful in clinical settings as well. Take time now to fill in your SRE before we continue.

> "There are risks and costs to a program of action.
> But they are far less than
> the long-range risks and costs of comfortable inaction."
> John F. Kennedy

The Schedule of Recent Experience (SRE)

INSTRUCTIONS:

For each life event item listed below please do the following:

Think back on the event and decide if it happened to you and when it happened. If the event did happen, indicate the number of times it happened by placing a number in each of the appropriate time periods. If the event occurred more than 4 times in a given time period, enter the number 4. The columns are as follows:

<u>O to 6 months ago   6 months to 1 year ago   1 to 2 years ago   2 to 3 years ago</u>

	0-6 Mo ago	6 mo-1 yrs ago	1-2 yrs ago	2-3 yrs ago
1. A lot more or a lot less troubles with the boss.	____	____	____	____
2. A major change in sleeping habits (sleeping a lot more or a lot less, or change in part of day when asleep.)	____	____	____	____
3. A major change in eating habits (a lot more or a lot less food intake, or very different meal hours or surroundings.)	____	____	____	____
4. A revision of personal habits (dress, manners, associations, etc.).	____	____	____	____
5. A major change in your usual type and/or amount of recreation.	____	____	____	____
6. A major change in your social activities (e.g., clubs, dancing, movies, visiting, etc.).	____	____	____	____
7. A major change in church activities (e.g., a lot more or a lot fewer than usual.)	____	____	____	____
8. A major change in number of family get-togethers (e.g., a lot more or lot less than usual.)	____	____	____	____
9. A major change in financial state (e.g., a lot worse off or a lot better off than usual.)	____	____	____	____
10. In-law troubles.	____	____	____	____

	0-6 Mo ago	6 mo- 1 yrs ago	1-2 yrs ago	2-3 yrs ago
11. A major change in the number of arguments with spouse (e.g., either a lot more or a lot less than usual regarding child-rearing, personal habits, etc.).	____	____	____	____
12. Sexual difficulties.	____	____	____	____
13. Major personal injury or illness.	____	____	____	____
14. Death of a close family member (other than spouse.)	____	____	____	____
15. Death of spouse.	____	____	____	____
16. Death of a close friend .	____	____	____	____
17. Gaining a new family member (e.g., through birth, adoption, oldster moving in, etc.).	____	____	____	____
18. Major change in the health or behavior of a family member.	____	____	____	____
19. Change in residence.	____	____	____	____
20. Detention in jail or other institution.	____	____	____	____
21. Minor violations of the law (e.g., traffic tickets jaywalking, disturbing the peace etc.).	____	____	____	____
22. Major business readjustment (e.g., merger, reorganization, bankruptcy, etc.).	____	____	____	____
23. Marriage .	____	____	____	____
24. Divorce.	____	____	____	____
25. Marital separation from spouse.	____	____	____	____
26. Outstanding personal achievement.	____	____	____	____
27. Son or daughter leaving home (e.g.,, marriage, attending college, etc.).	____	____	____	____
28. Retirement from work.	____	____	____	____
29. Major change in working hours or conditions.	____	____	____	____

	0-6 Mo ago	6 mo- 1 yrs ago	1-2 yrs ago	2-3 yrs ago
30. Major change in responsibilities at work (e.g., promotion, demotion, lateral transfer.)	____	____	____	____
31. Being fired from work.	____	____	____	____
32. Major change in living conditions (e.g., building a new home, remodeling, deterioration of home or neighborhood.)	____	____	____	____
33. Spouse beginning or ceasing work outside the home.	____	____	____	____
34. Taking out a mortgage or loan for a major purchase (e.g., purchasing a home, business, etc.).	____	____	____	____
35. Taking out a mortgage or loan for a lesser purchase (e.g., purchasing a car, TV, freezer, etc.).	____	____	____	____
36. Foreclosure on mortgage or loan.	____	____	____	____
37. Vacation.	____	____	____	____
38. Changing to a new school.	____	____	____	____
39. Changing to a different line of work.	____	____	____	____
40. Beginning or ceasing formal schooling.	____	____	____	____
41. Marital reconciliation with mate.	____	____	____	____
42. Pregnancy.	____	____	____	____

The Schedule of Recent Experience (SRE) by Marion E Amundson, Cheryl A Hart and Thomas H Holmes ©1981, "Reprinted by permission of the University of Washington Press."

To score your SRE, multiply the number of times each event occurred by the value listed for each item in the list below. **Please note: responses greater than 4 are scored as a 4.** Next, total the results to get your score for *each* time period.

VALUES FOR THE ITEMS ON THE SCHEDULE OF RECENT EXPERIENCE (SRE)

No.	SRE event	Mean Value
1.	Trouble with the boss	23
2.	Change in sleeping habits	16
3.	Change in eating habits	15
4.	Revision of personal habits	24
5.	Change in recreation	19
6.	Change in social activities	18
7.	Change in church activities	19
8.	Change in number of family get-togethers	15
9.	Change in financial state	38
10.	Trouble with in-laws	29
11.	Change in number of arguments with spouse	35
12.	Sex difficulties	39
13.	Personal injury or illness	53
14.	Death of close family member	63
15.	Death of spouse	
16.	Death of close friend	
17.	Gain of new family member	
18.	Change in health of family member	
19.	Change in residence	
20.	Jail term	
21.	Minor violations of the law	
22.	Business readjustment	
23.	Marriage	
24.	Divorce	
25.	Marital separation	
26.	Outstanding personal achievement	28
27.	Son or daughter leaving home	29
28.	Retirement	45
29.	Change in work hours or conditions	20
30.	Change in responsibilities at work	29
31.	Fired at work	47
32.	Change in living conditions	25
33.	Spouse begins or stops work	26
34.	Mortgage or loan for major purchase (home, business, etc.)	31
35.	Mortgage or loan for lesser purchase (car, TV, etc.)	17
36.	Foreclosure of mortgage or loan	30
37.	Vacation	13
38.	Change in schools	20
39.	Change to different line of work	36
40.	Begin or end school	26
41.	Marital reconciliation	45
42.	Pregnancy	40

The Schedule of Recent Experience (SRE) by Marion E. Amundson, Cheryl A. Hart and Thomas H. Holmes ©1981, "Reprinted by permission of the University of Washington Press."

An example of scoring might be as follows. In the past 0 to 6 months, if you:

Changed your residence = 20

Got a loan on a car and on new furniture is 2 X 17 = 34

Increased your social activities in five settings to find friends in your new home (remember that any number greater than 4 is scored 4) is 4 X 18 = 72.

Graduated from school is 26.

Won a Nobel prize is 28.

Took a vacation is 13.

Therefore your SRE score for 0 to 6 months is 193.

No doubt you noticed that some of the items would be considered socially desirable. You may have even initiated these events as part of your planning. Knowing that you would graduate, you chose to relocate and to take a well-deserved vacation.

Even in these instances, however, some change and adaptation were required. The emphasis in the SRE is your ability to adapt from what you had been doing on a regular basis. It is not measuring emotions, meanings or desirability. This is based on research showing that the more one is called upon to adapt to change the more likelihood there is of illness, increased healthcare visits or accidents.

Items on the SRE were chosen because research showed that the onset of symptoms or illness often occurred during the two years following these events. Therefore, a high score on the SRE might be a good reason to postpone for two years any of the events on this list that are under your control. For example, you might choose to delay getting a major loan, taking a vacation, moving across country or increasing social activities in so many settings.

Holmes found that 52% of individuals studied for a two-year period of risk experienced major health changes. Of the people whose SRE scores were below 150, 33% had major health changes. With SRE scores between 150 and 299, 48% of the subjects had major health changes. Are you ready for the big one? An astounding 86% of the people with SRE scores greater than 300 had major health changes!

In clinical settings I have used the SRE with almost all of my clients. People have appreciated the increased understanding of the amount of stress they have been coping with. It normalized their sense of feeling "stressed out." It has been valuable to them in making plans in areas of their lives where they were in control. In looking at your SRE score, consider how this should influence your future decisions.

Your current emotional status is another critical factor. In addition, you will want to establish how you currently cope with the various situations in your life.

This will include learning an easy way to measure progress. Among conditioned responses you will be building, perhaps the most important one will be giving yourself Positive Reinforcement for progress. Episodic measurements make that easier.

The next step will be choosing one technique at a time to add to your list of habits. Create a conditioned response with that one before moving on to another technique. This is not a race to the finish. It's about quality additions to your list of healthy options for Ideal Aging™.

With each technique, a simple *process* of keeping track of progress is going to be important. The one I've found to be most clinically useful is the BARE BONERS process. I created this initially as Bare Bones. Couldn't live with it. Had to add Positive Reinforcement for reasons that will be more obvious in that chapter.

This tool is solidly grounded in research. It's included here because it proved to be clinically useful with my clients. It is the process suggested for your use throughout the Ideal Aging™ book. Stated simply, it is **BARE BONERS**:

B egin
A
R ealistic
E ffort starting with:

B aseline – measures of today
O ptions – specific to you, your status, your written goals and a set time line
N ow do it. Do it now. Pick 1 or more options and repeat daily for 2+ weeks
E valuation – same measures as Day #1
R einforce (Reward; Refine) – because this strengthens permanent changes
S tart again at your new baseline – small changes get stronger with repetition

What will you measure? That will be clarified in each chapter.

The medical model of focusing on pathology has afforded us a large body of critical findings on the role of negative emotions in disease. Negative emotions will be important to measure. While quantifying these on a subjective level has all of the limitations of self report data, it can be helpful in getting a sense of the impact of new skills as you reduce your negative emotions in the interest of Ideal Aging™.

This model of disease is appropriately complemented by the Positive Psychology perspective. There have been many pioneers in this field across the years.

Norman Cousins gave us a delightful case report in his book *Anatomy of an Illness as Perceived by the Patient: Reflections on Healing and Regeneration*. By his logic, if negative emotions could make us ill, then the positive ones must have a healing influence. He had a vested interest in the theory. Several New York specialists had been consulted. One suggested he had little chance of recovering from collagen disease. In his words, he "was literally becoming unglued." He attributed his survival to lots of laughter, love, faith, will to live and plenty of companionship. The impact of his account on the scientific community was positive. He joined the faculty of the School of Medicine at the University of California at Los Angeles. A significant body of research began to accumulate showing positive attitudes were biochemical realities which can improve medical outcomes. *Head First: The Biology of Hope* is his informative report.

It was partly his influence on my work that led to my creation of a new scale for my clinical work. I'd been trained in the use of the Subjective Units of Distress (SUDS) to measure the improvement of negative states with such techniques as the Progressive Relaxation Response. That was a critical half of what needed to be measured.

I believed it was also important to measure positive emotions. To capture both positive and negative emotions, I created the Subjective Units of Feelings Index as the SUFI Report©. As is always the case, this is to be used only after medical clearance rules out physical causes for any symptoms.

It also seemed important to measure how happy or unhappy people were with various experiences. These could be used as scheduled Positive Reinforcement to make it easier to learn new thoughts and behaviors. For clinical use I created the Reinforcement Scale. It might not include those precious Positive Reinforcements that cause you to do your best dance. If not, add any of your favorite rewards to your Reinforcement Scale. You are also invited to email any suggestions for additions to this scale to **DrJoyce@StressPower.com** so they can be considered for inclusion in future publications.

In clinical practice it was quickly apparent that words conveyed vague levels of comfort or discomfort for different people. It was not always clear how to interpret the words, "I was really upset." During interviews in which each client tied their traumatic life events to a number on the SUFI Report©, we had a common vocabulary. It was a more meaningful measure which made the therapy process more efficient.

Also, through the course of psychotherapy there was greater clarity in the numerical response to "What is your SUFI© score right now?" than there was in a verbal description of the level of emotional pain in a given moment. That's why an abbreviated form of the SUFI Report© will be the suggested measure in several chapters of this book. Before proceeding further, fill in the following SUFI Report© and Reinforcement Scale rating any feelings you have experienced <u>in the past month</u>. The maximum negative measure is -10. The maximum positive measure is +10.

Subjective Units of Feelings Index (SUFI Report™)

-10   **0**   **+10**

Rate any feelings you have experienced <u>in the past month</u>.

Use -1 to -10 (*negative* #s) for discomfort.   Use +1 to +10 for pleasure.

Negative		Positive	
Anger	_____	Love	_____
Anxiety	_____	Hope	_____
Depression	_____	Equanimity or calmness	_____
Poor self-esteem	_____	Will to live	_____
Hostility	_____	Laughter	_____
Guilt	_____	Festivity	_____
Phobias	_____	Passion	_____
Fears	_____	Purpose	_____
Obsessions	_____	Compassion	_____
Compulsions	_____	Friendliness, social connection	_____
Muscular tension	_____	Joy	_____
High blood pressure	_____	Forgiving	_____
Headaches	_____	Gratitude	_____
Neck aches	_____	Appreciated	_____
Backaches	_____	Kind	_____
Fatigue	_____	Full of Pride	_____
Insomnia	_____	In the flow	_____
Obesity	_____	Loved	_____
Physical weakness	_____	Satisfied	_____
Job stress	_____	Happiness	_____
Other (explain)	_____	Other (explain)	_____
Total Negative Emotions	_____	**Total Positive Emotions**	_____

Reinforcement Scale
Rate how you feel at -10 (horrible) to +10 (ecstatic) when you:

- See a smile _____
- Get approval _____
- Are being heard _____
- Have something new _____
- Are being helpful _____
- Accumulate points _____
- Have a few moments alone _____
- Have a few moments alone with someone _____
- Meditate _____
- Pray _____
- Have company for dinner _____
- Make something _____
- Share _____
- Hear something new _____
- Visit a library _____
- Paint _____
- Cook _____
- Do something new _____
- Eat _____
- Hug _____
- Kiss _____
- Work _____
- Play _____

- Build _____
- Sew _____
- Travel _____
- Choose _____
- Plan _____
- Read _____
- Write _____
- Model _____
- Are watched _____
- Are heard _____
- Are touched _____
- See something new _____
- Have a party _____
- Have company _____
- Visit someone _____
- Are asked your opinion _____
- Use a tool _____
- Smell something new _____
- Follow through _____
- Are being read to _____
- Read to someone _____

7 Steps to Enhance Your Dance of Life • 23

Remember this: positive reinforcement is crucial to building new behaviors. That's especially true of Conditioned Responses. So it's important to know what reinforcements are unique to you. Again, add any that are unique to you that aren't on the Reinforcement Scale. Email your suggestions to DrJoyce@StressPower.com if you want them considered for future publications..

I learned about uniqueness of reinforcement most clearly by doing therapy with many different people on both sides of the continent over the years. One man's chosen reinforcement was to buy a poster – one that had been created by his favorite artist and which cost $5000! I was a starving student at the time so I was doubly impressed. A woman chose the freedom to pet her cat. Those animals ran free on the farm of my kidhood. The job of those cats was to keep the population of rats to a minimum. Again, I was duly impressed!

There's a message here: Know your druthers.

Your negative numbers on the Reinforcement Scale are things which might feel like punishment if you had to endure them. Your positive numbers are the keys to set you free. By using the positive items as reinforcement for steps taken to build new habits, you strengthen your resolve to grow. You increase the rate of new learning. You enhance the development of Conditioned Responses.

Some people have developed a pattern of working harder if that means they will avoid a negative consequence. If that's your style, use the negative items in the SUFI Report as a list of what you will have to do if you fail to keep your contract on schedule. For example, if you fail to keep a contract with yourself by the set deadline, you could be obligated to write a check for a painfully huge amount of money to your least favorite charity. But use avoidance of pain only for the short term. Working harder to avoid punishment might not be your healthiest option.

Increasing scientific data shows the broad health benefits of positive emotions. And most people would probably be happier when earning a reward for work well done than when running against a deadline just to avoid something negative.

If your best source of positive reinforcement isn't on the list above, add it. Be sure to make it realistic. And track it as it changes. It is the positive reinforcements you identify that you will use to turn the negative emotions and energy generally associated with stress into jet fuel for health and progress. The skills in the following chapter can teach you how others have recovered and excelled in spite of unavoidable stress.

Legions of rats and other animals have given their lives to science that we might learn how to empower ourselves up out of the depths of misery. And I've needed most of them to rise above more environmental stress than could fit easily into one text. Some of you have, also.

But what about accentuating your strengths while building new ones to buffer against unwanted angst? Not by way of denial of the pain of trauma. Amitai Etzioni may have a good point in saying that there is no such thing as "Good Grief" (in his article in the New York Times on October 7, 2006). It's more effective to weigh life's servings of suffering versus celebration. Then be intentional about tipping the balance in favor of the positive by adding pleasures where ye may. These things enhance your dance.

It certainly has been crucial along my path. For example, I've kept recordings of favorite comedians easily accessible for those times when the drive between home and something awful needed softening. And I believe I have used every other stress management technique I've taught—first, because I needed to and, second, because the pupil is usually the best teacher. I've learned this body of information on a need-to-know basis. I take my own medicine and apply this learning for my own Ideal Aging™.

Many giants in the field of healthcare have joined the new emphasis on making your strengths productive and your weakness irrelevant. New research has added clarity on what works along those lines. There are many ways to compliment recovery from negative effects of stress. Research is increasingly shedding light on what we can also do to balance the positive/negative scale. I've taught clients the value of making that ratio an improper fraction: Be intentional about making your positives more prominent and pervasive than your negatives.

Thanks to the efforts of Martin E. P. Seligman, we can learn how to develop enduring authentic happiness. His book, *Authentic Happiness*, condensed the research of decades. He is one of the pioneers in positive psychology. The flow of new research since his presidency of the American Psychological Association has put the arm of science behind techniques shown to aid in developing enduring and authentic happiness.

Bruce McEwen concluded that we can end stress as we know it. We can remain in good health by adding positive events to our lives. For him the term "allostasis" means "the resilience, the power, the seeming intelligence of our bodies' responses to an ever-changing world."

Marian Diamond did such stellar research with rat brains that she is one of a handful of scientists to get cubes of the brain of Albert Einstein. She has shown that branching growth of the dendrites, axons and spines of brain cells resulted from an enriched environment even in the very old rats. She believed this could be true for humans as well.

Lawrence Katz introduced the term "neurobics" as a play on the word aerobics. In *Keep Your Brain Alive*, he provides 83 neurobic exercises that are simple while solidly based on science. "Older and Wiser" can be a delicious reality.

Stellar scientists have found reasons to hope for healthy, happy and vigorous longevity. Their research helped identify ways of living for optimal performance and quality of life. New neuroscience helps clarify your choices. Given the accelerating expense to our nation of the health decline, it might also be argued that the impact of positive and negative emotions might set economic guidelines.

It is a joy to emphasize in this book the multitude of benefits that follow effective use of the energy of stress. It can create optimal health, happiness and aging. That will include teaching you how to go from misery to mellow in microseconds for the health of it. It will also include developing buffering strengths and making many of those conditioned responses.

Sometimes grandmother knows best. She may have been around long enough to have cleared some of the junk from the attic of her mind. She may have refined, fed and protected those elegant brain cells so effectively used across her life well lived that her old neurons are a veritable storehouse of lessons well learned.

If so, she could guide you to as much delicious, vigorous longevity as she shows. If not, she may be a model of what to change for the health of it.

My mother-in-law might be a prime example of both. She stayed tuned into the news of the world, challenged her brain such that she could carry on a vigorous conversation right up to her last breath and forgave those who asked for forgiveness of any real or perceived transgressions against her.

However, she had failed to care for her hypertension eventually suffering enough minor strokes to diminish her short term memory. One might say that served her well in the end when she couldn't remember being told that she had inoperable cancer. Just moments after being adamant that, "I'm not gonna die!" she walked with the assistance of a loved one across the room to her bed, laid her head on the pillow and took one last breath.

Would that we would all have vigorous longevity to the moment of one last, quiet sigh. Pain free.

In any case, begin by learning more about yourself and how you currently cope. Toward this end, several measures will be provided and others suggested.

Then you decide whether you need an intervention which is immediate, one that will prepare you for the future, or one meant to address historical matters. Set the goal of turning many of your new skills into new habits of health by developing a Conditioned Response. Change your brain, change your habits – that's what makes a conditioned response enduring.

Pavlov developed a conditioned response in dogs that learned to salivate to the sound of a bell. Humans, being smarter, can choose a skill of greater value. Most people in my clinical practice developed a conditioned response to Progressive Relaxation by using the technique twice a day for two to three weeks. Much smarter than salivating to a bell and more serviceable, wouldn't you agree?

Caveat: Smarter doesn't imply easier. Developing a Conditioned Response doesn't happen over night. There's work and time involved. That will be suggested and repeated because it is so pivotal. A Conditioned Response will require more work in the short term BUT it could save you a great deal of time and effort for the long haul.

Another Conditioned Response worth consideration is changing your worldview. The beauty of that effort is that your worldview is based on thoughts. That puts you in complete control. And almost everyone can find little steps of bad rhythm based on a negative perspective. Research throughout this book continually highlights the long-term benefits of dancing to the rhythm of hope, love, rewards, compassion, and gratitude. You'll learn that thoughts, alone, can change your brain architecture.

The initial work of identifying thoughts that hold you back might require the help of a good psychotherapist. Effective psychotherapy can be the best gift you ever give yourself. In any case, changing self-sabotaging thoughts could be a critical part of Ideal Aging™. Making the healthier thoughts new habits of thought can be especially empowering. Consider this in planning for peak performance in vigorous longevity.

Once you've chosen one technique to begin with, get started on rewriting the choreography of your dances for life. Learn how to reinforce change so it becomes self maintaining. Discover how you could act so your brain will resemble a "self-fertilizing garden." That could be a very good thing for Ideal Aging™ as you will see in the chapter **Smarter This Year**. Whenever information is clinical or speculative, I'll identify it. Otherwise, you'll find the scientist closely tied to his or her data.

Let your new dances begin.

PART B. FIVE DANCES TO LIVE FOR

Dance as if your life depends on it because it does. First appreciate how much you can do to improve your brain, improve your life! Now "plastic" is a wildly wonderful word.

Yes, of course, what you come into this life with makes a difference. But genetics only write about 50% of your life score. The choices you've made up to this point have had a great deal more to do with how much more you can do.

Now that you know that, you can plan ahead. It's never too early and never too late to have a positive influence on your brain. In the Introduction you learned how to Begin a Realistic Effort. That was Step 1. You also learned to measure where you are now. That was Step 2.

Part B expands the options you will organize at Step 3. You and your healthcare provider can be an awesome team in determining health and safety issues. Those take precedence. Let the dances of your life begin with **Brain Boost**—If it's Not Around, Why Am I? In some ways every component of this book could help you build a better brain. But this part will celebrate the brilliance of new neuroscience and tell you about how you can improve your brain's architecture. That will begin with the birthing of new brain cells (neurogenesis) and proceed with training old and new neurons to remain elegantly in service to you across your happy life. Part B discusses how you can be Smarter This Year.

Isn't it delicious to learn that developing the **Happy Habit** can improve all realms of your health? We have Martin E. P. Seligman and his colleagues to thank for vastly increasing research on how to develop enduring and authentic happiness.

An **Energy Elevator** could add to your quality of life. Maximum brain power and authentic happiness increase in value when you also have the energy to carry on.

Sex in seniors is another focus of increasing research. It's all good. **Sexual Saunter** is a dance of health.

We can look at **World Works** in terms of what each cell in you body needs. Equally important is considering spiritual, social, financial, philosophical and emergency perspectives. As your world turns for steady growth in all of these realms, remember to take measures of your progress so you can reinforce, reward and refine small steps along this evolving path.

Enjoy.

Student

Parent: "You can be really proud of yourself! I've seen you in action. You're very goal oriented. You study the situation, set a goal, decide on a strategy and work hard for long hours with little sleep. Not many people have the resources to do what you've done—such as completing 18 college credits in a quarter while maintaining a grade point average high enough to get into graduate school. You've given up a lot to get where you are. Hopefully, you are proud of yourself."

Student, softly: "Sometimes I just want to be normal."

(... after the shared chuckles subsided ...)

"I took a picture of my mailbox on a very sunny, beautiful day ... the mailbox I walked to every day to see if any school would take me ... and I made it my screen saver. Looking at that helps me remember how happy I am to get to do this work."

Phone conversation with a student accruing huge loans, March 2007.

1. BRAIN BOOST

Research at Harvard and Stanford showed that "this activity-dependent neurotrophin production formed more neural branches and connections, acting, in effect, like a self-fertilizing garden."
Lawrence C Katz, PhD and Manning Rubin in
Keep Your Brain Alive

The vast majority of this book on *Ideal Aging*™ could reasonably be in this section. Neuroscience is literally racing ahead like a house on fire, like a rabbit on hormones, like a tsunami, like free electrons in quest of bonding to another molecule of Truth, like reindeer circling the Earth to make all deliveries in one short night from a fat man in a red and white suit to every believer around the globe.

The most complex system in the universe is nestled between your ears. It's out of sight while it vigorously absorbs and emits more than any of the most stellar scientists even imagined possible until now.

To be Smarter This Year is no longer the gift of the very young. New research has identified many enhancers and suppressors of neurogenesis and neuroplasticity. And it shows that it is never too early and never too late to enhance your brain power.

There are two truths from research that work well together. They are complementary. On the one hand, research with post traumatic stress disorder (PTSD), shows that past trauma has residual effects on behavior and on the architecture of the brain.

On the other hand, a truism of research on aging states that, if you don't use it, you lose it. Does that mean that revisiting past horrors is the equivalent of "using" the memory which would make it persist? Not necessarily. Excellent research has found methods of harvesting the value of history and resolving much of the negative effects.

We are uniquely gifted to be alive in the age of instant information while research is focusing on defining optimal health. For example, research on the centenarians in Okinawa began in 1976 when the unusually high number of these elders was recognized in their own country. Only in 1995 did the World Health Organization recognize Okinawa as a World Longevity Region. Publications on the extraordinary health of these elders were only in Japanese. Translation of such research and internet access has hastened our shared education. More on this fascinating research will be presented later in this book.

Brain Boost integrates these perspectives. It will guide you through research on the most efficient ways of measuring what you have, showing you how to enhance your brain power, and teaching you how to move quickly away from whatever could suppress your best brain building efforts.

SMARTER THIS YEAR

"It's rather astounding when you think about it: a certain kind of sensory experience can permanently change the wiring in part of your brain!"
Lawrence C. Katz and Manning Rubin in
Keep Your Brain Alive

Goals

- Increase novel sensory combinations ... because that turbo-charges the brain cells you have by building a network of associations between more brain cells.

- Gather new learning throughout life ... because it's never too early and never too late to improve your brain which is highly plastic, can remodel synapses *at any age* and can give you peak brain function right up to your last quiet sigh.

- Fit neurobics into all daily routines ... because that can make your brain act like a "self-fertilizing garden" by stimulating neurons to create neurotrophins (their own brain food).

- Encourage growth of new brain cells ... because when you *replace* some of the ones you lost through disease, alcohol or other insults to your brain, they can thrive with proper stimulation.

- Stay engaged ... because social and intellectual networking improves your ability to cope with aging.

If I have a favorite chapter, this is it. In *Keep Your Brain Alive,* Katz and Rubin coined the term "neurobics" because neurobics can do for your brain what aerobics can do for your muscles. Giving your brain cells, the neurons, a workout as vigorous as aerobics can increase your brain power significantly. This chapter is a brief visit to the brilliance of their book with additional new research since that book was published.

I became fascinated with ways of changing brain architecture with the early writings of Marian Diamond and David Snowdon. They had shown that novelty and taking action on increasingly complex tasks were both critical to brain growth. Living in an enriched environment and actively doing things for new learning increases the branching and complexity of dendrites and spines of your brain cells.

Since learning this, I have entertained myself by inventing new and different ways to accomplish the same old tasks. For example, I'd try to pull the door with just sufficient force that, when I let go of it and rushed through, it would close and latch gently behind me. The measure of success was that I would make it through the doorway just before it would latch but not slam.

Sometimes I've been influenced by the struggles of others. Diane Schuur, "Deedles," is a famous jazz musician, winner of Grammies, guest more than once in the White House and palaces of kings, etc. Until you've heard her version of *Amazing Grace*, your musical experience is incomplete.

Deedles has been blind since birth. She accompanies herself on piano. Lovely woman with phenomenal talent. Just knowing her is enough to motivate higher levels of performance. Therefore, I occasionally shower with my eyes closed, walk around my home with no lights on, try to get the correct key into the right lock by touch alone, etc., attempting to experience being blind.

I learned to satisfy healthy brain growth, fitness, social connectedness and my green policy by simply taking buses. That's because I have a contract on myself. When I see the right bus, I get on and visit with other riders or read or think or write. Until I see the right bus, I keep walking. Some mornings I have gotten aerobically fit climbing a steep hill that is too many blocks long.

However, other mornings those same blocks have seemed longer and steeper than usual. I simply did not want to climb that hill! So I walked up hill backwards silently praying to the Cosmic Consortium: "Send the bus." If it came around the corner when I was close enough, I would run back downhill. Otherwise, I would rush uphill to the next bus stop. And I would be careful about when I admitted this to My Miracle Mate as the thought of such impropriety in business attire in the center of the city has tended to improve his posture too much. It was never part of my agenda to add to his duress.

Now that I've read the Katz and Rubin book, I can see that walking up a steep hill in the center of downtown could be considered neurobic. It required staying on the sidewalk without looking at it, not walking backward into people or traffic signs, not grazing a passerby with the briefcase in my arm that swung to the rhythm of my steps, stopping before the corner of the street, etc. These were all new and somewhat complex behaviors. It would be best if you just took my word for that rather than trying it. There's no need to create any unnecessary danger.

Katz and Rubin describe 83 neurobic exercises in their book. All of theirs seem safe.

Science behind your plan

At birth we have about twenty-three billion neurons. "Synapse" is the name of the connection between these brain cells. Until young adulthood the mass of the brain increases to nearly triple its size at birth.

Bear in mind that these statistics have been gathered on populations that have usually benefited from the stimulation of extended schooling and career changes en route to a young adulthood as sitters with, at best, armchair sports expertise.

One of the beauties of advancing technology is the increasing capacity to watch the brain at work with non-invasive techniques. A pioneer in this field, Richard Davidson, has been featured in *TIME* as one of the hundred most influential thinkers. For his innovative work, he uses electrophysiology, positron emission tomography (PET) and functional magnetic resonance imaging (fMRI) to study how the brain works, learns and changes. He is best known for his research on neuroplasticity.

"Over the hill around age X" is passé! It's much more accurate to think of aging, elegant, educated brains as having more filing cabinets that are filled with important information that's been distilled over the ages. Thus, elite skills are essential to appreciate and access the more vast accumulation of data.

Davidson collaborated with His Holiness the Dalai Lama in studying brain function in Buddhist monks who were highly trained in meditation. His research showed that their brains functioned differently when meditating. Also, when these individuals meditated, their brains functioned differently than the brains of less well trained individuals when they meditated.

Located behind the left side of your forehead is the left prefrontal cortex (left PFC). The left PFC is the part of your brain that regulates positive feelings like happiness and which causes you to approach the source of happiness. The left PFC showed the greatest change with deep meditation, especially in the monks who had extensive experience in meditation. Changes in the architecture of the PFC were noted subsequent to their years of practice in meditation.

Behind the right side of your forehead is the right PFC. That part of your brain is involved in handling emotions that are more distressing such as fear or disgust – feelings that cause you to withdraw. The limbic system is where the emotions originate. How they are expressed is regulated by many other structures. For example, the amygdala is important in processing emotions and memory. It's the "noise" generated by the activity of the many brain cells communicating among themselves that is studied by researchers such as Davidson.

What does all this have to do with Ideal Aging™? It disproves another popular myth that brain function declines steadily after early adulthood and that this is, in part, due to the death of brain cells. And this truth is much more complex while also being much more hopeful and empowering.

> Aging happens. Decline is optional.

Some of your most elegant brain cells have been with you all of your life. Most likely you have done at least three things to account for their elegance. You have nourished them well by Eating Smart so that the best nutrients were available in your system. You have Exercised Right to increase the circulation of these fine foods to your brain. Then you took an active role in learning-by-doing so your brain became a "self-fertilizing garden." As a result, your most elegant and long-lasting brain cells started out like upstarts on a new stage. They grew like healthy trees forming increasing numbers of complex *dendrites and spines*. Dendrites are branches of your brain cells. They accept new information, process it to form memories and create more *spines* which are like fruit hanging on their branches that help hold new memories.

As a result, the areas of your brain required for your area of expertise have gradually changed. Your brain has gone from the sparse nature of a field freshly planted with young saplings into a dense forest of neuron trees filled with the fruits of your labors as you continually acted on new learning. Nobody learned to dance by watching. It is moving your body to the sound of Mozart that causes the "self-fertilizing garden." It is fine-tuning the form of your dance to the Joy of Music that stimulates your brain cells to grow from little baby saplings at birth into the greater elegance that can come with Ideal Aging™.

Before you get the urge to drop this and put yourself down with any hint of a thought that you haven't done enough to nourish your brain cells into long elegance, remember:

<blockquote>
It's never too early and
Never too late
To turn your brain into a
"self-fertilizing garden."
</blockquote>

More on this after we revisit the rats.

Marian Diamond's research has shown increased branching and increased spines on the dendrites of neurons from rats housed in an enriched environment. Rats with toys and items they could voluntarily manipulate showed this brain growth. Rats in a neighboring cage—who could watch but had no opportunity to take such action—did not show brain growth.

Watching was not sufficient. Action was essential. We really owe it to legions of rats and other critters on this one. They have provided a model that encourages neurobics. If knowing this makes you want to be neurobic every day, that's terrific! It shows that you simply want more out of life.

The brain has special cells called glial cells. Glial cells give your brain structure. They provide support and nutrition for other brain cells. Diamond found a higher ratio of these glial cells to other normal brain cells in the brain of Einstein compared with men of average intelligence. This was also found in her rats which had benefited from living in the enriched environment.

The rate at which unused neurons are diminished varies considerably. Sickness, alcohol, some medications, malnutrition, hypertension, lack of exercise, depression and stress affect the rate of loss or shrinkage. The long held wisdom proclaimed that brain cells were particularly vulnerable to a rule of aging: "If you don't use it, you lose it." The research of Diamond and others sheds light on the other side of the brain portrait.

> Since the heart and soul of this book rests in positive psychology,
> I am happy to share another quote from Katz and Rubin:
> "The aging brain, however, continues to have
> a remarkable ability to grow, adapt, and change patterns of connections."

Doesn't that just make you eager to jump on whatever scientific evidence has shown will cause growth, adaptation and change at any age?!

Rats became more efficient learners after choosing to run on a running wheel. This was thought to be related to the effect of exercise in creating more brain food (neurotrophins). If that sounds like a contradiction in terms, this is how that works.

When you stimulate your brain cells by learning something new and by taking action with the new learning, it stimulates you brain to create nerve growth factors. These factors are called neurotrophins because they nourish your brain cells. Neurotrophins are essential for the formation of the new branching of dendrites and the new spines on the branching dendrites of your brain cells. This is one of the ways your actions send the message to your brain to GROW. And the more growth you cause through your learning and actions, the more you build a "cognitive reserve"—the term used to describe a form of insurance for coping with brain injury in the future and for a joyful, learned, vigorous longevity when you stay healthy and safe. It's all good!

Actually, the analogy of the aging brain to many well-filled filing cabinets is inadequate. A well-aged brain compares more easily to having a computer hard drive that is somewhat unlimited. The more files and folders you create in the memory of your hard drive, the more you need a sophisticated search tool to find the small details. At the same time, these files and folders can be cut, pasted, compacted and compensated. Communication between them is electric and at the speed of a few microseconds.

The more diverse and varied you build your complex spines and branches on your many dendrites, the more likely it is you will enjoy Ideal Aging™ with vigorous longevity. That's related to the fact that your brain is so plastic that it can learn to use other parts of your "cognitive reserve" if you are so unfortunate as to suffer some brain insult.

Your hippocampus, the part of your brain associated with learning and memory, seems to use two factors in deciding whether or not to store new information in memory. It looks for any emotional significance. It also checks to see if it is related to something you already know. Then it coordinates incoming information with the cortex of your brain. The cortex is what makes you unique. It handles memory, language, abstract reasoning and decision making, even your emotions. It has hundreds of specialized areas that are linked together by axons, the slender wiring that carries messages from one brain cell to the next. The bigger you build the network between these cells the easier it will be for your cortex to handle messages and association of messages.

Pavlov's dogs are the classic example of new associations. At the sight or smell of food it is normal for dogs to salivate. By ringing a bell at the same moment that food was presented—and repeating this for several days—Pavlov taught his dogs to salivate at the sound of the bell.

Neurobics is a similar process with a more humanly useful goal. By making new associations with as many senses as possible you improve your brain's power and flexibility. In part, that might be because your complex new associations add up to a smarter search engine for details you've put in storage.

So far the comments have focused on refurbishing the stage sets, lighting and wiring of those elegant brain cells that have continued to serve you well from Act I. Now it gets really exciting!

In 1998 Fred Gage found evidence of the creation of new brain cells in humans!

Gage studied the brains of people between the ages of 55 and 70 years old. At autopsy there were new brain cells in the hippocampus, the area of the brain involved in memory and learning. That startling news flew in the face of eons of believing differently. We were taught that the brain cells you had at birth were the only ones you would ever have. To make the stage darker, it was thought that you would lose most of those by disuse and/ or abuse. It was considered natural that the human brain only declines with aging.

Now it is suggested that new brain cells can be birthed at any age! And research by Gage and colleagues has shown exercise-induced neurogenesis in humans!

These new findings set the scientific community on fire to understand this delicious ray of new hope for human growth, repair and development. It has long been known that taking action to learn something new in an enriched environment will change the architecture of existing human brain cells. That means that what you do to acquire new learning will increase the elegance, size and storage capacity of the dendrites and axons on the neurons that you use. It also means that your active new learning could create some new synapses as well as influence how they communicate.

The findings of Gage added another exciting score to the neuron dance across the human lifespan—neurogenesis. Rats did it. Now humans are known to have done it as well. In fact, from hundreds to as many as ten thousand new nerve cells are birthed each day.

Neurogenesis includes the birth of new brain cells, determining what the cell's career will be, helping it grow to maturity AND keeping it healthy for Ideal Aging™. New research gives us increasing guidance on what all those stages of growth require.

Exercising Right and Eating Smart Deliciously on a daily basis influence all stages of the new brain cell's growth. It's enough to make me sleep soundly all night just knowing that restorative sleep is another way to enhance neurogenesis! Sleep deprivation suppresses neurogenesis.

However, even sleep research has yielded some surprises. Researchers in Italy found that gentle handling during "one night" of preventing sleep in rats significantly increased the number of surviving new brain cells "soon after sleep deprivation, as well as 15 days and 30 days later, in comparison to control rats that were allowed to sleep."

The results of that study are not presented here to encourage anyone to give up a night of sleep. However, in the event that this must occur, emphasize the role of gentle handling, even if you have to take that matter into your own hands.

Other ways of enhancing neurogenesis have been shown in animals. Aerobic exercise increased the number of new brain cells in rats. In a recent landmark study Gage and colleagues reported exercise-induced neurogenesis in living humans. This was found in the hippocampus, the part of the brain essential that is essential to memory and learning.

When compared to mice that could eat freely, mice that were only fed every other day did not create more brain cells. However, four weeks later more of their brain cells were still alive. Yeast, worms, zebrafish, flies, spiders, monkeys and rats lived longer with calorie restriction than when permitted to feed freely. The results are thought to be due to less age-related decline in immune function and to less production of inflammatory compounds.

It's not yet known how calorie restriction has an anti-inflammatory effect. It is suggested that increased measures of inflammation could be associated with the development of Alzheimer's dementia. That makes the survival of more neurons in mice with the combination of aerobic exercise and calorie restriction particularly compelling.

Scientists haven't discovered why about half of the new neurons die within a few weeks. In animals, good learners lose fewer cells than both slow learners and animals with no new learning.

Perhaps the best news of all is what rescues new cells from death. Learning does—and the more difficult the learning task is, the more cells are rescued according to research done at Rutgers.

Actively doing something in an enriched environment is essential for the survival of new brain cells. It also helps influence the job the new brain cell will have in your life. That suggests that some of the new neurons can be put into service in the area of our expertise. It is exhilarating to grasp how much we influence how our brain grows!

Neurobics are to your old and new brain cells what aerobics are to your overall health. Katz and Rubin suggest that you feed and exercise your brain cells in ways that encourage them to feed their own growth. That's how you turn your brain into a "self-fertilizing garden." That's how you grow bigger and more wiring and connections between brain cells for broader communication. That's how you build "cognitive reserve," the networking between brain cells that could give you peak brain performance across all stages of your life ... even to the last curtain call.

Novelty.

That word is so important to Ideal Aging™ that you can read more on it in many parts of this book.

Action.

Now do something for new learning because your aging brain is highly plastic. That means it has an amazing capacity to rewire itself, feed itself, grow, adapt and change patterns of how it makes connections *at any age* and in service to you as you influence it. That's deliciously empowering!

How to do it

Safety is the first factor. Confer with your healthcare provider. Know your environment well enough and assure that nothing compromises your safety.

In addition to smelling, hearing, seeing, touching and tasting, remember to include your emotions. So that's six senses you will be combining in new ways. Like physical cross-training that keeps your muscles fit and in balance, neurobics can help you enhance your overall brain fitness to make you Smarter This Year.

Use that last sentence two ways. Understand it as the early stage of creating a conditioned response or habit. As you strengthen the conditioned response, fewer and different brain cells will be active when you perform the new habit. These new brain cells will be more efficient and expedite this habit. Also understand that using fewer cells means that you will be creating fewer neurotrophins and not causing as much new brain growth. That is the core reason why novelty is essential for neurobics.

Your brain craves novelty. It thrives, nourishes itself and grows with novelty which includes doing some action to learn something new. The more complex the learning the better the impact on your growing brain.

Novelty is not Just dessert For your brain!

Creating new associations between behaviors and your six senses is the core of your neurobic program. That's how you will be making your "brain more agile and flexible overall, so it can take on *any* mental challenge, whether it be memory, task performance, or creativity" according to Katz and Rubin.

Once you try a new combination, continue it until it becomes easy, even automatic. Initially a wide array of brain cells and connections will be required for the new learning. This will create healthy new growth in your existing brain cells at the same time that it causes those brain cells to create more of the neurotrophins to feed themselves and their neighboring brain cells. This makes your brain cells stronger and more capable of Ideal Aging™. Once the novel combination of senses in this new learning becomes easy, your brain will change how it works. After you learn the new behavior, the brain activity shifts to different areas of your brain, uses fewer cells and is maintained without creating as many neurotrophins and new brain growth.

Try as many of the following examples as you wish. Then be as creative as safety allows in coming up with new ways of combining as many senses as possible to do old tasks in new ways.

Watching TV is passive. It is deadening to brain growth.

Remember, routines may save you time but they do not provide enough brain work for brain growth. Change your routines unexpectedly to make the most of your brain power. Remember that activity and novelty are both key to your success.

Smells. According to Katz and Rubin, what you learn associated with smells is learned quickly and lasts longer than associations with other senses. It's connected more directly with your cortex, hippocampus and other brain parts that process emotions and store memories.

Just imagining the smell of the turkey baking in the oven may flood you with many emotions. That's why baking a tray of cookies just prior to showing a home for sale is thought to improve the chances of selling and possibly even raise the final sales price to which the buyer will agree,.

Scent of a Woman is a terrific movie. In it Al Pacino provides a remarkable portrayal of a blind character whose sense of smell flooded him with complex memories.

Katz and Rubin suggest linking a new smell with the beginning of your day. Have a sealed container of mint leaves by your bedside. As you awaken, smell the mint. Brew a fresh cup of mint tea. Have that aroma with you in your shower.

Sounds. Without looking at the label on the CD try to identify the singer, the instrument playing, the melody, the harmony, etc. Listen to a story someone reads to you. Read a part in a play for readers' theatre. Learn to play an instrument. Learn a new language. Eat a meal in silence and listen to the sound of chewing, swallowing, etc. Start a conversation with someone you don't know and really hear what he says.

Sights. Go to work by a different route than usual. Get off the bus several stops ahead of where you want to end up. Use your memory of the lay of the land to take different turns so you see different things as you walk the distance. Notice how many people stayed on the bus, the color of the houses, the speed of the wings of the hummingbirds, the kinds of trees in the neighborhood, the brightness of the green grass, the number of bicycles along the way, the parents walking their children to school, the cloud formations, the ripeness of the blackberries, the trash that you can pick up and put in the nearest trash can, the yellow daffodils, the purple petunias, etc. If you make a wrong turn, that's a delicious opportunity to find your way home differently!

Touches. Showering or taking a bubble bath with your eyes closed is one example if that's safe in your bathroom. With your eyes closed, pick your clothes for the day. You can make it a silky smooth or rough knit day. You can tell them apart because they cause different brain activity patterns.

Katz and Rubin suggest keeping your eyes closed while using your fingers, cheeks, lips and feet for picking clothing because "they're all packed with receptors for fine touch." A fascinating study with monkeys showed increased brain growth in the areas controlling the fingers they used to get food. Similar findings with blind people reading Braille have been described. If being socially acceptable is important, lay your clothing out prior to your shower. After your shower, touch them with your feet, lips or cheeks to figure out which item adorns which part of your body.

Are you having fun yet? If so, refer to the chapter on laughter to see how much more you gain laughing as you go. And label the emotion. Katz considers emotions to be our sixth sense and critical for brain growth in neurobics.

Change hands for brushing your teeth, writing, combing your hair, opening envelopes, stirring the soup, etc. Change directions of the stroke of the brush as you apply makeup.

Tastes. Eat blindfolded. See if you can figure out the various seasonings. Try foods you've never experienced before. Go to a new ethnic restaurant and follow the chef's recommendations. Leave the salt out of your food. Add no sugar to anything. Try a new seasoning. As you will read in Eat Smart Deliciously, plenty herbs and spices have other health benefits in addition to neurobics.

My book on osteoporosis for teenagers will include protein drinks which taste better than milkshakes. So far I have fifteen flavors including one that tastes as good as your best cinnamon roll. Well, some say it tastes better because it has all of the flavor but it's healthy. All of these protein shakes are made with no fat and no sugar. If you have a favorite flavor you want included, please email it to **DrJoyce@StressPower.com**. Or just recommend one you think would be a good addition and I'll work on it.

Emotions. Your emotions can be your best guide. They improve learning and memory. Remember, the hippocampus of your brain uses the emotional parts of your experiences to decide whether or not to store new learning in your brain.

Create emotional experiences through the day. When someone visually impaired enters the bus, note how you feel about the person; the handicap; how the handicap affects them; about yourself; about the person who yielded a seat—or didn't yield; about watching the blind person find their way around the world without the benefit of sight which you might sometimes take for granted.

Watch the rare person racing around the gravel path barefoot. Imagine how that must feel. When I saw that, I couldn't take my eyes and ears away from the crunching sound beneath his bare, pink feet which looked too vulnerable for the pounding on sharp gravel.

Think of all the people you are grateful for and to. Refer to the chapter on Enduring Happiness. Imagine who you will write your gratitude letter to and look forward to reading it to them.

Novelty and combinations. Can you share the excitement of Katz and Rubin as they write: "It's rather astounding when you think about it: a certain kind of sensory experience can permanently change the wiring in part of your brain!"

> It is new and unexpected combinations of your six senses in action that can rewire your brain..

So, start your day to the sound of Mozart and the scent of lilacs with your eyes closed throughout your shower and dressing while you laugh with gratitude about your ability to choose … then study the new Ideal Aging™ you in the mirror to see how well you've managed without sight … just in case some material needs adjusting before you show your Joy to the World.

On another day, close your eyes as your reach in the refrigerator to find something suitable for breakfast. See if you can guess what you are eating before you open your eyes. Take turns with your mate being the one with your eyes closed and see if you can guess what you are being fed.

My surrogate grandmother gave me a recipe for Six-Week Bran Muffins. If the dough is handled properly, she said it could last in a refrigerator for up to six weeks. That's a lovely aroma to awaken to. And they are more healthy that the average bran muffin!

This is a modification of the recipe give to me by "Grandma" Velda Turnidge. I'm sharing it here to honor the lovely, compassionate woman who brought so much joy into the lives of so many people. I have not tested whether it will last up to six weeks. My family likes these so much that the batch has always been baked and consumed before that much time could pass—even though the recipe was doubled. We've enjoyed the freedom to dip into that large bowl of batter and have fresh muffins on a whim.

6-Week Multi-Bran Muffins

Mix together and let cool:

    2 cups boiling water
    5 teaspoons baking soda

Cream together:

    1 cup Olive Oil
    1 cup Sugar
    4 eggs

To the creamed ingredients, add and mix well:

    ½ cup wheat germ
    ½ cup oat bran
    ½ cup Soy flour
    3 ½ c Whole Wheat flour
    1 tablespoon salt
    1 quart nonfat buttermilk

Add the cooled soda water mixture to this mixture and stir well.

Stir in:

    4 cups All Bran
    2 cups cereal flakes with the highest fiber content you can find
    2 to 2 ½ cups chopped dates
    1 to 1 ½ cup chopped English walnuts

Store in tightly covered container in refrigerator – reportedly lasts for up to 6 weeks if you remember to NOT STIR this batter and take only from the top. That's not been tested.

TO BAKE:

    Spoon into greased muffin tins WITHOUT STIRRING.
    Bake at 375° Fahrenheit for 20 to 22 minutes.

Paper muffin cups in lieu of greasing the muffin tins makes them more portable. It is so easy to bake 6 or 12 and share with neighbors and friends.

These are also a set up for neurobics via novel combinations. First thing out of bed in the morning put a filled muffin tin in the oven and enjoy the aroma of fresh baked goods filling the room while you are doing your morning exercises. That combines the smell of healthy food with healthy physical fitness. Add your emotional sense by feeling pride in your accomplishment at the beginning of the day. If your exercise is aerobic, add the visual image of birthing new brain cells. Smell, touch, emotions plus sight—you've just combined four of your six senses while your day is still young. If this is also the day you are aerobic to the sound of music, you have it all by the time you are savoring the novel taste of your freshly baked muffins.

As other examples, with the window open as you learn a new dance step, notice the smell of fresh falling rain. Inhale the fragrance of lilacs in spring, or whatever fragrant blossoms there are in your part of the country, as you learn to pedal your bicycle while standing up.

Walk randomly around your neighborhood following the sights, smells and sounds that attract you. One day I did that for so many hours that I wasn't certain how to get out of the neighborhood I'd not seen before. All I knew was that I had walked about three miles south, another mile or so east, maybe six miles north, probably three miles west AND…the thought of taking even one step in the wrong direction after all that distance was quite unappealing! I asked the first person I saw which way to walk to get back to the Crossroads Mall. The poor man was so alarmed he could hardly mumble, "Oh! That's too far! You can't walk there from here!" My feet and legs agreed with him. My mind knew I was Car-less in Bellevue. So I described the circuitous route I'd just walked. He told me where to go. I owe him a gratitude letter!

Take a different bus route.

One day I was on a bus. The bus driver drove past the usual stop at Park & Ride. I thought that was weird. I knew it was weird when she signaled a left turn at the next traffic light. Realizing her error, she had decided to drive down through the parking lot and up the other side so as to not leave any riders stranded at the bus stop. Compassionate she was. A problem she created!

She was driving one of the long articulated buses. The parking lot was full to brimming over! After it was too late to back out, she realized our bus was trapped. As she let us off the bus, I requested that she radio ahead to be certain the next bus remain at this bus stop, if necessary, as the young man in the wheelchair had an important medical appointment. He wheeled around unfamiliar territory to find the flat access uphill to the bus stop while I ran straight up some flights of steps to be sure to catch the next bus. As we rode away on the next bus, I heard the bus driver say into his radio, "Yes, I got the wheelchair. But did you know there's an articulated bus at the base of the Park & Ride lot?"

Katz and Rubin suggest using lovemaking as the "ultimate neurobic workout." Novelty can enhance sexual arousal. They suggest letting your imagination go wild with all senses. "… wear silk, strew the bed with rose petals, burn lavender incense, have chilled champagne, massage with perfumed oils, put on a romantic CD … and whatever else turns you on."

> "To think that a good sexual encounter also helps keep the brain alive
> is almost too good to be true. But it is;
> more than most 'routine activities,'
> sex uses every one of our senses and,
> of course, engages our emotional brain circuits as well."
> Katz and Rubin in Keep Your Brain Alive (italics theirs)

After sex, your computer pales in comparison, agreed? Fewer senses involved, But don't underestimate your computer. It is unique in its capacity to facilitate brain growth.

The computer gives immediate reinforcement for correct responses. It provides endless opportunities for new learning. Some simple games give large bonus scores to reinforce for speed. Playing them to raise your score can improve your reaction time on skills used in that game. Spend time learning new software for your computer.

There is a term in brain science that is worth learning. "Long-term potentiation" or LTP is the change in the synapses, the places where one brain cell exchanges messages with a neighboring brain cells.

With the right conditions, when a synapse has had enough repetitions, you "get it." Thereafter, that synapse more easily exchanges information with neighboring brain cells. It is amazingly strengthened in its response. That is LTP. No one knows why LTP lasts a long time. It is part of learning and memory. It is the stuff of getting messages between brain cells easily in microseconds.

New memories might result from the new connections between these brain cells. It might even result in the formation of new neurons.

The same things you do to create LTP also tell your brain to increase the neurotrophins that your brain cells need to survive and thrive. The LTP is part of the building of the net of associations between many brain cells to increase how flexible your brain is. The neurotrophins might help protect brain cells from damage from such things as a stroke or brain injury.

46 • Ideal Aging

This means that the things you do to improve how your brain works today and tomorrow might also be seen as a form of insurance. At the same time you are causing brain growth, you are causing your brain cells to create a form of protection against damage. The more LTP the better insurance you've purchased.

Measuring Goals

By keeping track of when and what you do for novel and complex changes in behavior, you will be more aware of how much you are stimulating your brain. Your goal is to turn your brain into a "self-fertilizing garden" so it will increase in complexity, flexibility and adaptability as long as you focus on new learning. This means that you will continually add activities with new learning every day of your life and change your neurobics frequently to Keep Your Brain Alive.

This form can help you monitor your wise choices.

Day & Date	New activity & new association with sense(s) Smell Sound Sight Touch Taste Emotion

Summary

This might be the hottest topic on Earth! It certainly is for me. It is delicious that you can put together novel sensory experiences and actions to change your brain for the better. You have always influenced your brain architecture. Now you can make a plan based on science that could build a better brain! The newest research shows that the brain is highly plastic. This plasticity means that it can rewire to adapt to change at any age. Your ability to rewire your brain means that you play a much more important role in defining your unique Ideal Aging™ than was ever known until recently. Just by reading and pondering what you have read thus far has gotten this rewiring process started. This is a good thing.

> It's never too early and never too late to "permanently change the wiring in part of your brain."

Being intentional and strategic about how you rewire your brain could elevate you to a new level of peak performance. What is peak performance? My personal prediction is that new definitions of Ideal Aging™ will evolve. More people will take increasing control over how they age. The information explosion, computer software and brain-plasticity-based models of learning will markedly increase human potential and enhance vigorous longevity. Research is already in progress in this realm.

This chapter ties in neatly with the one on Conditioned Responses. Choose the new learning that you want to make permanent. Associate it with smell because it will be learned quickly and the memory will last a long time. Also associate it with strong positive emotions. Emotions cue your hippocampus to store the new learning in long term memory.

This book teaches you to use positive emotions because they are associated with better health. See the chapters Connect, Enduring Happiness, Laughter and many others for a review of the benefits of positive aging. Associate your new learning with all six senses: seeing, hearing, smelling, tasting, touching and emotions.

Just add one or two neurobic activities one day at a time. Those other "routine" activities probably help you get through the day more efficiently. As soon as your new neurobic becomes easy, keep practicing it until it becomes automatic as a conditioned response. That's sort of like an auto-responder or a default option.

Meanwhile, create a new combination. Have fun! Positive emotions are particularly cost effective here because they improve memory and learning.

And remember: Many of your brain cells have become longer and more elegant as you have learned the many dances of life. Keep improving the ways that you cherish and nourish the elegance and the continued growth of these neurons throughout all stages of Ideal Aging™.

Celebrate Randomly that it is never too early and never too late to Build Better Brains. Put this information together with Daniel Goleman's theory that our emotions are "contagious" between brains when we Connect. That means that including positive people in your novel combinations of new sensual learning can make brain building more of a community affair than we had formerly guessed. In fact, Goleman suggests that we broaden our sense of social responsibility to include this awareness.

What a gift this Information Age is! What a gift to be alive in the age of technology. How fortunate we are to know more about how to enhance neurogenesis, neuroplasticity, long term potentiation and other factors of neuroplasticity. How empowering it is to be at the forefront of research identifying how to drive these factors to positive outcomes at any age.

I confess. I'm not a King-Arthur-era type. The rising tsunami of data about neuroplasticity for positive outcomes is better food than chocolate!

Smarter This Year requires active, complex, new learning and
such things as a surprise around every bend.
These are some of the unique individuals
who spent the entire year 2000 on a bicycle trek (O2K)
that went into and out of 45 countries on 6 continents
averaging 80 miles of pedaling per day ... because it required all of the above
and more.

Len Beil: I went to Seattle University on a basketball scholarship; graduated with a Bachelor of Commercial Science; and earned an MBA in marketing at University of Oregon. When I was 54 in 1999 I took early retirement from Seattle University where I was the Executive Assistant to the president. I quit my job to go on my dream bicycle trip around the world in 2000.

A day before Christmas in 1993 I received a flyer announcing an around-the-world bicycle trip in 2000! I sent in my deposit five days later and was second by one day to sign up, six years in advance. I think I made the best $29,000 investment ever for that trip. I also raised about $125,000 for minority and single parent scholarships at Seattle University for the trip. I decided to go for the adventure of a lifetime. And it was all of that!!!

Ideal Aging™ requires both setting goals and living one day at a time. I set goals annually in: Relationships; Marriage; Work; Education; Finance; Travel; Health/Physical; Material Things; and Community Involvement. While keeping these goals in mind as my compass, I work at living each day to the fullest. I strive to make a difference in the world by helping others and being a good citizen. I do extensive volunteer, board and church work. I feel blessed to have good health and wonderful loving and supportive family, friends and community.

Stell is a wonderful wife, friend and companion. We were married in June 2001. We rode around the south island of New Zealand on our honeymoon later that year. While we are both retired we are both very active as Master Gardeners, Mentors for Master Gardeners, and active volunteers at our parish. Ideal aging™ is being able to continue to grow and do the things you love. It is living a balanced life mentally, spiritually, emotionally, and physically. It is being excited about life, being thankful for today and yesterday and hopeful and confident in tomorrow. It is being in control of my life and what I do. Do all you can to take good care of the body, mind and spirit God has given you. Exercise, read, challenge yourself mentally and physically and give back to the community. Love deeply your family and friends; reach out to them when they are in need and be open to family and friends helping you when you are in need. Find your passions and follow them whether it is reading, biking, hiking, starting a new career or whatever.

Jane Hostvedt: I grew up in Wisconsin in a middle class, supportive family. At 18 years old I fell in love, got married and had a baby. Not necessarily in that order. I became a single mom after 13 years of marriage. I have not re-married. My career was in banking. In 1986, I started a mortgage business, owned and ran it for 15 years and sold it to a bank in 2002. I am still working for the bank that bought my company. My daughter is now 35 years old.

I cycled everywhere as a kid but then work, raising a daughter and other life things got in the way. I started cycling again at the age of 40. I am in a Rotary club that supports an organized bike ride called the Courage Classic. It is a 3-day, 3-mountain pass ride that raises money for Mary Bridge Children's hospital. After accepting a dare to ride it the following year, I bought a bike and trained for that ride. I enjoyed my reconnection with a bicycle so much that I just kept riding. The organizer of the Courage Classic was also putting together the O2K ride. I received, in the mail, a brochure, about O2K. It said "Ride 20,000 miles in the year 2000, around the world". That was in 1996. I had successfully raised my daughter, financially gotten her through college, started a mortgage company and worked many, many hours as a self-employed, single mother. **It was my turn.** My turn to do something fun and really big, just for myself. I wrote for more information and sent in my non-refundable deposit within a week.

Ideal Aging™ includes good health mentally and physically. Live a balanced life. Do exercise that you enjoy daily, get enough rest, and eat healthy, natural food. Keep in touch with friends and family, i.e., phone calls and hugs. Keep your heart open to love and your mind open to learning new things. Be happy and have a little red wine

Joan Irwin: Born in Wyoming to missionary parents with the Arapaho Indians, I lived on a reservation until age 5 when we moved to Long Island, NY. I was raised in a three generational family with my father's parents. After marriage and four children, I attended college including earning a PhD in Psychology. In addition to Private Practice I worked in assorted institutions with geriatric psychiatric patients; mentally retarded and autistic residents in a developmental center and a Special Education Program.

In late 1999 I sold my home, downsized and took off on O2K to see the world from the saddle

Smarter This Year • 51

of a bike! In 1995 I had seen a documentary on a group of disabled cyclists who were taken on a trip around the world, and I thought how cool it would be to find a trip for "Senior" cyclists around the world. The following year a friend shared a copy of the League of American *Bicyclists'* magazine, and there was an ad for O2K. I made some inquiries, and a decision to go for it. I didn't need much persuasion. It was a leap of faith.

Ideal Aging™ would be defined as maintaining my spirit of adventure with health and vitality, and keeping on exploring for new experiences, even in the face of the usual stuff life throws at us. In order to do this, I need to care for my body, (good food, exercise, vitamins, red wine.) I need to keep on learning, creating something, being with family and friends whenever possible, and continuing to have fun.

At age 71 I decided to move to the Black Hills of South Dakota and start a new business, a Hostel in the town of Lead. I found a fabulous home where I live, and take in visitors from all over the world. **MainStreetManorHostel.com** has details. I volunteer as a Board Member for the Historic Homestake Opera House, which we are restoring, and for the Historic Lead/Deadwood Arts Council promoting a variety of Arts in the area. I still cycle and ski, and play a little tennis. I have taken a renewed interest in reading philosophy, and a new interest in quantum physics. I like to read biographies of famous people who inspire me. Movies and theatre have long been a passion. I hope to do more bike touring in the off-seasons, when tourism is light. Bike tours have always been a turn-on, and some of the most fun I've ever had. I've met great friends who continue to be in my life.

Jim Higbee: This is my family at the finish line and the completion of my 20,371 mile dream of riding around the world. It had been my dream since 6th grade to ride the world.

Bicycling became a part of mine and my family's life. Just 8 riders rode the entire 20,000 miles as advertised on Odyssey. To do so required riding the optional rides on our days off. Sometimes 14, 18, or even 20 days straight in the saddle. We helped each other, encouraged and bolstered each other on. Trueheart (the youngest rider on O2K) rode a double with racer Bob on the last day to help Racer Bob get in. Bill Bliss and I did it by riding all the designated O2K routes on days off. Even though I was successful in business and have a wonderful family, for 35 years bicycling and logging miles was how I measured life. Now that I am paralyzed (from an accident after the O2K), life is measured in how much energy there is in my body on any given day just to be with my family and their activities. My aging now is so much affected by my paralysis of body, not the healthy mind.

Recently I started a travel business out of my home office. A wide variety of travel needs can be booked at very competitive prices at **YTBTravel/Jim53**.

Jim McDonald   Ideal Aging™ is being able to get older without losing basic functions of mind and body. It is my firm belief that both are tied to physical fitness and proper diet. My advice is therefore to eat a "healthy diet" which along with vigorous exercise keeps you at the recommended weight for your height and body type. Along with the exercise and weight control, exercise your mind by studying topics that you have an interest in. You can learn more about who I am and why I did the O2K at
www.spotsworldtour.com/whoami.htm.

Diane Sumter

Diane earned a BS in Exercise Gerontology from the Pennsylvania State University in 1991. She is a certified fitness instructor. Her undergraduate research project looked at flexibility, ability and balance in women over the age of 50 participating in low impact aerobics vs. water aerobics. Her interest in helping the elderly population maintain independence and health has lead her to pursue a career in Occupational Therapy. After the O2K bicycle ride around the world, she got carted to the altar in a rickshaw pulled by a bicycle pedaled by her father.

Pat Hansen: There must be some truth to the saying "life starts after 40". Having finished raising my family, I set out to pursue my dream of working for an airline and seeing the world. I spent 11 years with Alaska Airlines, working in various positions and eventually being chosen for one of their highest awards "Legend of the Year".

Thinking I had fulfilled my dream, along came another one. An opportunity came to me in the year 2000 to go around the world covering 44 countries, 6 continents and 365 days. I was a key staff person for Odyssey 2000 keeping tract of 247 cyclists for one full year.

The energy generated from Odyssey 2000 led me to start a non-profit organization called "Emerald City Lights Bike Ride". I designed a bike route and a fun filled day for cyclists to be a part of helping to feed families in need. As we go in to our 3rd year we have fed over 50 families, over 200 adults and children. My passion in the years ahead is to be able to feed a family each day and promote good health through exercise and organic eating. I look forward to devoting myself to this endeavor full time when I retire next year at the age of 66.

From emails of peripatetic pedalers.
There were 247 riders plus staff and volunteers on the O2K; profiling more of them is for another book.

CREATE CONDITIONED RESPONSES

*"As a physiologist who has studied stress for many years,
I clearly see that the physiology of the system is often
no more decisive than the psychology… We are uniquely smart enough
to have invented these stressors and uniquely foolish enough
to have let them, too often, dominate our lives.
Surely we have the potential to be uniquely wise enough to banish their stressful hold."
Robert Sapolsky, PhD in Why Zebras Don't Get Ulcers, 3rd Edition*

Goals

- Find out what reinforces you … so you can use that to learn new behaviors

- Identify high value reinforcement … so you can begin what you have delayed

- Learn how and when to reinforce effectively … to increase the intensity, frequency and duration of desired behaviors

- Develop your unique system of reinforcement … to create Conditioned Responses

- Build self-reinforcing statements into your self-talk … because that gives you 24/7 access to positive self-empowerment

The focus of this chapter is on recognizing strengths in the conditioned responses you already have. It is anticipated that you will want to change some of those and add some new ones. We'll also look at how conditioning takes place. In the **Chill** chapter you can learn how to create a cued conditioned relaxation response. It warrants a whole chapter because it one of the most broadly applicable skills.

A friend of mine was writing a paper on obesity. He said that obese individuals should avoid grocery shopping close to when they had eaten because they would tend to buy more groceries, eat more food and gain more weight. These obese individuals were said to have a "response inhibition deficit." That means that once obese people got started on a particular behavior, they didn't stop as readily as non-obese folks.

Was that ever a relief! All along I had thought that my obesity was a result of trying to regain my dear Grandma by ingesting the entire world of food. That Freudian perspective had fueled guilt for years. Now, at last, I was free of that torment. My obesity was simply a behavioral style. "No wonder I'm obese," I reasoned. "I'm just doing what obese people do."

And then I remembered. I'm a Cognitive Behaviorist. I teach people how to change thoughts and behaviors.

Oh.

Science behind your plan

Therefore, I created a handout for my clients. It started with the medical model of pathology.

Problems of self-control usually fall into one of two categories. Either a person engages in a behavior pattern that is self-defeating or injurious, such as eating patterns leading to obesity, workaholism, excessive smoking or drinking or other form of drug abuse, aggressive behavior, or indiscriminate and/or impulsive sexual behaviors. Or a person suffers from lack of self-control from engaging in certain behaviors only very infrequently such as inability to study, the failure to initiate social contacts, a low frequency of helping others, not being assertive and sexual inactivity.

That's half of the truth. The other half is celebratory.

Celebrations can be free. People find time to do what they really want to do. They want to do what they enjoy. They enjoy doing what they do well. This might be a good time for you to go to **AuthenticHappiness.org** and take the VIA Character Strength Survey. It measures 24 character strengths. After you complete the survey, you will learn what your signature strengths are. Look at the top three. You can return to the website episodically to review and re-measure.

It is a source of delight to measure your strengths, to enjoy using them at every opportunity and to enhance them. Building buffering strengths has become the backbone of my clinical work. It is delicious to have the increasing database on techniques associated with lasting happiness. See the chapter on **Enduring Happiness** for more of those details.

Positive Reinforcement will be explored. It's important to remember that learning new behaviors is not an overnight miracle. You will need to continually practice and work until you know you have a conditioned response. Then you'll have to persist with practice and work episodically in order to establish LTP. That is essential to maintain the new behavioral pattern. Once you develop a Conditioned Response, it will happen as automatically as washing your hands after using the bathroom. Do you remember how long it took for you to first learn that?

The first focus is on types of reinforcement. Then the effects of different ways of reinforcing behaviors for change will teach you how to effectively use reinforcement.

The most basic part of self control is you reinforcing yourself. That's worth restating differently. Behavior which is reinforced is repeated. Whatever immediately follows a behavior that is repeated is the reinforcement or reward.

Watch an amateur comedian. As soon as laughter follows his words, the comedian says it again. Watch someone tell a great joke that gets tons of laughs. He might repeat the punch line or launch into another joke.

I had the pleasure of telling the stellar urologist, James Gottesman, that part of his healing power was his capacity to elicit giggles. He grinned as he immediately leaned against the wall and did several additional hilarious one-liners!

Study your behavior. Are you more responsive to the reinforcement of material goods? Or to other people's reactions? Or to what you think? Over time increase your reliance on what you think because it's free, you are in total control of your thoughts AND you're the only person who will ever be available to you 24/7 for the rest of your life.

Watch a trained animal or even a pet. Isn't it amazing what they'll do for a pat on the head, scratch on the tummy or a biscuit?

There is a quote in this book (aren't you going to tell them what it is or tell them where to look for it?) of the individual appreciating the power of aerobic exercise. It shows the power of self-talk. We will focus on what you say to yourself because it's free, easy and completely under your control.

Using the BARE BONERS process, you may discover that you have not been using reinforcement to your best advantage. You may have been defeating your own best efforts when you do not give yourself a reinforcement of sufficient value. Restated in the positive, you strengthen your LTP most efficiently when you give yourself a realistic reward of significant value as determined by your standards and resources.

Self-improvement behaviors fit in this category. I've seen people devour 600 calories in high-fat, high-sugar foods in just a few minutes. It takes an hour of extreme exercise to burn off 600 calories. Most people don't burn it off.

Downing the food is usually its own immediate reinforcement because of the pleasure in the taste, texture and smell. After a few minutes you also have the joy of fullness.

Exercise is immediate pleasure only if you recognize the benefits and label them. For example, re-read the quote (where is it?) of the friend appreciating aerobic exercise. The conversation (what conversation?)reveals many uses of reinforcement through expectation of positive results, labeling them when they occurred and sharing the sense of well-compensated achievement so that the social reinforcements added value to your efforts to change.

There's little if anything to be gained by thinking that self-control is simple will power or backbone. People who appear to have no difficulties in most areas of self-control may be seen as "strong." However, it must be stressed that what those individuals possess is not strength or moral fiber, but rather a *fortunate learning history that empowers them, probably with little effort, to behave in self-enhancing rather than self-defeating ways.*

If you're one of those people, congratulations! Celebrate your gift of a healthy learning history.

The problem with the person with less self-control is usually not that they are putting in too little effort. Rather they simply have not yet learned to use the most effective tactics.

Some years ago a fine, intelligent young man came in to get help. He had not been able to get himself to do regular exercise although he could list the reasons why he should. He wanted to do exercises! He was putting himself down regularly for NOT improving his physical fitness with exercise.

We started there. Books to read were part of his homework assignments. He learned more.

After a few sessions on becoming more accepting of himself, he burst out, "Look! I've had it with changing my self-talk so I like myself better. I just need to do the exercises."

"Excellent insight! Let's change our approach to this. Tell me your daily routine?"

Every day he got up, fed and groomed his horse, went to work, returned to the home for dinner then fed and groomed his horse again. On questioning, he was clear that the horse would come to no harm if it were groomed only once a day.

"Great," I said. "I think it might be helpful for you to make a contract with yourself. For example, you could contract that you would feed and groom the horse as usual in the morning, go to work and, on returning home, you would only be allowed to attend to the horse in the evening if you earned that privilege by doing your exercises."

His posture visibly improved. "Sounds a bit Draconian to me!" he growled.

"Well, then. There it is! I think we've got it," I said as I made a mental note to go home and look up Draconian. That word never came up on the kidhood farm but his posture changes had said tons.

He was visibly happier the next visit because he kept his contract. The reward of tending his horse twice each day was too high in value for him to give it up.

Telling yourself that you lack will power is a real downer. That's compounding negatives. Too many other people will do that to you. Increase the positive value of the reinforcement. It's more effective. It's more fun. That's a better score for your dance of life for Ideal Aging™. It'll give you a more positive Subjective Units of Feelings Index (SUFI) Report. Once it becomes a conditioned response, go on to new learning. If possible, do some of the learning on a computer. It could more efficiently rewire your brain for better functioning because computer learning provides immediate reinforcement for the correct responses and is nonjudgmental.

How to do it

The BARE BONERS process is critical here. For example, if adding aerobics on a daily basis is your realistic goal, measure what you are doing now.

Begin – today. Tomorrow never comes. Ideal Aging™ starts now.

Set time on   Monday   _____
              Tuesday   _____
              Wednesday   _____
              Thursday   _____
              Friday   _____
              Saturday   _____
              Sunday   _____

A

Realistic – Do you have recent medical clearance to do aerobics?

Schedule 5 minutes to warm up then 5 minutes to stretch, 30 or more minutes at an aerobic pace, and 10 to cool down and stretch.

Or schedule an amount of time that equals your average last week.

Effort starting with what your baseline activity is. _____

Baseline – How many minutes were you aerobic yesterday? _____

How many minutes were you aerobic last week? _____

On average, how many minutes were you aerobic last month? _____

Options – Will you start with a brisk walk?   _____
             Or stair climbing?   _____
             Or a machine?   _____

Create Conditioned Responses • 59

Alone? _____
With a buddy? _____

N ow do it. Do it now. Pick 1 or more options and repeat daily for 2+ weeks

E valuation—same measures as Day #1

R einforce, Reward, Refine—to strengthen permanent changes.

S ame thing from the beginning with as little as a 5% increase per week.

This is critical timing for an essential question: If you're not doing it now, what accounts for that? _____

Years ago I bought a pair of exercise leotards thinking that would make it more likely I would get on my exercise machine. But I noticed I wasn't putting them on. So I put them on as soon as I was out of bed each morning. At the end of the day I removed them and went to bed without doing any exercise. I made a contract on myself: The exercise tights could not come off of my body until after exercising. So I slept in them. Can we agree that this was going nowhere?

On reflection it was clear that my *To Do* List was too enticing for me to even get on the machine once I was awake. "Well, then. There it is!" First thing in the morning, roll over, go the bathroom, get on the machine and wake up later.

That worked.

Adding multiple choice to activities I did during the time on the machine strengthened it: read, listen to a new CD with earphones, meditate, phone somebody who didn't mind heavy breathing … in short, either entertain myself or work on the
To Do list while the aerobic time flew to the rhythm of my dancing limbs.

Fortunately or unfortunately, sometime I lose track of time while on an exercise machine. I've been known to stay much longer that I had planned … even for over an hour.

Like the quote earlier in the book (what quote, there have been lots of them), during times of special grief it was labeling the benefits of exercise that got me on the machine and held me there. Here are some examples of things to say to yourself to get started and stay aerobic. Say them out loud to increase their power.

"I only have to keep the rhythm about ten minutes for my brain to be more clear."

"Good for me! My brain is working better."

"I've done 10 minutes; it's only about 12 more minutes 'til my mood lifts."

"I'm getting my antidepressant."

"I'm working off the chemistry of stress."

"There's a lion in front of this machine and that's my lunch."

"I've been doing this long enough to improve my heart health."

"I'm increasing my insulin resistance."

"My mitochondria are burning fat right off my body even as I read."

"Aerobic people have more fun."

"I'm building a level of fitness that will help me bicycle longer distances."

"Well, my stars! I lost track of time. I've been here 43 minutes. I'll stay two more."

"I'm aerobic 40 minutes four times a week; that could increase new brain cells!

Since reinforcement is the factor that will make this self-maintaining, these are some examples of two different categories of reinforcement.

Examples of Nonverbal Reinforcement

Smile of approval	Being seen	Listening with earphones
Being heard	Novelty	Minutes alone with someone special
Individual attention	Food	Being watched
Ruffle hair	Hug	Being listened to
Being helpful	Kiss	Good book
Accumulate points	Artwork	Pat on head or back
A few minutes alone	Work	Having a party
Company for dinner	Travel	Being asked
Making something	Choices	Choosing the reinforcer
Sharing	Seeing it	Using the reinforcer
Visiting a library	Planning	Following through
Painting	Reading	Being read to
Touch	Novelty	Making models
Eating	Modeling	Drawing
Something new	Cooking	Eating out

One of the nonverbal reinforcements has so much more power than the others that it is repeated above. See if you can find it here. It also is a focus in **Smarter This Year** and other chapters.

Sometimes people get stuck on the nonverbal rewards. They do have their value. However, it is far more powerful in the long run to acknowledge, use and accentuate the verbal and social reinforcement. Reliance on verbal rewards is especially critical when you are home alone with best thoughts. These are a few examples.

Examples of Social Reinforcement – Verbal

I really appreciate your willingness to …   … ride the bus with me.

It's very generous of you to …   … rearrange your calendar to do aerobics with me!

You're doing just what I asked, so …   … we'll be finished work early.

Measuring Goals

These are built into the BARE BONERS process. Keeping a chart helps. Use the one in the **Exercise Right** chapter.

Summary

Conditioned Responses you've learned across your life have allowed you to put much of your life on auto pilot. You can think of them as time savers. This is good. Frees up those long elegant brain cells of yours for new learning, new dance steps. Sets you free to roam the bigger stage, take the curtain calls, learn new dances, put those new steps on auto responder, glide with glee and count on the furniture to be moved as if by stage hands.

By reflecting on how long you spent perfecting some of those dance steps into your routine you can appreciate that your new Conditioned Responses will require your same careful attention initially. Brain imaging shows that new learning involves many different parts of your brain. These parts of your brain become quiet once a behavior becomes automatic. That means that every time you create and maintain conditioned responses you increase your brain power and enhance your elegant brain cells.

Start with small steps. You will repeat them until that critical moment when you've created LTP. Then they happen automatically. Little if any thought will be required at that point. The new behaviors will have become your default options, your auto responder.

Once you've become conditioned, the initial work is done. You'll be eons ahead of Pavlov's dogs because you will have chosen a conditioned response for its use in Ideal Aging™ because you simply want more out of life.

Those benefits can prevail with episodic rewards, reviews and refinements. You will have changed your brain and changed your habits. This is one of many ways you can be older and wiser.

By pairing the new learning with emotions you will strengthen it. Recall that your hippocampus, the part of your brain involved in learning and memory, uses your emotions in deciding whether or not to put the new learning in memory.

Have fun. It will enhance your new learning. So, enjoy the learning of the dances.

Lisa Dufour

Senior Deputy Prosecuting Attorney and TV Producer

I feel really good about what I do because I represent children. Previously in TV I focused a lot on children's programming. My interests haven't changed but I'm just working at them from a different angle.

My definition of Ideal aging™ includes keeping your interests alive, feeling vibrant, being able to focus on what you can do to help others. I try a couple of times a year to make a list of where I want to be in a few years and what I want to accomplish. Writing things down helps focus on what you're doing with your time.

I want to spend quality time with my husband and children. I want to continue working in a fulfilling area, probably still focusing on women and children and do volunteer work.

I want to travel more to exotic locations. We've been to China, Cambodia, Egypt, Greece, Turkey, Singapore, Hong Kong and Thailand. I want to go to India, Morocco, Italy and Spain.

Staying active physically and intellectually is important. Hard work and not wasting time on things that don't matter in the long run is important.

A lot of people spend several hours a day watching TV. I've never done that. I enjoy intellectual programming. But I don't watch soap operas and things that just time drains.

I've had several mentors. In high school it was my math and drama teacher. As I was starting into college, I had a woman that had emigrated from Europe. She had been a dancer in another country and was working in a box factory in Aberdeen. But she still was very much alive. She worked with me in community theater.

My children have been highlights of my life. Being able to help someone mature into a citizen that can give something back to the world, be honest and be creative. I have five.

Other highlights have been incredible experiences on trips that I'll remember forever. Being able to be places that have played huge roles in history, like the Great Wall of China, just freeze moments in your mind. I've learned to slow down and really develop relationships with other people and not just be work focused.

I think it's totally wrong that you go downhill at 30. I'm 50 and enjoying life more now than I ever have. I think when you're young you don't really appreciate the complexity of life. You're more into personal gratification and things that are happening to you right then. You don't look at long-term effects. You don't have the long-term relationships that you have at an older age. I have friends that I've had for 40 years.

I find it much more enjoyable because you have more background and more ways to look at things, a deeper perspective culturally, historically, politically and across the board.

It is harder to remember some things but then you have so much more in your brain. At 50 you've met tens of thousands of people.

I totally agree with the priorities of the Bill and Melinda Gates' Foundation … helping other people.

Don't give up. It's just a journey.

Sharing philosophy and travels by phone on February 14, 2007.

CONNECT

"[W]e are wired to connect."

"The brain-to-brain link allows our strongest relationships to shape us on matters as benign as whether we laugh at the same jokes or as profound as which genes are (or are not) activated in T-cells, the immune system's foot soldiers in constant battle against invading bacteria and viruses.
That link is a double-edged sword: nourishing relationships have a beneficial impact on our health, while toxic ones can act like slow poison in our bodies."
Both by Daniel Goleman in *Social Intelligence*

Goals

- Be assertive in a responsive way … because this can result in a win-win situation with both parties feeling better about themselves

- Listen actively … because what you got might not be what you heard

- Touch judiciously … because a touch that is welcomed can be healing

- Avoid toxic relationships … because they can slowly poison your body

- Hang out with positive people … because that can enhance the health of both of you

"I'm really angry with him," she said. "He doesn't bring me flowers any more."

"Does he know you want him to?"

"Yes! After all the years we've been together, he has to know that."

"When was the last time you told him how much you like getting flowers from him?"

"I shouldn't have to tell him that. He should know me well enough by now to figure that out!"

Connect • 67

If these were unique comments heard only in one private session, they wouldn't be quoted here. Many people wish someone else would read their minds in order to brighten their lives in just the right way. Celebrate it when somebody does that for you! But counting on it is setting a trap for yourself to be disappointed and for the other person to fail by your standards.

Some difficulties come from cultural differences. I nearly lost a dear friendship because I sat with my foot propped up with the sole of my shoe toward her. She believed that was an insult to the Buddha within her … a belief few people in our culture hold dear. I didn't know.

When you don't say what is in your heart, it remains a deep, dark secret. Sharing what is near and dear to you is giving the listeners a drummer so they can decide if they can dance to that rhythm. Can you still respect them if they say no?

So often I've heard patients and friends say they can't ask for what they want because they don't want to put anyone in the position of feeling obligated. Oh, good grief, the games people play! One of the beauties of the Jakubowski and Lange book, The Assertive Option: Your Rights and Responsibilities, lies in the assumption that each one will be safe in making a request because everyone is equally safe in granting or not granting the request. It's been a source of joy across the years helping so many people broaden and deepen their love and respect for others through being responsive to but not responsible for others.

That also requires mastering the art of listening. It is one of the best gifts you can give and receive. How often do you really listen to hear the fine details of what the other is saying? Only when you know someone would be offended by your placing the sole of your shoe toward them can you avoid offending the Buddha within … and undo an unintended hurt.

A colleague and friend suffers with post traumatic stress disorder (PTSD.) She remembers when she removed her shoe once and was surprised to find it filled with blood. Lack of awareness of pain is one of the symptoms of PTSD. She had walked all the way home on a piece of glass. As it cut into her foot causing the bleeding, she felt no pain. She lurches away when anyone attempts to touch her in any way. Even the touch of anyone's hand on hers is threatening if she did not invite the touch.

Connect.

Assertiveness, active listening and touch can strengthen bonds. Using each one with deep mutual respect between you and another person can build bonds of friendships that last. There is an art to balancing the use of each one.

Remember that our brains are wired to connect. That means the emotions of others are "contagious." Reduce to the bare essential the amount of time you spend with toxic relationships. They can slowly poison your body. Cherish time with positive people as this can enhance the overall health of both of you.

Science behind your plan

Assertiveness. Books on assertiveness flooded the market for several years. Many are still selling well. Research still shows that being assertive can enhance self esteem, improve ability to negotiate, decrease risk for depression, increase social supports and create win-win situations.

Nobody can read the whole library. If you have a favorite book on assertiveness, send an email about it to **DrJoyce@StressPower.com** and it will be reviewed to see if it fosters deep mutual respect for all parties. If so, I'll reference it in the future.

My clinical bias is to recommend only one book on the topic—The Assertive Option by Jakubowski and Lange. At least one thing distinguishes this book. The authors clearly advocate being responsive to the other person's reaction to what you say and do. The response of the listener defines whether or not you have been assertive. This is not about right or wrong, it's about having the kind of deep mutual respect for each other that values honesty and fluid communication.

Your goal is to be responsive to but not responsible for the reaction of the other person. This is not about blame. It's not about someone making an error of judgment. It's about communicating effectively with care, compassion and deep mutual respect.

Do you see how empowering that is to both people in a conversation? It means that a wide range of responses is expected, respected, valued and used.

On the one hand each of you can become assertive in expressing yourself and in asking for what you want. On the other hand each of you can be comfortable with differences and can count on each person to be her own best judge of what works best for her. No mind reading is required or even tolerated.

> "One of the ultimate goals of assertion is developing caring, honest, and accepting relationships with others."
> Jakubowski and Lange in *The Assertive Option*

According to Jakubowski and Lange there are three options: assertive, nonassertive and aggressive behaviors. How your listener responds determines which one of those you have been. This is how you can tell the difference. This is how you empower each other to improve communication.

Assertive behavior:

- Is self enhancing;
- Is usually other enhancing as well;
- Is an honest and relatively straightforward expression of thoughts and feelings;
- Is socially appropriate;
- Takes into account the feelings and welfare of others;
- Benefits the assertive person through an improved feeling of well-being;
- Improves the assertive person's ability to achieve significant social rewards; AND
- Benefits the receiving person through an increased understanding of the thoughts and feelings and wishes of the assertive person.

Nonassertive behavior:

- Is self-defeating;
- Is defeating to the receiver who only has a best educated guess of what you want and need; AND
- Is associated with negative outcomes for you and the other person – such as frustration, resentment, lack of satisfaction, irritation, etc.

Aggressive behavior:

- Is coercive;
- Violates the rights of others;
- Has an unnecessarily negative impact on the welfare of others;
- Is self defeating: AND
- Defeats the other person.

The same sentence said with the same tone of voice during the same time of day to the same person, etc., could end up with a different response from one time to the next. That's OK! That just means that you modify your response to that person's reaction.

For example, the woman wanting flowers began with, "I really appreciated all those times you came home with flowers saying, 'It's a flower kind of day!' It was fun."

When that got no response, she added, "I'd really like it if you would surprise me like that again some time this week." It gave him more specifics of what she wanted and when. He was delighted because he knew what would make her happy; all he had to do was repeat a behavior he knew well. She was happy initially because she was heard. Also, she was happy again when she got what she asked for.

Assume always that the other person has equal wants, needs, rights and responsibilities.

Therefore, her response is her gift of honesty. If the response is no response, she may be distracted with "stuff." Sometimes that means you must be clearer in what you are saying.

If his response is "Thank you for asking. However it's not a good time for me," then you know your request was heard AND that the other person has enough respect for both of you to do what they need to do.

Passive and Active Listening. Often the best response is active listening. Thomas Gordon described this in his Parent Effectiveness Training book. It is a valuable book at any age. Just substitute "self" and "other" where he uses "parent" and "child" and read it for the concepts and process. It's on the bookshelves of most of the clients I've had the pleasure of helping. Well, actually, one dear woman said, "Yes, Dr. Joyce, I got the book when you asked me to. It's under my bed holding my bed up along with all the other books you recommended."

Gordon describes twelve roadblocks to communication that could have unintended effects. In response to these roadblocks the listener may become more submissive and compliant. Or he may become more resistant, rebellious or argumentative. These barriers to conversation tend to lower the listener's self-esteem and reduce motivation. They reduce your ability to influence others and increase your likelihood of blaming the listener.

Interestingly, these roadblocks are used in the vast majority of conversations. Some are valuable in quiet times. They become a significant barrier to communication when one or both persons have a problem or a strong sense of need. That's why it's particularly important to avoid communication roadblocks in times of stress.

According to Gordon, these twelve roadblocks can divided into three major categories:

A. Judging—this is probably the major barrier to good communication. We have been socialized to judge, to approve or disapprove of the statement or actions of the other person. This tendency can be worse with someone with whom you are emotionally involved.

1. Criticizing;
2. Name-calling;
3. Diagnosing;
4. Praising evaluatively;

B. Sending solutions—these tend to end the exchange of information.

5. Ordering;
6. Threatening;
7. Moralizing
8. Excessive/inappropriate questioning;
9. Advising;

C. Avoiding the other's concerns—these tend to dismiss the other's concerns and take the conversation off track.

10. Diverting;
11. Logical Argument; and
12. Reassuring.

You may be thinking that you use many of these on a daily basis. You may even be asking how it could possibly be a problem to praise someone or reassure them. Then, too, how could a logical argument be out of line?

Remember, your tactic is to be responsive to but not responsible for the emotional state of the person with whom you're communicating. That is one of the reasons that Gordon's P.E.T. Parent Effectiveness Training book is a fine companion piece with The Assertive Option. Some of these styles will probably work fine when both of you are feeling good. When you feel needy and the other person is available, it's probably most useful for you to be assertive. When both are distraught, it might be best to be assertive enough to suggest talking later. When you are available and the other individual is feeling troubled, build your skills of passive and active listening.

These conversational bad habits
Can be corrected by
Substituting such skills as
Passive listening,
Active listening and
Assertiveness.

Listening is unbelievably underrated. Once I've trained clients to use passive listening, they're both relieved to find out how easy it is and delighted to see how often the speakers heal themselves with no additional help.

"Sometimes active listening merely helps a [person] accept
a situation that he knows he cannot change."
Thomas Gordon in *Parent Effectiveness Training*

Some years ago I entered the front door saying firmly, "We need to talk." Looking like he feared the worst, my son came promptly to the living room. His mood shifted somewhat as he listened. "You need to be sure you do not take my mood personally," I assured him as I listed a few of the smaller financial, career and other worries on my mind. I was an unemployed single mother of a medically fragile teenager without adequate medical insurance and rapidly running out of funds.

He just listened, made direct eye contact, nodded occasionally. That's passive listening.

When I changed the topic to what to fix for dinner, he softly said, "I think we ought to eat at …" I've forgotten the name of the place we could walk to that served unlimited salad and spaghetti for so little money. Maybe that's why they went out of business. In any case, I reluctantly agreed. Only small talk drifted between us.

About an hour later, he softly asked, "How are you feeling now?" Coming from him that was a bit of a scary question. Since he was barely old enough to crawl, he'd been the kind of wise old soul that led social workers to suggest that he become a psychiatrist when he grew up.

"Better. Thank you so much for being such a good listener."

"I think you just need to know you are going to pass the licensing exam."

Hit the nail on the head, he did! Right down to the core emotion of fear as well as the irrational thought behind it.

That's active listening. Allow room for the emotions of the other. Accept and acknowledge their feelings. Believe that the speaker usually has what it takes to heal the self in the presence of loving acceptance. Hear the salient point. Paraphrase it.

People like my son who seem to do than naturally from the moment of their first salient thought make it look easy. Others have to learn that listening effectively actually is easier that struggling with the twelve roadblocks listed by Gordon.

The twelve roadblocks tend to trigger feelings of inadequacy, anger or dependency in the speaker. Then he or she may become more submissive and compliant. Or she or he may become more resistant, rebellious, or argumentative. One or both of you may suffer lower self esteem and less motivation as a result. Therefore, the listener will probably feel and act less empowered. The listener is more likely to focus on the evaluation outside the self.

And then there's the matter of touch.

> "...loneliness and isolation can literally 'break your heart.'"
>
> "The most simple and direct type of human communication does not need words."
>
> "In some patients, indeed, pulse taking had the power to completely suppress arrhythmias that had been occurring."
> All by James J Lynch in
> *The Broken Heart:*
> *The Medical Consequences of Loneliness*

James Lynch's research of clearly shows that we have a biological need for human companionship and touch. The death rate is higher among the unmarried than it is for married individuals regardless of age, sex or race.

Some of his research observations took place in coronary intensive care units. While watching people with their loved ones in that setting he was affected by how several people expressed their final good-bye. A brief physical contact just before leaving seemed to say it all—whether by silently holding the patient's hand, holding their foot or gently touching another part of their loved one's body.

Lynch reported that human contact was very important to patients in the coronary intensive care unit. As a loved one's health hung in the balance, a wife's touch could stabilize a failing heart. The simple act of a nurse taking a patient's pulse could improve the heart rate.

How to do it

Assertiveness. For all of the wisdom in this section on how to be assertive I give complete credit to Jakubowski's and Lange's The Assertive Option, published in 1978. I highly recommend their book still. They teach being assertive with body language as well as with words.

There are several reasons to focus on the basics. Say please and thank you. Get permission. Voice your opinion. Give compliments. Accept compliments with a gracious "Thank you."

I have a confession. To me a car is nothing more than a tool. (Stick with this. It's related.) My car gets me to the few places I cannot access on foot; on a bike; or on a bus, train or plane. So I have no idea how many weeks it was after the neighbor washed my car before he had to tell me about it because I never noticed that it was cleaner.

Is it your experience that it's kind of like that around your home as well? The one who rids up knows how long it took to make the place tidy, clean and beautiful. Frequently that goes unnoticed by any other resident. Being oblivious to the new cleanliness seems to be simple human nature. I believe it is not determined by gender, age, lack of social graces or anything else.

I feel fortunate to have experienced this from several perspectives. That has helped me develop more compassion from many sides.

In my early years, it was just expected that making the home livable was my obligation. The only thing that was noticed was what I missed. When I hired someone to clean my house, it was so wonderful to come home to that I made a point whenever possible of expressing my gratitude about all that had been done. One difference was that I had written the task list so I knew what to appreciate.

It was a bit troubling to me that I failed to notice when housework had been done by anyone living with me. Cleanliness, order and beauty are small but crucial elements of making my home my castle. I'd have thought I would've noticed when a nice guy did something without being asked! I wanted to change my ways and be more perceptive.

My husband made that easy. He has an attitude! See if you can agree with me on that. The first thing after we're out of bed in the morning he asks at least two questions: "What do you want for breakfast?" "When do you want it?" Well, sometimes he also asks if I need a lunch! Now, that's an attitude, don't you agree?

You can see that that's a set up. See, I used to just grab some bread and fruit on the way past the kitchen and eat on the way to the office. With this Mate, gratitude came easily. These are the basics.

> "Thank you for asking."
> "Thank you for cooking."
> "This is delicious!"
> "Wow! What a work of art. Let me get a picture of that plate for my book."

"What's your day look like?"
"I'd like to give you a hug. Is this permissible?"

Empathy is not quite as basic. It involves expressing awareness of someone else's feelings. You will need to be responsive to how he receives that information. Sometimes, "Wow! You're really angry!" is heard with relief as the other person feels understood. Other times it's more comfortable to hear, "I think I'm picking us some anger." This avoids those tender moments when the listener really wants to be the one who decides how to label his emotion. It lets him know his feelings are important and have been noticed while it also leaves the labeling in the listener's control.

So often people say, "I know just how you feel … " as they ramble off into their similar story. That actually works sometimes. Other times it's seen as a kind gesture. In a clinical setting I've often heard it described as offensive. Although it is a common effort to connect, it's difficult to imagine that any one person actually can "know" how another feels. I prefer leaving the labeling up to the feeler.

Escalating is simply being responsive to your listener's response … or lack thereof. Starting with "No, but thank you for asking," should work. If it doesn't, the next step might be gentle Voice-of-America English as you say, "Thanks, but no." If the other party persists, you might resort to saying tenderly, "Since I've already said no twice, I'd appreciate it if you would stop asking." Escalating done infrequently but with compassion, humor and mutual respect can be an act of beauty in a relationship which enjoys sharing each other's enthusiasm in moments of passion. If it became a pattern, it could become a drag.

Confronting someone can also be done with deep respect and beauty. Just recently a precious friend and mentor said she really needed our phone calls to be limited to twenty minutes because otherwise she feels pressured about what she planned to accomplish that day and tends to fret about that during the week. "So, next week we have to stop even if we're in the middle of a sentence!"

"Consider it done," I chuckled with gratitude. We'd spoken on it before but the specifics and sense of urgency made it crystal clear. I love clarity and purpose. That's totally empowering.

"But how will we make ourselves do that?"

"Count on me. I'm expert at that. My whole professional career has required me to end on time in order to not keep the next folks waiting." And so it shall be. Do you see what a gift she gave me? As soon as I knew her need, the solution was easy!

Besides confronting the issue, she used I-language. Here's the format:

"When we … (linger on the phone too long),
the effect is … (I don't finish what I intended to do)!
I feel … (frustrated and tend to fret during the week)!

I'd prefer ... (that we end at twenty minutes even if we get cut off mid-sentence.)"

Power to both parties. Delicious!

Fortunately, or unfortunately, I am also over-trained in dealing with emotional and other issues. In my office when something really important came into the last minutes of the session I might consider it the wisest choice to go over a few minutes. So I haven't achieved total compliance. But I am empowered by knowing the rules so I have an evolving capacity to do the right thing.

I hope these snippets out of The Assertive Option empower you, too. Done with deep respect for all parties, this style of assertiveness is mutually delicious for healthy growth and social bonding.

Passive and active listening. All of the wisdom on this topic comes from the Thomas Gordon (1975) book, P.E.T. This book sold so well and was read and used effectively by so many people that some folks began to have a problem with the use of the word "problem." But that's testament to the power, simplicity and value of the concepts in his book. I'll just substitute a different word here.

Gordon has boiled it down to a system that is easily learned with practice and with verbally rewarding your progress. When all you do is listen effectively while you watch someone heal themselves, the joy inherent in the process can help strengthen your long-term potentiation (LTP) to make this habit endure.

Your attitude is probably the most important part. As you are learning and practicing passive and active listening, be certain that:

- You want to hear;
- You want to be helpful;
- You accept the other person as she is;
- You trust the other person to heal herself;
- You know that emotions are temporary; and
- You respect and cherish the other person's responsibility for herself.

Passive listening with this attitude is hearing what another person is saying while making direct eye contact, nodding and making appropriate changes in facial expressions to assure the other you are listening. Active listening includes all of these things and adds three more. Try to understand what the speaker is feeling. Try to understand what the message is. With active listening, the only things you may say are two kinds of feedback: Only what you think the speaker is feeling AND only what you think the message means to the speaker.

Nothing more. Nothing less.

Unfortunately, under stress people regress. That means you might fall back on using one or more of the roadblocks to communication when it could be more effective to use active listening. The beauty of assertiveness is the respect each party brings to the other. So, when it's not easy to just listen, it might be best to simply say "I want to hear your point of view. It's not timely right now. With your permission I'll delay this conversation until 5:30 PM or later when I've cleared my slate of a few things. Is this permissible?" That's an example of the balance between assertiveness and effective listening.

Touch. The same is true for the potential healing power of touch. As Lynch makes clear in his book, even the simple touch of a nurse taking a patient's pulse can stabilize it. At the same time some people find touch aversive. My colleague with PTSD found blood in her shoe after walking all the way home feeling no pain. She takes offense at being touched. Her experiences highlight the need to be judicious with touch.

I was number seven of seven children born in poverty on a farm. Being one of four girls cuddling through a cold winter night in a small bedroom with frost on the inside of the window was a source of warmth and comfort. It was a healthy habit. Hugging came naturally to me. So did laying my hand on the shoulder or wrist of a stranger. However, my friend and colleague with PTSD taught me to get permission first.

The examples of touch discussed so far are all free. The only reason all examples are free is because that puts you in total control at all times. At any time in any place you can afford to give yourself the healing gift of touch. It's been a source of joy to reinforce clients who had become so accustomed to using touch for healing that they would be seemingly unaware that their one hand was massaging the other as they cried through memories of trauma. There's ample research supporting the healing power of massage and other forms of touch as well.

Link and Loop. Surround yourself with positive people. You can catch their emotions just as you can catch a cold. New technology has accelerated neuroscience. Some of these tools are: functional magnetic imaging (fMRI); positron emission tomography (PET); and quantitative electrophysiology. Richard Davidson used these in collaborating with His Holiness the Dalai Lama. Davidson has been a leader in describing how internal states of consciousness are tied to the objective data of brain electrical activity.

Goleman believes that research using these sophisticated tools makes our brains comparable to Wi-FI. It suggests that we are constantly picking up information by brain-to-brain bridges which carry two-way traffic.

> When a functional link between two brains occurs, there's "a feedback loop that crosses the skin-and-skull barrier between bodies."
> Daniel Goleman in
> *Social Intelligence*

Emotions can be picked up by your unconscious mind as rapidly as 17 milliseconds. That's less than two-hundredths of a second.

These exchanges can escape our awareness but the impact is huge. Goleman says "These take on deep consequences as we realize how, through their sum total, we create one another." The only system in your body that keeps you in tune with and influenced by the feelings of another person is your social brain. "Our social interactions even play a role in reshaping our brains through 'neuroplasticity'."

Just like other experiences, social linking and looping influence the number, size and shape of neurons and how they develop connections at a synapse. Increased complexity in social interactions induces new learning. Goleman suggests that this could induce neurogenesis at any age. For these reasons he argues for putting daycare centers in assisted living facilities for the mutual benefits to children and the elderly.

Powerful and lifelong effects on our brain can result from our relationships. This means to Goleman that positive influences and repair of neuroplasticity are possible across your lifespan. And you can enhance the lives and brains of others by being positive. What a lovely new perspective on social responsibility!

Goleman counsels against spending unnecessary time with negative people because, whether anyone is aware of it or not, the linking and looping does affect the other party as shown by growing social neuroscience evidence. He encourages hanging out with positive people to exchange an influence which could have a healthy affect on them, even on their brain architecture.

This could put a whole new meaning on your role in social responsibility. Goleman's theory supports the Jakubowski and Lange requirement that assertiveness takes place with deep mutual respect for the welfare of all parties. For compassionate people who are driven to be of service to others, it might increase their motivation to develop enduring authentic happiness in themselves. It might increase the value of positive emotions for their potential to enhance the immune response, physical wellbeing and brain growth of their friends and family.

Measuring Goals

On a daily basis do the short form of the SUFI Report™. Rate the times you were assertive, listened effectively or touched from -10 for negative outcomes to +10 for positive outcomes on how successful you were. Do the same for how the other person seemed to be affected. Set a goal to live in deep mutual respect while being responsive to but not responsible for the reactions of others.

Using the SUFI Report™ to measure linking and looping might also be useful. However, there are several problems with attempting a measurement at this point. First, Goleman's theory is too newly published to fit like a well worn glove. Also, as described by Goleman, so much of this takes place below our conscious awareness. Therefore, I'll include below a form primarily to stimulate discussion on his new theory of social intelligence and how we might get maximum awareness and benefit from studying it in ourselves.

Subjective Units of Feelings Index (SUFI Report™)

-10   **0**   **+10**

SUFI while being assertive: _____   SUFI after being assertive _____

    What did you say? _____

    What did you do? _____

    How did your listener respond? _____

    Was it a win-win outcome? _____

    What, if anything, would you do differently next time? __

SUFI while listening effectively: _____   SUFI after listening effectively _____

    What did you say? _____

    What did you hear? _____

    How did the speaker respond? _____

    Was it a win-win outcome? _____

    What, if anything, would you do differently next time? _____

SUFI with touch: _____   SUFI after touching: _____

    How did the other person respond? _____

    Was touch helpful? _____

    Was it a win-win outcome? _____

    What, if anything, would you do differently next time? _____

SUFI with linking and looping: _____   SUFI after linking and looping: _____

How did the other person respond? _____

How did either of you determine that you were linking and looping? _____ ____
_____

What, if anything, would you do differently the next time? _____ ____
_____

Choose one person to practice with. Start with assertiveness, effective listening or touch. Your goal is to make just one little change at a time. That might mean setting a goal of giving 10 compliments today. Or it might mean remembering to accept a compliment with a simple smile and nodding of your head. Or you might decide to ask permission before taking someone's pulse. Whatever you choose to change, measure it and practice it until it becomes second nature before choosing another skill to practice. And enjoy rewarding yourself with compliments on your progress in Ideal Aging™.

Summary

Jakubowski and Lange raise assertiveness to world class level. This is, in part, because their definition of assertiveness includes being responsive to but not responsible for how your listener reacts. That sets both of you free to bond with deep mutual respect. It expects that each of you can ask for what you want because both of you feel comfortable saying and hearing, "Thank you for asking but that wouldn't work for me." It assumes that you can count on your friend to let you know if your slip is showing. It provides a safe haven for an honest opinion with or without agreement.

My clinical bias is that your feelings are your very best friends. They belong to you as a form of guidance. They often do not need to be shown to others or even expressed. You might just get the best results by using your emotions as you would road signs. "I see I'm still listening (on Main Street) when I'd prefer to be dancing (on 5th Avenue)." When you explore your emotions to understand what thoughts are associated with them, your emotions can set you free. Turning onto 5th Avenue ("May I have the next dance?") could suffice. In that case, your emotions have served their purpose.

This exploration is how you identify the changes you desire. Assertiveness is how you ask for them. Pairing these skills with effective listening can be a beautiful balance.

Practicing Gordon's passive and active listening similarly strengthens your bonds of friendship. It saves you the trouble of problem solving for the speaker who knows more about the situation than he can readily explain. That frees you up to give the speaker your undivided attention. Through listening to themselves speak, most people come to their own best resolution with no further help.

Sometimes we connect best without words. At times the most effective bond is the healing power of touch. Still, some people find touch aversive. That's why being judicious might mean asking permission prior to even taking someone's pulse.

Developing enduring and authentic happiness takes on much greater significance with advances in social neuroscience. The same could be said for surrounding yourself with positive people. His review of this literature convinced Goleman that our social brains can link and be shaped by feedback loops which cross the skin-and-skull barriers between brains.

Goleman's theory of social intelligence clearly supports Jakubowski and Lange in requiring that interactions be based on deep mutual respect. He suggests that we share a level of social responsibility to be positive and surround ourselves who contribute positively to relationships.

The good news is that it's never too early and never too late to enhance your brain architecture through linking and looping with positive people. That seems like a clear, cogent and convincing argument in favor of connecting often with brains in nourishing relationships. Enhancing the immune response and architecture of each other's brains can be an enticing new social responsibility.

Susan Curington
Owner and Manager of a certified sustainable forest.

I own and manage 120 acres of timber. Under my management this forest has become certified sustainable. My background is in healing arts, massage therapy, women's spirituality and teaching meditation. I spent three and a half years in Dharamsala in India. I grew up on a farm.

Ideal Aging™ would be to follow the example of my grandmother who lived to be 100 years and three quarters. She lived alone happily until about 96. Her example was about good attitude, faith, prayer, gratitude, looking for beauty and not tolerating negativity. She was a hard worker physically and had good clean air to breathe most of her life. So I think how I treat my body is how it will treat me.

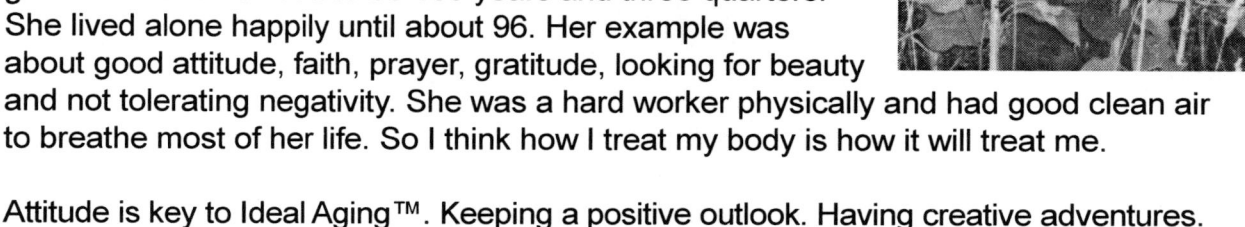

Attitude is key to Ideal Aging™. Keeping a positive outlook. Having creative adventures. Risking. I have struggled with hormones. I went into menopause at age 37. I'm struggling a bit with my physical body and grateful to live in this century where there are natural hormone replacements. I think having creative outlets, pleasure, play, happy relationships and a satisfying spiritual life are all key to aging and keeping an open mind.

Prayer and my friendship network are my answer to hardships. I have a very strong emotional safety net in my life. I value personal vulnerability, personal honesty and creating a sanctuary of friends before I need them. It's also extending a listening ear to my friends and practicing compassion when they face their own hardships.

My husband, Les and I are setting up our financial life to be stable while passively producing income. Then we can do philanthropy, spend time with grandkids, creative projects and whatever else we're here to do.

While I feel our efforts are currently improving the world I want to make changes on a grander scale. First, I'd change so there is renewable blue energy, solar energy, wind energy and anything nonpolluting to try to turn back the global warming situation and do massive replanting. I'd do what human beings can do to mitigate the damage done already and turn it back. I would completely eliminate herbicides and pesticides because I believe a lot of the problem with cancer is toxicity. I'd return to organic gardening with full financial and social support. I would encourage changes in our political systems. I would support large groups of people to get trained in non-violent communication. I'd work with Unitus (see www.unitus.com) to eliminate poverty at grassroots level. I think that adds up to world change. So a little bit of everything—ecological, personal, spiritual, political, sociological.

To improve their individual worlds, people should turn off the TV. And take a walk in nature.

As one ages, patience is key to Ideal Aging™. I'm getting increasingly patient and becoming more easily surrendered to things that cannot be changed. I've had a lot of close relatives die within a short span of years. In that depth of grieving there is just an amount of surrender that is priceless.

I once asked, "Grandma, what's really important in life?" She thought about it and answered, "Soap. Never run out of soap or salt." That's from her days on the prairie when it was miles to a store. The last thing she said was, "Eat a piece of chocolate every day."

It's also important to do aerobic exercise everyday. And get enough sleep and good, hard, physical exercise.

Hugs from my sweetie pie husband increases my happiness. Touch is really important. I notice an effect on my general happiness and well being if I'm touch-deficient for any reason.

From a tender telephone talk on January 29, 2007

CHILL

"…some key truths. First, you don't need to be stressed out…"
Bruce McEwen, PhD in *The END of Stress As We Know it*

Goals

- Learn to do progressive relaxation … because the resulting reduced cortisol could help keep your brain fit

- Practice progressive relaxation until you have a conditioned response … so you can go from misery to mellow in microseconds, improve your performance and enhance Ideal Aging™

- Relearn progressive relaxation episodically to develop heightened awareness of muscle tension … because that helps you use your emotions more effectively

Science behind your plan

This is one skill for which no legions of rats have been run ragged. Humans are blessed with being the subjects of a multitude of studies on various forms of progressive relaxation. And what a gift this skill, used to its fullest potential, is to humankind!

Progressive relaxation research started with Edmund Jacobson. He thought that emotions were stored in tense muscles. He taught that tensing and then relaxing these muscles could afford relief. That's especially effective if it is done with opposing sets of muscles.

For example, you could start with making a fist to tense the muscles in the front of your hand. After relaxing those muscles, you extend your fingers in the opposite direction to tighten the muscles in the back of your hand. Pausing to focus on the tension and the contrasting relaxation in each set of muscles is critical to this process.

Abbreviated forms of Jacobson's technique have been researched extensively. Progressive relaxation has been found effective in treating allergies, arthritis, phobias, anxiety, depression, muscle tension, high blood pressure, headaches, neck aches, backaches, gut problems, fatigue, sleep disorders, chronic pain, etc. Progressive relaxation is recommended as a first-line of treatment for insomnia.

Various relaxation techniques have been shown to produce dramatic changes in brain activity. Jacobs and colleagues found that within five minutes the brain waves change to those similar to early stages of sleep. Similarly, meditation has been shown to improve brain function, to improve immune function and possibly to maintain more thickness in portions of the brain cortex with advancing age.

One advantage unique to progressive relaxation is the potential for increased awareness of tension in one or more muscles. Sensing tension in its early stages increases the power of the relaxation response. When this sensitivity to tension is paired with a thought cue to relax and is practiced until a conditioned response is developed, improvement in relaxation is very effective and can be rapid.

> *"I am SO good at handling stress when there's no stress there!"*
> Mary C

Mindfulness meditation has some similar health advantages. As the research of Richard Davidson has shown, it has been associated with changes in the left prefrontal cortex, the part of your brain which registers happiness.

One difference with meditation is that it does not develop the cued conditioned response. Nor does it focus on building an awareness of the difference between tension and relaxation in opposing muscle groups. It's the building of this awareness that facilitates earlier intervention with anxiety, fear and other forms of tension which are so prevalent in Western cultures.

This is an immense advantage to learning progressive relaxation techniques. Early awareness of muscle tension means you can study the thoughts associated with the tension while those thoughts are fresh. Those thoughts are associated with the emotion held in tense muscles. Understanding which emotion is expressed in the muscle tension helps you use these emotional cues more effectively in decision-making in any setting.

Also, the earlier you intervene by changing your thoughts, the more profoundly you can the effect change. That means you can use progressive relaxation for greater impact before your tension builds.

How to do it

Which muscle group you begin with doesn't seem to matter. The important thing is to allow adequate time to label and focus on the difference between exaggerated tension and the difference when the muscles are suddenly relaxed.

To get the most benefit from this technique, consider creating your own tape of instructions that will guide you through the systematic tensing and relaxing of opposing sets of muscles. It can be pretty special following your own recorded voice through these exercises.

Before beginning, get into a comfortable position in a warm setting. Although people in my workshops have fallen asleep during this technique while sitting up in a metal folding chair, most folks would rather be lying down. It is important to have all body parts supported, especially your back and neck. I prefer to use my recording after I am in bed as part of my bedtime routine. If you have any injuries, leave those muscles out of this routine altogether.

Start with taking a deep breath, holding it and slowly letting it out. Each time as you exhale, say the word "relax" silently to yourself. Repeat that a few times. Work your way through opposing set of muscles labeling the tension and relaxation as you go. It's this pairing of the label and the tension that will help you recognize tense muscles more easily than you have before. Similarly, as you associate the label with being relaxed you are building that conditioned response. Pause for about ten seconds for each tensing and relaxing.

It might be best to begin with your hands, arms and shoulders. Use only gentle tension in bending your neck to each side and forward. Bending you neck backwards is not recommended. Frowning will tense some of your facial muscles. Opening your mouth wide might be a safe way to tense your jaw muscles. Use caution in tensing your back muscles. This time when you take a deep breath, make it abdominal and hold it before slowly letting it out. Tighten your abdominal muscles as you would to do a sit-up, then as you would to flatten your stomach. You will feel your body rise from the surface when you tighten you buttocks and ease back down when you relax. Raise you knees slightly to tighten the front of your thighs and straighten your knees to tighten the back of your thighs. Work your legs by raising your feet then pushing your heels into the floor or bed. Curling your toes and then pulling them toward your chin will focus on opposing sets of muscles there.

It's at this point in my recording that the focus is totally on relaxation, warmth and comfort. This is emphasized by repeating the deep breathing, holding the breath and silently thinking the word "relax" with each breath out to strengthen the conditioned response.

If you prefer, you can obtain audio recordings from resources listed at the end of this book. My CDs of this technique are available on **StressPower.com** and on **IdealAging.com**. Develop a conditioned relaxation response. It is an invaluable goal. It can improve your performance as well as your health. Getting a conditioned response is much easier with a recorded version of progressive relaxation, be it your own recording or a recording obtained from a commercial source.

Easier does not imply quick. It will take practice, practice, practice to become conditioned. Remember that a child doesn't master walking with the first step. But being ambulatory is clearly worth the sustained effort.

When my clients used my recording of progressive relaxation twice a day, they reported having a conditioned response in about two weeks. Individuals who used it once a day just took longer to become conditioned.

As soon as a conditioned response was achieved, it was strengthened by using the progressive relaxation recording once a day for a few more weeks, then once a week or so thereafter to maintain the strength of the conditioned response. That's relatively easy to do by simply making it part of your bedtime routine. About fifteen minutes is the time required to complete progressive relaxation as I recorded it.

The reason I recorded this initially was to make it easier for my clients to get started quickly. The assumptions were that 1) most people with a recording could learn how to use progressive relaxation on their own and 2) they could also develop a conditioned response with regular use.

They had the potential for substantial savings of time and money for the health of it. We began with the understanding that I would teach it in my office if their measures at home did not show adequate results. The combination of motivation for improved health as well as independence in learning without paying for an office visit apparently worked very well. Hundreds of clients were able to build a conditioned relaxation response on their own.

To quote one elegant woman recently, "It is just peachy!"

Measuring Goals

Progressive relaxation to develop a conditioned cued response is ideally suited to using the SUFI Report. Review this in the Introduction.

Subjective Units of Feelings Index (SUFI Report™)
| -10 | 0 | +10 |

What is your SUFI score right now? _____

Track your SUFI Report before and after using it twice each day.

	SUFI Before Progressive Relaxation	SUFI After Progressive Relaxation	SUFI Before Progressive Relaxation	SUFI After Progressive Relaxation
Monday				
Tuesday				
Wednesday				
Thursday				
Friday				
Saturday				

Keep paper and pencil by your bed for recording this measure before and after each use of progressive relaxation. This will tell you how well it is working each time you do it. After using it a few times, take episodic measures of your progress. Note your SUFI score, silently think the word "relax," and then record your SUFI score again. When your SUFI score drops significantly just by thinking "relax," you are well on your way to having a conditioned relaxation response.

Being able to relax from just thinking the word "relax" could give you the added grace to exceed your previous level of performance in your career and/or socially and/or health. You know how sometimes in the middle of a sentence you freeze? People are staring while your chin and tongue are poised in mid-air because you suddenly seem to have mashed potatoes for brains!

With progressive relaxation developed into a cued conditioned response, you could be back

Chill • 89

in your game in the time/space of one word simply thought. Since thinking one word is much more efficient than saying it, how long could that take? It might take several microseconds after establishing that conditioned response. By using it every day, every day, every day for fourteen days.

Since several microseconds is a lot faster than what you experience now, would it be worth the effort? Could that be helpful? Once you establish long-term potentiation (LTP), a habit or conditioned response, you will have learned how to go from misery to mellow in a few microseconds. That could set you free to excel socially as well as in your career. At the very least this could reduce the amount of time your brain is ordering up more cortisol which suppresses neurogenesis.

But be warned: easier does not imply quick. It will take repeating the practice often enough for it to become conditioned (strengthen LTP). In my clinical experience, clients clearly found it to be worth the sustained effort to master this cued conditioned relaxation response for the health of it. That was true even before we knew about human neurogenesis.

Summary

Decades of research show progressive relaxation has many health benefits. It can improve sleep more effectively than prescriptions and its effects on reducing insomnia also last longer. Progressive relaxation can reduce blood pressure and acute or chronic pain.

When it is used sufficiently to create a conditioned relaxation response, progressive relaxation becomes extremely useful anywhere, any time. It can reduce strong emotions such as anxiety. After mastering the technique, you could achieve that relaxed state before anyone other than you noticed your tension. This could reduce the amount of cortisol you produce as well as the length of time your precious body parts are bathed in it. This could also enhance your social and career performance. It could also protect more of your brain cells from the ravages of cortisol.

The practice that will be necessary can be seen as a short term investment of time. You can be enjoying each period of relaxation in return for a long term gain of health with increased potential for peak performance. What this means is that it is clearly worth the sustained short term effort to master this cued conditioned relaxation response.

One of the unique aspects of progressive relaxation is that it increases your awareness of tension in your muscles. This make is easier to explore the thoughts and emotions associated with that muscle tension so you can make decisions in your best interest without being unduly influenced by your emotions.

This increased bodily awareness also makes it easier for you to use the conditioned relaxation responses before your tension builds. That means it can be more effective.

SLEEP

...sleep deprivation "reduced the numbers of new neurons by 60%."
Ruben Guzman-Marin and Dennis McGinty in Sleep and Biological Rhythms

Goals

- Sleep through the night with minimal awakening ... because restorative sleep could create new brain cells AND maximum brain function

- Develop a bedtime *routine*...because this prepares you mind and body for sound sleep

- Change any dysfunctional attitudes ... because thoughts influence sound sleep

- Be asleep within 30 minutes of going to bed ... because this could improve restorative sleep

- Get between 7 and 8 hours of restorative sleep each night ... because that range is associated with living longer

- Learn a conditioned relaxation response ... because this can reduce arousal when initiating sleep and during the night

- Awaken refreshed and feel alert during the day ... because this can improve your happiness, health and productivity

- Use the bed and bedroom only for sleep and love making ... because this creates a conditioned response

Science behind your plan

Since sleep disturbances can both cause and be caused by disease, medical clearance is critical. A few facts clarify the magnitude of this problem.

Statistics

Sleep deprivation has become a public health concern. Insomnia affects one-third to one-half of the population. Most frequently mentioned causes of insomnia were stress, loneliness and bereavement. Quality of life suffers as much due to insomnia as is reported with chronic medical disorders. Increased healthcare visits are one result. Sleep deprivation results in poor psychomotor and cognitive functioning, increased absenteeism and decreased performance at work. In economic terms about eight percent of this cost falls under the umbrella of health insurance. About eighty-eight percent of the cost is borne by employers.

Approximately eleven percent of interviewees in a European study reported nonrestorative sleep. The several life habits that contributed to sleep deprivation included drinking coffee daily, alcohol intake during the day, eating close to the time of going to sleep and doing activities in bed that required concentration, such as crossword puzzles. A long delay in going to sleep was associated with nonrestorative sleep. Physical fatigue and irritability during the day were also the result of this problem..

Less time sleeping, less deep sleep, difficulty maintaining sleep and decreased physical and cognitive functioning during the day have been associated with advancing age. The damage to quality of life is huge. Getting adequate restorative sleep is critical to maintaining quality of life and minimizing the impact of brain disorders. Melatonin has a significant role in promoting restorative sleep and influencing the circadian factor of sleep. Taking delayed-release melatonin at bedtime can be effective in improving the quality of sleep without also causing morning drowsiness.

Sleep Architecture

Rapid-eye-movement (REM) and non-REM are the two healthy neurobehavioral conditions that occur during sleep. When first going to sleep, light non-REM stages precede the progressively deeper stages 3 and 4 of non-REM sleep. The deepest stages of sleep, stages 3 and 4, are sometimes referred to as "slow-wave" sleep based on the EEG patterns.

It's during the first half of the night that most of the stages 3 and 4 sleep occur. This is also the type of sleep that people attempt to "make up" when sleeping late. REM and non-REM alternate about every 90 minutes. Toward the morning waking hours non-REM sleep decreases while REM sleep become longer and more intense as measured by how complex the dreams are in recall and by the frequency of eye movements.

Across one's lifespan non-REM and REM sleep stage 2 is pretty consistent. This is the stage of sleep most likely to enhance memories which are dependent on sleep for processing and integration. With advancing age, stage 1 non-REM sleep tends to increase while stages 3 and 4 tend to decrease. Adolescents tend to have a later time of sleep onset. Sleep onset becomes earlier with aging. Similarly, adolescents tend to have a later time of awakening than their seniors experience.

Pain, shortness of breath, side effects from medications and other health issues may be interfering with sound sleep. When treatable disorders, such as sleep apnea, are improved, this may be necessary and sufficient for improving quantity and quality of sleep. No matter what the cause of sleep deprivation, learned thoughts and behaviors can make it persist beyond the actual cause.

It is noteworthy that the amount of sleep is reported to have decreased by as much as two hours per night in the last half of the twentieth century. Pre-industrial sleepers are reported to have had a "night watch" between two phases of sleep. After being asleep some hours they would be awake for two or more hours before resuming the second phase of sleep. It was during this night watch that people would make love, snack, meditate or talk in the halcyon days prior to industrialization. Except, of course, when they were fighting off predators! But the two phases of sleep with a "night watch" between them raises a few questions? What really is "natural sleep?" Why is sleep maintenance insomnia so prevalent today?

Insomnia, according to the Diagnostic and Statistical Manual IV, Text Revision (DSM IV-TR), is "difficulty in initiating or maintaining sleep or ... nonrestorative sleep" and is "causing clinically significant distress or impairment in social, occupational or other important areas of functioning."

It is equally important to get enough sleep to awaken easily with joie de vivre and sufficient energy for peak performance. To do that, it will be helpful to understand what scientists are saying about sleep.

Sleep and being awake are so basic to human nature that they are sometimes taken for granted. Most of us know why we are awake during the day. It's the "functions" of sleep that are too complex to pin down. As you read the information below about the "functions" of sleep, remember that there is not yet a consensus on what sleep does. These statements are based on what research has shown as well as theories about what sleep does for animals. However, we do not yet know how sleep is actually related to physiological changes in our bodies. Here are some of the best theories on the function of sleep.

Functions of sleep

Environmental matching – One theory is that having a set time of stillness helps match us to our ideal environment. This perspective holds that being awake during daylight is human nature because we rely so much on our vision. Animals that rely more on other senses are better matched to night time activity. For example, bats fly in the dark because they do not require visual information to avoid running into walls.

Physical restoration – While it is not known how these physiological changes are related to sleep, scientists have found differences worth further research. Studies have found insensitivity to insulin, impaired glucose metabolism and immune function deficits associated with sleep deprivation. European adults were studied from age 18 to 40. Sleeping fewer than six hours was a significant predictor of obesity at ages 27, 29 and 34. This is an association in a community sample but it leaves open the question of what caused the obesity.

With increasing obesity and decreasing sleep, several studies have focused on the role sleep may have on weight gain. Sleep plays a major role in balancing energy. Leptin is a hormone that helps communicate to your brain about your calorie intake. It has a natural circadian rhythm that is higher during sleep, partly in response to your calorie intake. It decreases your appetite. Another influence on the amount of leptin in your blood is the length of time one is asleep. It is decreased with sleep deprivation. When leptin is high, the stress hormone cortisol is lower.

Sleep duration similarly increases the amount of ghrelin – a hormone which increases your urge to eat. After two days of getting only four hours of sleep, healthy young men had eighteen percent less leptin, twenty-eight percent more ghrelin, twenty-four percent more hunger and twenty-three percent greater appetite. The increased food intake showed a preference for sweet, calorie-dense, high carbohydrate and salty foods. Other hormonal changes with sleep deprivation can include elevations of the stress hormones cortisol and thyroid stimulating hormone.

Sleep had been seen as essential for protein synthesis because it is so energy intensive. We now know that protein synthesis is about as effective during quiet and awake periods as it is during sleep.

Sleep deprivation is another topic for which legions of rats have run ragged and beyond for human welfare. While living on a treadmill belt they suffered sleep deprivation for four days. For three seconds out of every fifteen seconds the belt moved at their walking pace. This compared to the control group whose belt only moved for fifteen minutes of every seventy-five minutes. The control group experienced eighteen percent less total sleep and thirty-three percent less REM sleep whereas the experimental group was permitted only very brief sleep episodes through the four days. Since the time in movement and total distance traveled was equal for both groups, differences between them could reasonably be attributed to the lack of sleep.

The sleep deprived rats created 50% fewer new brain cells. Sleep deprivation also reduced maturation of the new cells to 47% with sleep deprivation as compared to 72% in controls. With the combination of fewer new brain cells and reduced maturation, Guzman-Marin and McGinty estimate that sleep deprivation "reduced the numbers of new neurons by 60%." Stress as a factor was ruled out because stress hormones were not elevated.

These findings suggest that basic structure and growth of brain cells require adequate sleep. That process increases during non-REM sleep, especially "deep" non-REM sleep. Insulin-like growth factor (IGF-1) promotes both protein synthesis and creation of new brain cells. Growth hormone (GH) shows a major increase each day at sleep onset. Neurogenesis might be promoted by both GH and IGF-1. Both are greatly reduced with chronic sleep deprivation in rats.

Decreased size of the hippocampus, the part of the brain noted for memory function, has been noted with disease and with aging. Sleeping in fragments happens with both illness and aging. For example, several researchers have found shrinkage of the hippocampus with major depression. Treatment of PTSD with Paxil was associated with 4.6% increase in the average size of the hippocampus. This treatment also improved verbal memory even after 9 to 12 months of being off the drug. Guzman-Marin and McGinty believe that decreases in the size of the hippocampus "results from disease, rather than [predisposing] patients to disease." Interestingly rats also grew more new brain cells with long term antidepressants. With brief antidepressant treatment, rats did not increase the rate of creating new brain cells.

Peak performance – As anyone who's lost a night of sleep has probably experienced, sleep deprivation reduces capacity to seize the day. Again, there's a good research base showing that people who get adequate sleep do better on cognitive and emotional learning tasks than their sleepy neighbors.

French insomniacs had poor self-esteem and were less efficient at work than people who slept well. Improvements in some forms of memory depend on sleep. This is true on a cellular and molecular basis where nerve cells communicate at the synapses. It's also important in integrating new memory at a systems level. The process of enhancing visual memory and motor sequencing continues for three to four days after initial learning. Interestingly, these improvements in performance across time only develop during sleep.

It is clear that procedural memory is improved after periods of sleep. An example of procedural memory is riding your bicycle.

In one fascinating study, sleep increased the chance of getting novel insight. Subjects were taught a complex method for solving a numbers task. They were not told that a simpler solution existed. Gaining the insight to this hidden rule after sleep was more than twice as likely as after staying awake. The researchers concluded that sleep not only strengthens memory traces, it also restructures new memories in a way that sets the stage for new insight into hidden rules.

> "Enhancement of performance seen over time seems to develop only during sleep."
>
> And "Sleep enhanced the probability of gaining novel insight into the task."
> Robert Stickgold in Sleep-dependent memory consolidation.

Brain imaging studies have shown that different areas of the brain are activated for a specific newly learned task after a night of sleep. Apparently sleep alters the entire strategy of how the brain uses new learning to enhance performance by making it more automatic.

In fact, part of your memory depends on sleep. For example, to keep new learning in a form that is useful for the long haul, changes have to happen to the architecture of your brain. See the chapter Smarter This Year for much more detail on this. For long term memory of some tasks brain cells communicate differently and different brain cells assume part of this function. Stabilizing these memories includes changes in the brain cells as well as alterations in the system. These changes develop automatically over time with no awareness on your part. But sleep is required for these architectural and systems changes to occur. That gives special meaning to the saying "sleep on it."

Survival – Sleep deprivation and/or loss of non-REM sleep in rats could result in impending death in as little as two to three weeks. Skin lesions, changes in temperature regulation and weight loss were also observed in spite of increased calorie consumption. A syndrome developed that suggested sleep "may be necessary for effective thermoregulation." Mortality is an issue for humans at both ends of the continuum. Research has shown that some individuals are "short sleepers" who apparently show no ill effects with as little as five hours of sleep. Anything less than 5 hours or longer than 9 hours of sleep per day is associated with increased risk of death. A study in France showed that insomniacs not only had more accidents while driving, they had a "3-fold greater risk of having 2 or 3 serious road accidents."

In short, adequate sleep is necessary to stay healthy and safe. And staying healthy and safe increases your chances of getting adequate restorative sleep.

Sleep Process

Sleep is pretty much involuntary. When our body circumstances and our environment are conducive, sleep occurs. It is regulated by two processes – homeostasis and circadian factors.

Sleep "drive" is influenced by the homeostasis factor. The length of time you spend awake is one of the strongest influences of the strength of that drive. The longer you are awake, the more urgently you feel a need to sleep. The EEG delta waves you produce during non-REM sleep and the theta waves when awake are in proportion to your sleep drive.

The 24-hour, or circadian factor, is another powerful and multifaceted influence on our sleep drive. This is driven by our biological clock and varies across a 24-hour day. This is neurobiological. It is part of being human.

These internal rhythms respond to environmental cues referred to as zeitgebers, or time givers. Light is the strongest time giver. It can completely suppress the secretion of melatonin.

All systems are affected. The endocrine system shows predictable changes. The amount of cortisol in your blood rises rapidly in the morning. Some are tempted to say the increase in cortisol reflects the stress of getting out of bed. Certainly the cortisol measures across time reflect your body's response to real or perceived stress. In contrast melatonin tends to be at its highest before your regular bedtime, levels off during sleep and is at its lowest some time prior to your regular time of awakening. In healthy persons, the core body temperature varies to a daily rhythm, dropping as you sleep to the lowest reading about 1 to 3 hours before your regular time of awakening. The temperature of the brain decreases during non-REM sleep and increases in certain regions during REM sleep.

The homeostatic and circadian factors regulate sleep in interactive processes with a "sleep switch" in the hypothalamus (the ventrolateral preoptic area of the hypothalamus, or VLPO). It receives messages from the "master regulator" of our awake states through the hypocretin system. This involves the neurotransmitter hypocretin or orexin. It is keeping the homeostatic and circadian factors in balance that ensures restorative sleep at night and effective daytime functioning.

The suprachiasmatic nucleus (SCN) in your brain is the main pacemaker of the circadian factor. Melatonin, a neurotransmitter, is a slave to the SCN. The SCN dictates increasing or decreasing production of melatonin as well as other neurochemicals. About two hours prior to your regular bedtime your pineal gland begins the process of increasing the amount of melatonin in your blood. This is associated with feeling sleepy. Melatonin normally reaches it highest level between 2 and 3 AM. This coincides with an increased tendency to maintain sleep. Melatonin is thought to inhibit the circadian factor of being awake.

Melatonin synthesis is regulated primarily by the 24-hour light/dark cycle. Melatonin synthesis and release are increased in response to darkness and decreased when your retina perceives light. Thus, melatonin is sometimes characterized as the "hormone of darkness." Although the significance is unknown, melatonin is also a powerful antioxidant. There is some evidence that sleep problems are related to insufficient production of melatonin.

How to do it – What's a sleeper to do?

After ruling out any medical causes for poor sleep, there are four categories of options. Your homeostatic sleep drive has several known influences. Circadian factors are addressed by focusing on the major zeitgeber–light … and its opposite, darkness. Cognitive Behavioral Techniques on average have shown up to sixty percent improvement in sleep onset and maintenance. Research has found about eighty-five percent improvement in sleep efficiency as well as thirty to forty-five minutes of increased sleep time. These strategies address practical, behavioral and environmental changes which effect sleep. Other information aims at addressing your internal chemistry. These are based on research showing how to improve the quantity, quality and maintenance of sleep.

Your sleep "drive"

Get regular exercise – aerobic is best. To influence your homeostatic drive for sleep increase your level of physical activity during your time awake. Exercise creates a "sleep debt." It tends to improve sleep onset, enhances phases 3 and 4 "deep" sleep which is restorative and helps maintain sleep.

Depression is associated with diminished quantity and quality of sleep. Aerobic exercise thirty minutes three times a week has shown an antidepressant effect equaling a commonly prescribed antidepressant. Aerobic exercise also reduces the chemistry of stress and inflammation. That adds to the list of reasons to exercise regularly.

However, complete your exercises at least four, possibly six, hours prior to your regular bedtime. Exercise raises your core body temperature. Done too close to bedtime it will interfere with your body's circadian rhythm for temperature which requires that the brain be cooler to facilitate sleep.

Do not nap. Unless your healthcare provider suggests otherwise. And except during those wonderful times of your life when you are enjoying early onset of sleep, better than 85% maintenance of restorative sleep AND you awaken with joie de vivre and sufficient energy for peak performance. On those delicious days a nap of no more than 20 minutes around the middle of your day could be restorative without interfering with your getting a good night of sleep.

The rule is that your drive to sleep is increased by the amount of time you are awake. So, be judicious if you nap. Whenever you are having difficulty going to sleep and staying there through the night such that you are not in top form during the next day, nix the nap.

Stay in bed only for the amount of time you usually sleep … while maintaining the same time of awakening seven days a week. Thus, if you awaken daily at 6 AM and achieve peak performance with seven hours asleep, set your bedtime between 10:30 PM and 11 PM. Lingering in the bed without sleeping could reduce the quality of your sleep on subsequent nights. The range between 7 and 8 hours of sleep per day has the strongest association with health. By the same token there is evidence that some individuals can thrive on fewer than seven hours. Research is pretty clear that risk of medical problems and even death increase with both too much and too little sleep. Monitor your 24-hour activities over the course of a week to determine the number of hours of sleep that results in your having restorative sleep and best performance during waking hours. Maintain the same awakening time and set your bedtime to assure you are in bed only long enough to get the amount of sleep that is restorative.

Circadian Rhythms

Wake up at the same time _every day with bright light_. The *most powerful* way to improve sleep is to set a regular time for awakening with exposure to light…and stick to it *every day including weekends*. That's what makes it repeatable. Especially because the timing of light and dark have so much influence on sleep onset, sleep maintenance and alertness during waking hours.

By getting up at the same time every day you maximize the natural circadian factors influencing sleep and wakefulness. Bright light on awakening signals the decrease of melatonin, the hormone (you called it the hormone of darkness of p 102) associated with feeling drowsy. Bright light during the two hours prior to your regular bedtime will advance the evening time that melatonin will be increased and will delay sleep onset.

Simulate dawn. That means gradually increasing the amount of light in the thirty to forty-five minutes prior to getting up so the lighting in your bedroom is as close as possible to daylight. This will increase the value of the regular awakening even if your light exposure is only 250 lux as might be typical in a home.

Go outside on awakening. Within thirty minutes of your regular time to get up get at least thirty minutes of sunlight. The amount of light on a cloudy Seattle morning is somewhere between 1,000 and 10,000 lux (how light is measured). That exceeds what has been found in "bright, well-lit" offices at 400 to 600 lux. And most homes achieve 100 to 300 lux. So, you can see why going outside will give your eyes a stronger light signal than can easily be managed in a bedroom. Sunny mornings are even more effective.

Simulate dusk. A feeling of sleepiness is increased by dimming the lights gradually during the two hours prior to your regular bedtime. This darkness signals your body's natural release of melatonin so sleep onset can occur within 30 or fewer minutes after going to bed.

Stay in darkness through the night. Since safety comes first, if a night light is necessary, keep it as dim as possible. Dimming the lights during the few hours prior to bedtime is the beginning of this. If your bedroom isn't dark and there is no way to make it dark, consider using an eye mask. Even the amount of light in a dim room perceived through closed eyelids can give a mixed signal to your brain that delays or diminishes production of melatonin.

If you get up in the night, do not expose yourself to bright light. Use the minimum light needed for safety.

Cognitive Behavioral Therapy

Wake up at the same time _every day with bright light_. The *most powerful* way to improve sleep is to set a regular time for awakening, expose yourself to bright light and stick to it *every day including weekends.* From a Cognitive Behavioral perspective it is one of the adaptive conditioned responses. The regular time of awakening is a form of stimulus control.

By getting up at the same time every day you maximize the natural circadian factors influencing sleep and wakefulness. By awakening to bright light you signal the decrease of melatonin, the hormone associated with feeling drowsy.

Use your bedroom only for sleeping and making love. This form of stimulus control establishes a conditioned response so that sleep onset and maintenance is enhanced. When you read, knit, watch TV or do other activities in bed, the bedroom loses the association with sleep or lovemaking. Remember, Pavlov only associated food with the ringing of the bell to teach his dogs to salivate at the sound of the bell. There was no confounding activity. Keeping this association of your bedroom with ONLY sleep and lovemaking is what increases the positive influence on sleep onset and maintenance.

Think and believe sleep promoting thoughts. By understanding how many ways you can improve your sleep, you are more empowered. Perceived control has been shown to generate less anxiety than believing that nothing you do will improve your situation. By remembering that research findings are probability statements – not everyone needs exactly 7.9 hours of sleep – you can be more comfortable in establishing the ideal amount of sleep that will result in your awakening easily with joie de vivre and sufficient mental and physical energy to make the highest and best use of your day. By recalling that it is not unusual to awaken briefly during the night, you can experience less arousal if you do awaken. By telling yourself that the bright light in the morning will enhance your awakening and being alert with good functioning, you can more easily return to sleep assured of your welfare. By establishing a conditioned relaxation response, you will have heightened awareness of arousal and increased ability to decrease it rapidly. By making a mental appointment to handle the next day anything you think of in the night, you can stay calm knowing the situation will be handled … or at least that you've set an appointment to worry about it later. By realizing that everyone sleeps differently (I've been told by one of his students that Buckminster Fuller only slept three hours out of twenty-four and look at how much his brilliance contributed to the world: the geodesic dome is but one of his inventions), you can begin to view an occasional short night as a potential to use more of the hours of a given day differently.

Use progressive muscle relaxation. This is a first-line of treatment recommended by the American Medical Association for sleep deprivation and insomnia. This is one of the most effective non-pharmacologic ways of improving sleep. It reduces arousal caused by your autonomic nervous system. It also reduces arousal caused by sleep-sabotaging thoughts. The simple act of following the instructions for progressively relaxing opposing sets of muscles tends to still a busy mind as it focuses on the instructions and the growing sensation of being more relaxed. Since the whole technique takes about twenty minutes, it easily fits into the desired thirty minute window for sleep onset.

To markedly increase the power of this technique, use it frequently enough and long enough to establish a conditioned response. When you develop the conditioned response, a simple thought cue to yourself can afford you deep relaxation in minutes. Pavlov taught his dogs to salivate at the sound of a bell. This conditioned response is a similar mechanism but smarter. At the thought of the cue to relax, you can reduce arousal very quickly. That make this conditioned response a gift you can give yourself with any awakening in the night. Developing a conditioned response is simple but can be time consuming. By using the technique twice a day, most of my clients developed a conditioned response in about two weeks. Using it only once a day took longer to build the conditioned response but still did so. That means you can save time by using this technique as part of your bedtime routine every night. Use it during the desired thirty minute window between getting in bed and falling asleep. See the chapter on relaxation for further details.

Go to bed at a regular time. This establishes a conditioned response to begin sleeping in response to time. It takes advantage of the circadian factors which make sleep at bedtime the natural outcome. There is some literature suggesting that going to bed only when sleepy improves sleep as long as the regular time of awakening is adhered to.

Have a routine before bedtime. As part of the routine of gradually turning down the lights, do the same type of things every night. For example, take supplements if that's part of your self care. Floss your teeth. Do four minutes of brushing your teeth with an electric toothbrush that effectively removes plaque. Meditate. Journal on gratitude. Write down three things that went well today and what caused them (more on this technique in the chapter on **Enduring Happiness**). Massage your feet. Or your hands. Whatever is relaxing for you.

If that includes reading, find a comfortable spot out of the bedroom. Use low light. Only read something that is sleep inducing such at Henry David Thoreau's *On Walden Pond.*

Be sure no clock is visible from your bed ... unless you find it helpful in decision making. No research has been done on this topic. Clinical findings suggest that many people have a tendency to worry about the effects of loss of sleep if a clock is visible. Some people find it easier to return to sleep when there is no sensation of time. My colleague who is an expert in sleep research finds it easier to decide which action to take if he can see what time it is. Sleep laboratories report that people consistently underestimate how much time they actually are asleep. Therefore, it would seem that you can tailor this to your own style of getting the most out of a night of sleep. If you can use the clock for your own best decision in the night, keep if visible. If you look at it and think troubling thoughts that disturb your sleep, hide it until you learn to think self empowering thoughts.

My niece decided to set the alarm for several hours ahead of the time she was required to get up so she could think, "Great, I still have four hours to sleep." She repeated that pattern for three hours, two hours and one hour…to celebrate how much time she had left to sleep. That was during her adolescence. She outgrew the pattern.

The point is if you see the clock when you awaken and think thoughts that help you return to sleep, it may be a useful tool. Do what is best for you until more research come in.

Decrease liquid intake for several hours prior to bedtime. Be certain to get plenty of fluid early each day. With a little experimenting you will soon know how far ahead of bedtime you want to restrict fluids so you are not awakened by a need to go the bathroom.

Keep your bedroom temperature at or below 66° F. The circadian rhythm of your body's temperature includes a drop during sleep. The brain requires this lower temperature. It's been said that at 58° F dust mites cannot move. In a room at that temperature you are less likely to be disturbed by those pesky dust mites making night moves on your tympanic membranes. That could improve your sleep. Room temperatures at or above 82° F with high humidity resulted in less efficiency of sleep and more episodes of being awake.

Other

No stimulants. Remember that caffeine has a half life of about 7 ½ hours. This might be grounds to eliminate it from your life. Certainly avoid it all together past noon.

This also includes avoiding any media and games during your bedtime routine. These have the potential to energize when you need to be slowing your mental, emotional and physical paces.

Do not smoke.

Avoid alcohol. When consumed prior to bedtime alcohol does make it easier for some people to go to sleep. However, that effect wears off in a few hours causing awakening in the night. It makes sleep non-restorative by increasing slow-wave sleep, decreasing REM sleep and interfering with the second phase of sleep.

Have a light snack such as warm milk at bedtime. This has been shown to promote sleep onset. It also satisfies the suggestion to have a small, light snack at bedtime to avoid being awakened by hunger. Avoid heavy foods for about three hours prior to bedtime.

Melatonin. This is the "hormone of darkness." In individuals whose bodies create a normal amount of melatonin, taking additional amounts has not been shown to be effective. However, people vary in how much their body produces. Generally the amount produced declines with age. In people who produce too little melatonin to experience sleep onset within about thirty minutes, research has shown some benefit to taking up to 0.5 mg of time-released melatonin. When given 3 mg by mouth for up to 6 months added to prescription medication for sleep, elderly insomniac women had better sleep quantity and quality. They went to sleep faster and awakened less during the night. They also functioned significantly better the next day.

Melatonin taken at bedtime was not associated with sleepiness during the following morning as often occurs with prescription medications. These effects were more prominent in individuals who secreted low levels of melatonin than in individuals whose natural melatonin was within the normal range. Even 0.1 to 0.3 mg has been found to cause sleep during the day.

> "Recent studies show that melatonin plays an important role in the circadian regulation of sleep and has a significant sleep promoting activity."
> S. R. Pandi-Perumal and colleagues in
> *Experimental Gerontology*

Measuring Goals

Both daytime and nighttime activities must be assessed because they interact to affect the quality of each time period. Activities just prior to regular bedtime improve or lessen the quality and duration of sleep. The amount of time it takes to fall asleep, how many times you awaken during the night, what you do during night-time awakening, how long you are awake with each awakening and any sleep decreasing activities such as snoring, pain and movements are important to assessing quality of sleep. Time of awakening and how that is achieved are equally important. Activities during the day are important to track. Any sleepiness or naps during the day should be noted.

Daytime Activities

Awakening Time_____   Is this your usual time? Yes ___ No ___

If no, is it earlier? ___ Later? ___   By how much? _____

Night time Activities

What time did you get in bed? _____ What is your usual bedtime? _____

When preparing for sleep, were you tired? Yes ___ No ___

Were you anxious? Yes ___ No ___   Could you let this anxiety go? Yes ___ No ___

If yes, how did you do that? _____ If not, why? _____

Environment

When did you start to dim the lights?_____ Was your bedroom cool? Yes ___ No ___

What was your evening routine? _____

Did you properly limit your fluid intake? Yes ___ No ___

Did you have a light snack or warm milk at bedtime? Yes ___ No ___

Did you use the bedroom for anything other than sleep or lovemaking? Yes ___ No ___

Other Options

Exercise:
Did you exercise for 30 minutes or more today? Yes ___ No___ How long? _____
Was your exercise aerobic today?   Yes ___ No ___

Caffeine:
Did you ingest caffeine today?   Yes ___ No ___   How Much? _____

What time today was your last intake of caffeine? _____

Smoking:
Did you smoke today?   Yes___ No ___   How much: _____

Alcohol:
Did you consume alcohol today? Yes ___ No ___   How much? _____
What time was your last intake of alcohol? _____

Sleep • 103

Summary

Potential benefits of good quality and sufficient quantity of restorative sleep are:

- Creating new brain cells
- Improving memory and learning
- Stabilizing weight and metabolism
- Appreciating a delicious quality of life
- Awakening easily with joie de vivre
- Enjoying better health with less inflammation
- Having a stronger immune response

Although a few people appear to be functioning with as little as five hours of sleep, the long term effects of this are unknown. Research has found a higher risk of death with fewer than five and more than nine hours of sleep per day.

The most powerful way to improve sleep is to have a regular time for going to bed and for awakening *every day ... including weekends.* Reducing light exposure during the two hours preceding regular bedtime enhances the onset of sleep. Use of a dawn simulator for gradual introduction of bright light at the regular time for awakening improves physical and mental energy during the day.

Cognitive behavioral techniques are effective for approximately eighty percent of subjects with sleep deprivation. The most effective interventions include developing conditioned responses such as using the bedroom only for sleep and lovemaking, developing a cued conditioned relaxation response to counter arousal and learning the style of thinking that helps you sleep.

2. HAPPY HABIT—FOR THE HEALTH THAT IS "CONTAGIOUS"

To keep your brain fit, keep it happy.

If that sounds simple, take heart in knowing that it can also be easy and fun. Following the model of Norman Cousins can be rewarding in more ways than one. Do what it takes to add laughter to your life. Use the biology of hope to your advantage.

Chronic stress can reduce neurogenesis, decrease the percentage of new neurons that survive and thrive and make you more vulnerable to diseases. That is why it's important to have a full tool box of skills to alleviate long term stress. Planned happiness is one of my favorite skills. Science says some real risk reduction can clearly come with positive emotions.

The goal of the Happy Habit is to create as many microseconds as possible of the kind of body chemistry shown to enhance overall health. Stress has many faces. Mild to moderate stress improves performance on many levels including some improvements in cognitive functioning. It is prolonged stress that can wreak havoc with your **Bones, Brains & Beauty®**.

Is "happily ever after" one of your goals? We don't yet have research proving that that is attainable. However, Seligman spearheaded research that has identified what others have done to develop enduring authentic happiness.

With the new technologies plus instant information via the internet, social neuroscience research is mushrooming. The findings even on the "normal" population prove we have more to count on and less to fear than had ever been known. Some of the new research findings are simply exhilarating!

Richard Davidson researched some extraordinary monks trained in Asian perspectives and practices. He found that monks with a history of long term meditation had increased the thickness of part of their cortex in comparison with people who had not meditated. These areas of the cortex of the long-term meditation monks were also thicker than the monks who had meditated only long enough to show some thickening in these same areas. The brain area showing increased thickness was the left prefrontal cortex (PFC)—the part of the brain identified as associated with happy emotions. Mindfulness meditation is a way of being in the world. It includes greater awareness in the present moment, seeing clearly and just observing. What's not to like about science showing that it's never too early and never too late to improve the architecture of your brain as well as the power of how it functions?

Happiness, creativity, hope, love, positive character, positive reinforcement, institutions that enhance positive emotions … these elements are associated with many good outcomes beyond just feeling good. Daniel Goleman proposed to His Holiness the Dalai Lama that your body's immune system provides an ethical system which might appeal to the three or four billion people on planet earth that have no religious beliefs. The largest body of data details the bad effects of negative emotions on health. A growing body of research addresses the healing power of positive emotions.

Conditioned Responses can have the most enduring power. This has been demonstrated with the placebo effect in which subjects have the described expected outcome whether they are given the drug under investigation or an inactive pill.

Even the immune response can develop a Conditioned Response. This has been so convincingly demonstrated by Robert Ader that there was only one reason to not chock those results up to the placebo effect. His initial research was with rats, sheep and other animals. At the same time that the animals were injected with medication that suppressed their immune system, they were also injected with a placebo. This "conditioned" their immune system to react when the placebo was given alone.

This was similar to the famous dogs of Pavlov but had a broader potential use. Unlike other animals, people enjoy the placebo effect when they experience a favorable outcome which they assumed would occur. For example, people with hypertension did worse when medications were stopped than when the medication was replaced with a pill with inactive ingredients.

Belief affects biology … including that of people with whom linking and looping share the impact.

"…a full life consists in experiencing positive emotions about the past and future, savoring positive feelings from the pleasures, deriving abundant gratification from your signature strengths, and using these strengths in the service of something larger to obtain meaning."
Martin E. P. Seligman in *Authentic Happiness*

LAUGHTER

"Indeed, laughter may be the shortest distance between two brains, an unstoppable, infectious spread that builds an instant social bond."
Daniel Goleman in *Social Intelligence*

Goals

- Combine comedy with new learning … to facilitate that learning, memory and creativity

- Watch a comedy video for one hour … to improve your immune response

- Develop a list of jokes and one-liners … to enhance your social interactions

- Get ten minutes of solid belly laughter … to help relieve pain

- Enhance positive social interactions … to connect with emotions that are "contagious" and healthy

Dr. Norman Cousins. author of *Anatomy of an Illness as Perceived by the Patient: Reflections on Healing and Regeneration,* gave the invited address at the American Psychological Association (APA) in 1985. The room was meant to hold thousands of people. It was standing room only. With no notes he kept the room rolling with laughter.

Years ahead of that APA address, I'd been "tricked" into reading it. "*Anatomy of an Illness!* The story of a man who laughed himself well. Dr. Joyce, you gotta read it!" the nurse said.

Nodding politely as she handed me her copy I was not sharing my thoughts. "The story of a man who laughed himself well? I don't think so! I'm a scientist. Show me the random controlled trials. Give me the gold standard of the industry. Science or silence. No way am I going to read this. First, it's a case study and second, laughter as medicine just doesn't cut it."

And then I remembered: a scientist doesn't diagnose prior to the evaluation.

Science behind your plan

Read *Anatomy of an Illness*. As you know, I don't give doctors orders. Even if I did, I wouldn't in books. So this is just an invitation to you, Dear Reader, to linger longer with an erudite, witty, wonderful soul who played an active role in directing his life away from the brink of death. His is a fresh breath. Norman Cousins brought us the science about the impact of positive emotions on health. He wrote a textbook on *The Biology of Hope.*

Cousins had been 40 years the editor of the *Saturday Review*. He was an intelligent and informed consumer of health services. He was in considerable pain when physicians diagnosed ankylosing spondylitis, an inflammatory disease.,. One specialist had estimated that he had "one chance in five hundred" of surviving this illness. According to Cousins, his collagen disease was causing him to come unstuck. He had an investment in the outcome.

Since he had read that negative emotions caused disease, it was his logic that positive emotions would heal. Among his assets were his physician who was excited to partner with Cousins in his plan; an outsized will to live; creative problem solving; plenty of friends to supply love, hope and faith; and a lot of information on the chemical changes caused by negative emotions. He also had so much pain and anxiety that testing his hypothesis about laughter would have been a stretch without a systematic program. Films and TV shows filled the bill.

> "It worked. I made the joyous discovery that
> ten minutes of genuine belly laughter
> had an anesthetic effect and
> would give me at least two hours of pain-free sleep.'"
> Norman Cousins in *Anatomy of an Illness*

When the pain returned, the movie-induced laughter cycle was repeated. Readings from books on humor added to this systematic program of laughter for pain relief.

There also were measured changes in his body chemistry suggesting an improvement in his immune system's ability to decrease inflammation. For Cousins, these repeated measures of reduced sedimentation rate support "the ancient theory that laughter is good medicine." Sedimentation rate is the measure of inflammation that was used to follow the course of his illness. His had become elevated to the point of being considered critical. It dropped at least five points from when it was measured before and for some hours after each session of laughter. Even though this is a case study it set the stage for further research on the physiology of laughter.

Laughter was among the self-designed interventions he attributed to saving his life. He accepted an invitation to be on faculty with the School of Medicine at University of California in Los Angeles. Dr. Norman Cousins' insight has played a major role in advancing the science of laughter and healing.

Lee Berk and colleagues found healthier immune responses associated with one hour of watching a comedy video. Some of these benefits lasted up to twelve hours. Although their data have some findings that are similar to those associated with exercise, they did not show increases in beta-endorphin, prolactin and norepinephrine. Their research found reductions in cortisol, growth hormone, and epinephrine. Other physical changes were improved immune function including increased white blood cells.

Blood glucose was measured In individuals with adult-onset diabetes prior to and two hours after their eating a standard five hundred calorie meal. After eating on day one, they heard a non-humorous lecture. Day two they attended a forty-minute comedy show after eating. Laughter was associated with a lower blood glucose reading in diabetics after they had eaten. From this Keiko Hayashi and colleagues concluded that diabetics could benefit from daily laughter as an inhibitor of elevated blood glucose after eating. This was a small sample. These authors acknowledge the difficulty in determining whether this difference was due to the energy expenditure of laughing or to the effect of positive emotions on the neuroendocrine system.

Appreciation of humor involves complex interactions of various parts of your brain. Many steps are required to "get" the joke. The parts of your brain that are stimulated are different for visual humor, such are cartoons, than for spoken comedy. That means humor which provokes laughter could be an effective neurobic exercise (more in the chapter **Smarter This Year**). Memory and learning are improved when the presentation is comedic.

After the surprise of incongruity, your reinterpretation of the event provides the humor. Allman and colleagues found that humor produces actions in many parts of your brain that are similar to those of other rewards. Both activate the reward system which releases dopamine. They believe that being able to appreciate humor "is related to the ability to make rapid, intuitive assessments, a skill that would be particularly adaptive during the complex social interactions typical of our lives." Humor also is associated with some changes in your autonomic nervous system. You may show heightened arousal in anticipation of or release of tension when what you see or hear is incongruous with previous experience.

Watching a comedy film prior to doing a novel task increased creativity. Several studies have found that laughter is associated with psychological benefits including improved self esteem, better coping skills and elevated mood.

A ten to twenty percent increase in the energy you burn and in your heart rate is a possibility with laughter which is genuine and given voice. This is in comparison to your resting rate of pulse and energy expenditure. Researchers suggest that up to forty kilocalories could be burnt with fifteen minutes of laughing depending on how hard and long you laugh. However, this doesn't hold a kilo-candle to activities such as aerobics and some household chores that can increase your energy expenditure up to 100 percent . But maybe every little calorie helps, especially if social and emotional benefits top off your efforts.

Ninety-four percent of healthcare providers surveyed in Alaska believe that laughter is good medicine because it supports a comfortable community for learning, relieves stress and enhances learning. The virtual Giggles Theatre was started in 2005 to afford children with catastrophic illness some relief through laughter with programs available on the internet.

Medical settings have begun to include laughter in their total care. Harborview Medical Center in Seattle added it to their provision of compassionate medical care. On a weekly basis staff, patients and people who drop into the Patient and Family Resource Center keep the laughter echoing down hallways and byways. Tita Begashow invited people to the first session in 2000. Kevin Wilhelmsen, a clinical nurse educator of psychiatry at Harborview, works with her in adding to the farce. Elva Dodd has been a member of this laugh group for five years. She believes "Laughter does discourage pain" as reported in *The Seattle Post-Intelligence*.

As the body of research continues to grow and clarify what elicits mental, emotional, social and physical health benefits, increasing numbers of people and companies are choosing to take laughter seriously. And it's free. That makes it a particularly valuable routine to choreograph for Ideal Aging™.

How to do it

Research has used comedy films, cartoons, jokes, etc. In addition to these, Cousins used books of humor read to him by friends. A couple I've worked with laughed themselves silly over crossword puzzles.

Clinically helpful have been recordings that can be played easily, even repetitively. There are several routines by Bill Cosby that I have pretty much committed to memory from the many times and situations in which they bridged the gap between knowing what was ahead and getting there.

Another valuable clinical tool is to collect funny scenarios throughout your life. While waiting for more definitive research, remember that laughter enhances memory, learning and creativity. Enjoy finding as many sources of laughter as possible.

Measuring Goals

Start with measuring your laughter on a daily basis. Look for frequency, intensity and duration of laughter. Make note of who is with you when you laugh.

How many times did you laugh? _____

How long did you laugh each time? _____

What effect did it have on you? _____

Who was with you? _____

What about the situation made it funny? _____
_____
_____

What one-liners or short jokes can you commit to memory to share when the time and people are right? As you gather new ones to share, write them down here.
_____
_____
_____
_____
_____
_____
_____
_____

Also do an abbreviated SUFI measure at the end of the day. Refer to the description of this tool in the Introduction. In an overall sense of how you feel about the day, give yourself a score between -10 and +10.

Subjective Units of Feelings Index (SUFI Report™)
-10   **0**   **+10**

Your score at the end of the day _____

Look for the relationship between your SUFI score at the end of the day and the frequency, intensity and duration of your laughter during the day. As the amount of time you spend laughing increases, your SUFI Report should become more and more positive.

Summary

Laughter may be a powerful medicine. Neuroendocrine, sympathetic nervous system response, social and emotional changes are all associated with full-bodied laughter given voice. Laughter can reduce muscle tension, increase the oxygen in your blood, give your heart a workout, and increase endorphins.

These changes show some similarities to those associated with exercise although burning fewer calories in comparison to exercise. But a good laugh while hanging onto the overhead loop in the aisle of a standing-room-only bus is more convenient than being aerobic. Of course, some of you can get aerobic in that situation by simply hanging on while alternating between rising on your tiptoes and doing a squat to strengthen your leg muscles. I leave it to your discretion to decide which will have the most positive impact on your image as well as your mood.

However, there is a certain wisdom, if you choose to burst into raucous laughter in the aisle of any bus (or on the street corner for that matter), in being sensitive to those around you. Hopefully they can share your comedic relief. Goleman assures us that emotions are contagious. At the very least, it's preferable that they are not offended by it. Laughter can be good medicine for immediate relief when you need it most, especially when sensitivity to the gravity of the situation and needs of others in your environment are respected.

Being full of laughter tends to improve your social attractiveness. People are more prone to want to be where the laughter is. Using laughter to increase your social supports could be all good. According to Goleman, our brains are wired to connect and laughter may be the shortest bridge to form and strengthen social bonds.

ENDURING HAPPINESS

*"Daddy, do you remember before my fifth birthday? From when I was three until when I was five, I was a whiner. I whined every day. On my fifth birthday, I decided I wasn't going to whine anymore.
That was the hardest thing I've ever done.
And if I can stop whining, you can stop being such a grouch."*
Nikki, 5 years old
As quoted by Martin E. P. Seligman in *Authentic Happiness*

"The vast psychological literature on suffering is not very applicable to Nikki. A better psychology for her and children everywhere will view positive motivations–loving kindness, competence, choice, and respect for life–as being just as authentic as the darker motives. It will enquire about such positive feelings as satisfaction, happiness, and hope. It will ask how children can acquire the strengths and virtues whose exercise leads to these positive feelings. It will ask about the positive institutions (strong families, democracy, a broad moral circle) that promote these strengths and virtues. It will guide us all along better paths to the good life."
Martin E. P. Seligman in *Authentic Happiness*

Goals

- Awareness of your Signature Strengths … because using them helps you thrive

- Better interactions with your world … because you're easier to negotiate with

- Stronger friendship bonds … because you're more expansive, tolerant, creative

- Higher quality romantic relationships … because positive emotion predicts marital satisfaction

- Less pain … because happiness increases endorphins

- Better physical health … because happy people tend to have more healthy habits

- Vigorous longevity … because positive emotion predicts living longer with less deterioration

- Improved immune response … because happiness has a good influence on your stress chemistry

- Enhanced performance … because positive emotions broaden your intellectual resources, increase productivity and are associated with higher income

Science behind your plan

Many of us may be more indebted to Nikki than first meets the eye. That short conversation with one small daughter helped Seligman define his mission during his presidency of the American Psychological Association. Building on giants in the field who had gone before, Seligman worked to advance the scientific base of mental health and well-being.

The impact of positive emotions has been found in remarkable studies. Part of the brilliant work in the Nun Study by David Snowdon analyzed early writings of the nuns. In the happiest fourth of that group, ninety percent were alive at the age of 85 and fifty-four percent were alive at age 94. In the least happy fourth of nuns the percent alive was only thirty-four percent at age 85 and a shockingly low eleven percent at age 94. One of the amazing elements of these statistics is the association of longevity to expressions of positive emotions in one essay which the nun had written decades prior.

Equally impressive is the ability to predict outcomes from women's college pictures taken as much as 30 years earlier. Harker and Keltner found wellbeing and positive outcomes in marriage were associated with the presence of a Duchenne smile captured in one photo in college yearbooks. This smile is named after Guillaume Duchenne, a nineteenth century neurologist. His detailed study of muscles in the human face convinced him that false or half-hearted smiles involved only muscles around the mouth. Smiles reflecting true happiness involve several additional involuntary muscles. A happy smile cannot be faked because it requires these involuntary muscles. It is remarkable that the Duchenne smile reflecting authentic happiness in one photo predicted wellbeing and good marriages 30 years later.

As the research of Davidson has shown the left prefrontal cortex (PFC) has shown marked and sustained increased activity during the bliss experienced in monks. It is meaning, pleasure and mental engagement that add up to happiness.

Positive psychologists studied interventions to increase happiness as well as treat suffering. Increasing someone's "buffering strengths" is certainly as important as decreasing stress.

The Diagnostic and Statistical Manual of Mental Disorders (DSM) of the American Psychiatric Association has been of significant value in the treatment of mental illness. Seligman coauthored the *Character Strengths and Virtues: A Handbook and Classification* as a complement to the DSM. By classifying and describing human strengths and virtues, he established the goal to enhance thriving, to discover and empower buffering strengths.

Seligman offers powerful tools for building enduring happiness that is authentic and, by its own right, healing. His book, *Authentic Happiness,* provides tremendous detail and an erudite integration of extensive research which has evolved to appreciate the role of positive emotions.

Also, it seems that Seligman's experience as a grouch has increased the value of his interpretation of groundbreaking science on both ends of the spectrum – immersion in misery versus pervasive happiness. The sufferer of the malady has heightened opportunity to take the measure of the stress of grouchiness. The grouch also gets to see the impact on self and environment when using the leverage of judicious change.

What a refreshing perspective! Focus on your signature strengths rather than spending a lot of resources correcting your weaknesses. In other words, make your strengths productive and your weaknesses irrelevant. Ask not what the world needs. Ask what makes your heart sing. What lifts your face in an involuntary smile? Do that. Because people like to do what they do well.

What a gift his contribution to developing stress power is. For surely it's impossible to be both stressed out and authentically happy. Let the wise counsel of research in the field of Positive Psychology help you evolve into being joyfully, more meaningfully alive.

At AuthenticHappiness.org you can take multiple surveys to increase your self awareness, compare yourself with others who take these surveys, track your progress over time as you raise the bar in defining optimal as well as authentic happiness for yourself and contribute to the valuable database on the role of positive psychology in improving quality of life. That's a huge return on investment in your own health as well as the health of fellow citizens of the world. You might want to stop at this point and return to this page after you go to AuthenticHappiness.org to learn more about yourself and the new science of positive psychology.

The centuries of focus on illness have saved countless lives and reduced suffering worldwide. What a gift to be alive as the focus shifts for so many scientists—to include study of the hardy in quest of expanding the definition of optimal health.

Research by Seligman on learned helplessness has helped us identify environmental influences which will change an active animal into one which is helpless. These include insolvable problems.

Unfortunately, I learned that in a case study that I wouldn't have published even if a journal would have begged for it. In our undergraduate psychology lab we were assigned the task of training the (ever-present) rat to pick up a marble and put it through a small hole in an overturned end of a tin can.

Stick with this. It's a sad but clear portrayal of poorly applied reinforcement.

All other classmates accomplished the task easily and quickly. They simply gave their rat a pellet of food for successive approximation. That means the rat got food for each baby step in the right direction.

However, my lab partner and I focused more on talking about the trials and tribulations of our lives than we did on our rat. We were oblivious to any baby rat steps in the correct direction. Our granting of pellets to the hungry rat was random. The poor thing went off to the far corner of the cage to huddle, urinate on itself and quiver.

Years later I take little comfort in knowing that we at least did not subject that rat to the inescapable trauma other experimental rats have known. What we did was influence an active animal to act helpless.

Interestingly, Seligman found that about twelve percent of an animal population will start out helpless. But thirty-three percent never give up, no matter what!

That's rich food for thought. By recognizing how hardy people become invulnerable, resilient and strong in the midst of the level of stress that renders most mere mortals helpless, you have lengthened your list of options. You've invested in your future by creating a multiple choice list of ways you can empower yourself.

What are these elements of hardiness described by Seligman?

- Disputing catastrophic thoughts
- Future-mindedness
- Hope
- Interpersonal skills
- Courage
- Capacity for flow
- Faith
- Work Ethic
- Positive motivations–loving, kindness, choice, competence and respect for life
- Positive feelings–satisfaction, happiness and hope

See other chapters to broaden your reserves for tough times and happy ones. The stronger your positive emotions the greater will be your intellectual, interpersonal and physical health base for handling threats and capturing the best opportunities.

Happy people live longer, have less disability, suffer less pain and have the kind of health habits associated with lower blood pressure and more protective immune systems than less happy people. Increased happiness is also associated with higher quality goals, improved performance, more persistence, greater productivity and higher pay. Imagine that – such a huge Return on Investment from simple happiness! If happiness is simple.

Seligman sees happiness as scientifically difficult to define. Thus his focus is on three "routes to happiness" and satisfaction: 1) pleasure, 2) engagement and 3) meaning in life. None of these are seen as transient or superficial. When all five senses are intensely stimulated, the brain's pleasure system is activated. Total engagement in tasks to the point of loss of a sense of time and other contingencies brings satisfaction and authentic happiness. Making your signature strengths productive and your weaknesses irrelevant in social, career and entertainment activities is the strategy for achieving a meaningful life.

Lyubomirsky, King and Diener found that happiness causes success and being more engaged socially. By the same token, success and being socially engaged cause happiness.

Happy people that are socially engaged tend to be more altruistic. In dealing with people in need, happy people were more empathic and contributed more money.

In two hundred twenty-two college students the happiest ten percent had a richer and more fulfilling social life that the average people lacked. Happiness "causes much better commerce with the world." It affords a win-win situation as it helps bond friendships, enhances love, improves physical health and magnifies achievement. Judgment is appreciating complex contingencies. Happy people excel at this.

Seligman's formula for happiness is:

$$H = S + C + V$$

H is the enduring level of happiness which it is your challenge to raise. Even if you have inherited traits such as pessimism and fearfulness, you can learn to change for long term and authentic happiness.

S is a so-called set range which could inhibit increasing your level of happiness. However, there are forces under your control that could overpower this influence.

C includes some circumstances that could exert a positive influence on your happiness such as living with (but not focused on or attached to) wealth in a democracy, maintaining a satisfying marriage, decreasing negative events and the negative emotions you feel about them, cultivating a rich and fulfilling social life and strengthening religious beliefs that promote hope and afford meaning and purpose in life.

V signifies voluntary control of internal events. Hardy individuals often exert control over those external circumstances alluded to above. But these factors are subject to maximum control. This is often poorly understood and even more frequently far under-utilized. So let enduring authentic happiness begin – whether about your past, your present or your future!

To keep your past in a balance that facilitates enduring, healing, authentic happiness start with creating two lists.

To rid up and reduce the power of past trauma, create your list of traumatic events. Include the names of individuals involved. Be sure your name is on that list. With this list begin the process of forgiveness – of all individuals on the list, especially yourself. This helps you rewrite that history and let go of the power of angst and bitterness. See the chapter Forgive for more details.

Your second list is about gratitude. Both positive and painful events contributed to the beauty of who you are today. Capture the elements of progress in both happy and horrible moments. Crystallize the learning and growth from both kinds of experiences. As you continue to lengthen this list, you can magnify and multiply your satisfaction with and celebration of most of what has been.

For yourself, spend five minutes at either end of a day creating a list of at least five things in the past twenty-four hours for which you are grateful. This could markedly increase your happiness and satisfaction with life.

Because you know the value of feeding and nourishing your social network, do at least two things. First, begin now to tell people in any given moment why you are grateful to have them in your life.

Second, identify someone you may want to thank in a more meaningful way than you have. Spend the time to think back through why this individual is significant to you. As suggested by Dr. Seligman, record your testimonial on one laminated page. Without revealing the reason for the visit, take this with you. Read it aloud to this person with full expression and with eye contact while allowing time for the other person to react. What more precious gift could one give to self and others than sharing in this depth?

Future enduring happiness is strengthened by hope and optimism. Even pessimists can increase theirs.

For starters take an existential perspective on trauma. Label pain and trauma as temporary situations and lapses in skills in which you normally excel. For example, realize that you would have done better with more sleep.

On the other hand congratulate yourself and see your extraordinary traits and abilities as permanent factors associated with successes. This faith in your own abilities will result in your increased efforts with each success. Optimists stay on a roll when things go well and believe that each success will enhance all future endeavors.

It is noteworthy that optimists stay upbeat by observing their own strengths. Too frequently we are socialized to put down ourselves and others. As long as your self-praise is realistic, wouldn't it be healthier to overdose on complimenting yourself for your strengths and progress? By observing that good outcomes are a result of who you are and what you have done, you strengthen your productive behaviors while also increasing your happiness for the health of it.

Hope floats anyone's boat. The beauty of seeing good outcomes as caused by permanent and universal forces while misfortune has temporary and specific causes is the fabric of hope.

Pleasures are enhanced by taking time to be mindful of them. Linger with the awareness. Savor the pleasure.

Besides being a major source of pleasure, novelty sets your neurons abuzz … and causes them to increase the neurotrophins which build dendrites and spines and newer, more complex connections. The complexity of your new learning will improve how you will build your elegant brain cells. See the chapter on **Smarter This Year** for more details.

When new events are spaced judiciously, they can retain the aspect of novelty. Surprise also helps keep them novel. Part of the value of a rich social network is that friends can incorporate this element of surprise for each other.

Seligman's assignment to Have a Beautiful Day involves setting aside one day per month to "indulge in your favorite pleasures. Pamper yourself. Design, in writing, what you will do from hour to hour."

My way to guarantee a Beautiful Day involves putting a bright red border around the chosen day and creating a multiple choice list of personal pleasures lengthier than could ever be accomplished. When the day arrives I proceed on whim to do exactly and only what raises my cheeks in an involuntary and authentic smile (a Duchenne smile). That same day closes with the glee and gratitude of having been free to satisfy me from a cornucopia of excellent options. They were excellent options because I wrote the list.

Mihaly Csikszentmihalyi teaches increasing happiness with "flow." Time stops, your sense of self disappears, your goals are clear, challenge and skill are part of the task, you feel in control and you are concentrating so effectively that your involvement in what you're doing is deep and effortless. Is it any surprise, then, that your greatest moments of productivity are in the flow? The chapter **Flow** tells more.

Katherine Dahlsgaard led the reading of traditions in writings from across 3000 years and many civilizations to find the six virtues all endorsed. Those six virtues are:

- Wisdom and knowledge;
- Courage;
- Love and humanity;
- Justice;
- Temperance; and
- Spirituality and transcendence.

Strengths of character form the routes to achieving these virtues. Your strengths of character that you are aware of owning, that you celebrate and that you use daily and broadly—these are your *signature strengths*. Seligman's formulation of the good life: "Using your signature strengths every day in the main realms of your life to bring abundant gratification and authentic happiness."

How to do it

Seligman conducted a random controlled trial delivered over the internet. Participants were asked to complete their tasks in one week. They used one placebo and five interventions that were thought to decrease depression and increase happiness. All six groups reported more happiness on completion of the one week task, including the placebo. Only three of the interventions lasted beyond that first week.

"Three good things in life." Participants were asked to write down three things that went well each day and their causes every night for one week. Their other task was to explain the cause of each of the three good things. Individuals doing this exercise were happier one month later than they were prior to this study. Their happiness persisted at three months and at six months.

"Using signature strengths in a new way." At AuthenticHappiness.com. participants were able to take a character strengths inventory online. Individualized feedback was given on their top five "signature strengths." One of these top strengths was to be used in a "new and different way every day for one week." These individual also were happier at one, three and six months after participation than they had been prior to being in the research.

Even though everyone had been instructed to do their exercise during the one week of the research only, many continued on their own beyond that time. Those who experienced the most benefit had continued to do these exercises beyond the one week in spite of explicit instructions. The authors hypothesize that these skill are "self-maintaining" because they improve with practice and are fun. This is in contrast to the changes required for weight loss or body sculpting that consume a great deal of time and are slow to show results. Writing about the three good things in life with associated causes and using your signature strengths in new ways is quickly self reinforcing.

"Gratitude visit "was the third technique that produced large positive changes. Increased happiness was evident at the end of this task. However, the increased happiness lasted just one month. Since there's likely to be more than one individual in your life that's been especially kind to you while still insufficiently thanked, consider repeating this exercise on a monthly basis. The act of hand delivering a letter of gratitude to someone special, reading it to them with full emotional expression and leaving a laminated copy creates precious memories and bonding for both of you. In some instances it can also shed new and healing light on some old history.

"Happily ever after" might be possible based on continued use of these techniques. "Shotgun" efforts which use more than one of these approaches could be even more beneficial.

It is significant that improved happiness occurred with three techniques and, with two of them, lasted up to six months **even though it was accomplished via the internet without the benefit of the therapeutic relationship.** Seligman believes that the effects may be even more powerful in the hands of a skilled clinician or coach.

Summary

Authentic and enduring happiness involves using your signature strengths in new ways. It also involves writing about the causes of good things that happen in your life each day. Even though happiness following a gratitude visit only lasted one month, it could easily be repeated with additional loved ones. The beauty of all three skills is that since they are fun, they are self-reinforcing. They don't require practice because they come naturally. In fact, participants in this research kept doing them even though they were instructed to do them for only one week. People who kept doing them against advice showed more enduring happiness than those who stopped at one week as instructed.

What this research provides is an evolving scientific database behind what had been thought to be helpful. Giants in the field had laid the ground work. Nikki's words of wisdom were a tipping point. And positive emotions are associated with improved physical, intellectual, social, career and emotional health.

Remember, one smiling photograph predicted marital satisfaction and well-being as much as 30 years after that photo appeared in the college yearbook. The amount of positive emotions expressed in one essay for entry to the convent predicted longevity in the Nuns decades later. There is healthy purchase in authentic happiness.

While more techniques of creating enduring and authentic happiness are clarified by research, these three methods can be a powerful complement to countering depression and decreasing stress. The Nun Study suggests a positive outlook may be a critical predictor of vigorous longevity.

Joycebelle Edelbrock
Author, Publisher, Coach, Consultant and Founder of GoodStoryADay.com

Today is February 4, a sunny gorgeous day in La Jolla, California.

I'm a woman…

… who loves being a woman and has used my femininity throughout my life to get what I want, not from the standpoint of being obnoxious or being too sexy or being immoral or anything else. If you own this book, send an email to **Joycebelle@ GoodStoryADay.com** and write "Beauty E-Book for *Ideal Aging™*" in the subject line—I'll give you a free e-Book edition of *Love Your Beauty* so you can learn more about loving your beauty. It's just if you are a woman and being who you are, then you can please the world. That's what I've always attempted to do more subconsciously than consciously. I really find if you follow your passion, you're happy. If you're happy, you're healthy and you are in love with life. That is what I am—in love with life and goodness.

I grew up on a farm in Michigan. I had a one-room country school education. When I was in the fifth grade, I was still a non-reader. In the sixth grade I got a new teacher. She was a college professor who had traveled all around the world. She was a dynamic, remarkable individual. She took our class, which consisted of five girls and one boy, to the heights of education. Somehow in the sixth grade I learned to read very, very rapidly. I had the same teacher for three years so by the time our little class entered high school there were no limits to our successes. By then, there was virtually nothing we needed to learn and we got an A in every subject.

My mother was my mentor because she was such a remarkable person. We lived on a farm—far away from everyone. She was so close to her children. She never treated us like we were little kids. There was no subject that we couldn't talk about. She had a thirst for knowledge. Therefore, she read everything. If she was reading Shakespeare, every night we would get Shakespeare. If she was reading poetry, Keats or Walt Whitman, we got that every night. This closeness brought love. Thus, I've always been loved. I think that is a really important factor. I've always loved everyone.

My mother looked more like a movie star than a farmer's wife. She dressed much of the time with the big hats, gloves, high heeled shoes, stockings with the seam that came up the back of the leg that was always remarkably straight. Every time we would walk down the street, people would turn and look at her because she was so attractive. You never imagined that she would also plow, milk cows and work on the farm. So this duplicity of existence has always been a part of me.

I love *National Geographic*. It became my window to the world. I dreamed of traveling to far away places. I have traveled at least half the world over and have the other half yet to go.

I recently started a program called *GoodStoryADay.com*. It's an internet program for children from prenatal through age 19 in which I give a good story each day specific to their age. It's the culmination of everything I ever wanted to do. Number one, I love to work with children. I have two children. The 20 years that I was Mommy, I was a full time Mommy even though I supported the family. I decided I was going to work hours in which my children were occupied and not work when they were not occupied. While they were sleeping or at school, I would work very fast, furiously, and efficiently. Therefore, I made time to go to their ice dancing, water ballet, football and hockey games. I could be at school when I needed to be. I enjoyed that tremendously.

A contributing factor to my lifestyle is that I've always had an abundance of energy. I've always had the ability to do without sleep and go at any extremes that I need to go to, to get something done whether it's four or five days without any sleep at all except little catnaps. And physical activity is also important. I still jump in the ocean, and still go diving.

I became involved in publishing when we started a company that was producing underwater photographic equipment. We wanted to market this by writing articles, stories and books on underwater photography or the results of the underwater photography. Every time that we would use a picture, we would tell what photographic equipment we used—which we manufactured—as well as what kind of film—which we also sold. Readers were sold on us from the articles. This is really a smart way of doing business. I have published magazines, books, manuals, CDs, DVDs and whole programs. I work with Robert Allen, the guru of business success. Mark Victor Hanson, the *Chicken Soup for the Soup*™/ Guy, calls me their out of the box coach because I don't think conventionally.

Ideal Aging™ is being—well, I love the word young from the standpoint that children are not inhibited. They haven't learned to think as the world thinks. This youthful sense of exploration and excitement is Ideal Aging™. You never lose that youthful sense of adventure and thinking. As far as thinking is concerned, I think I'm sharper now than I was when I was 16, 35 or 55. I think that's the essence of Ideal Aging™. Thinking projects onto your body so that it is active, it moves quickly, it functions well and you don't really pay much attention to it. Just like a child doesn't pay much attention to the body.

Having children would definitely be the

Enduring Happiness • 123

highlight of my life. Second to that would be hand feeding sea otters in the ocean. The first day that I met a sea otter, my husband had been working with Jacques Cousteau. It was a very cold morning that was dreary and gloomy. We got in the boat and went out to where the sea otters were. We got in the water and it was really, really cold. This was not a pleasant, happy thing to do except I wanted to visit with the sea otters. So I held a sea urchin in my hand and I bobbed in that water for some 45 minutes, not moving, so that my husband could get a picture of the sea otter coming up and taking the sea urchin out of my hand. I waited. And I waited and I waited. One little sea otter way far away went under water and came up maybe an inch closer to me. I was maybe half of a football field away. He proceeded to do this very, very slowly. All the other sea otters around me were watching this. He came a little closer … and a little closer …. It was kind of like giving birth from the idea that it doesn't happen instantly. It is a process, a procedure. He came closer and closer and closer to me. Finally, he was within a hand's grasp of me. I let the sea urchin fall into the water. He took the sea urchin, dove underwater, and went back to his position 50 yards away.

This was extremely thrilling because that was the beginning. From that point on for the next six months we worked with the sea otters to the point where they would come up and touch us. One yanked my mask off. I chased it to the surface and my contact lens was in the mask. I got the mask back, the contact back, put the contact back in, went back down and played some more with the sea otter. So that type of adventuring I also think is *Ideal Aging*™. At the time I was 35 or so. When I had my first child at 37 the doctor said I was like a teenager. You know my body wasn't like a middle-aged woman.

Once I was in love with adventure, sea otters, diving, climbing mountains …… . Then there were the years devoted to raising my children. I loved every minute! Then I became consumed with publishing and teaching how to publish, market, and prosper from your intellectual property. But now, I am completely passionate about *Good Story A Day*. I want to take this *Good Story A Day* to every child in the world, even the children that don't have computers. Even for children living on the street, we can have computers in a kiosk so that they can go to **GoodStoryADay.com** and get a good story each day to focus their lives on. Each story is centered on a good word for that day such as love, joy, peace or happiness. Whatever the good word is, stories appropriate for each age group relate to it. There's also a journal in which they can write. There's a joke. There's an image of goodness to delight them, a good quote to inspire them, a good question and a surprise prize. There are several mechanisms to keep the youth thinking about goodness in their lives each and every day. That's where my future is and it's a long future.

Once I met a lady who was planning to buy a house to die in. She said: "This house has a wonderful overlook of the ocean with a park between us and the shore. I can watch people from all over the world congregate there, bands play there and lovers kiss there. I'm now 60. I plan on moving into this place when I'm about 90. I'm planning on dying when maybe I'm 120. So, for those 30 years that I live in this condo

I can observe the world go by."

I want a timeline like that. I've always said that I was going to live to 120. But now that I have reached my 70s, I say I'm going to live to 140. I'm still middle aged. I thought by creating a timeline from 1 to 120 or 140 you can work in everything you ever wanted to do particularly after you're 60 and you've done all those other things. Then you do the planned portion of your life in which you are an artist. I started painting a couple of years ago. I have these marvelous big canvases all over my walls. I haven't started to sell any because I don't think I could turn lose of them, but they are incredible. I knew I could see what I wanted to paint, but I didn't know I had the dexterity to do it. I've drawn all my life because I'm a publisher and you have to draw ads, technical things, charts, graphs and so forth. That's trained my hand to paint. There's transference of every knowledge that you ever acquire. That too is *Ideal Aging*. Always doing something brand new. That brings excitement into your life. That's youth.

The other thing that I think keeps people staying young is reading, finding out about other people and finding out what's new. I read two or four books a week, several at the same time.

I think patience is a tremendous life lesson. I don't have a temper like I used to. I think there's a learning curve. I learned to love children more after I had children because I saw them from birth up. When I had children and went back to teaching, I realized that I was a much better teacher.

If I start to get depressed, sad, or angry at the computer or the car driving next to me or somebody saying something they shouldn't be saying whatever the situation might be, I just have learned to turn away from that and ask what is the opposite? Turn to that.

Look for goodness in your life always. Love intently. Eliminate the worry factor. It does absolutely nothing. Enjoy, smile, laugh. Even if you feel like the world has stopped living, even if you feel like the love of your life is gone. My husband died when he was 38 years old. We had just had a new baby. We were very successful, but the business disappeared with him because I wasn't going to run the business. I was going to be a mommy and yet I didn't have an income. I had given my name and all of my activity to my husband. Well, that's tragedy. The next day after his funeral I took my two stepdaughters and my baby to the zoo. We had a wonderful time. Later I asked the two little girls who were 9 and 10 if they missed their dad and they said: "No, he's always with us."

I think that when you look for good it will appear. Sidney Poitier said in his book *(The Measure of a Man, A Spiritual Autobiography)*: "The simple life on Cats Island in the Bahamas as a child gave me such appreciation of nothing." Meaning to me that the sand could be wonderful to play with. The leaves on the trees could be wonderful to play with. Acting is not play acting. It is finding the *real* in real life and when the art and the real life come together then that is true acting. Whatever emotion you want to bring up you have to go back and find that emotion in your real life. That's what I do all the time. In other words, if there is a problem, then I go back into either a time in which I was very happy or into the reality that everything created by God is good. That brings the resolution.

From a sunny interview with a beautiful woman on February 4, 2007.

NEW LINKING AND LOOPING

"Looping together in an upbeat register is, as
psychologists like to say, 'inherently reinforcing'—that is,
it makes everyone feel good."
Daniel Goleman in *Social Intelligence*

Just seventeen to thirty-three milliseconds is the time it takes to register your reaction when you connect with another person. That happens long before you are aware of what you are thinking and feeling about them and their actions.

I Feel Bad about My Neck, writes Nora Ephron. Does the title imply hilarity? If you're not so fortunate that you get to spend time laughing with Ephron, this might be a great book to bring to your reading club. If you're not in a reading club, this might be a good time to join one ... or start one. The laugh-out-loud time coupled with talking about what you've read could be good for your brain as well as your happiness.

"Permeable" is not how most of us would describe our minds. We tend to think of ourselves as fiercely independent. New neuroscience expands that view. While we are connected to another, each of us helps create the mental life of both of us.

It turns out that our brains are wired to be empathic. Our default option is to cooperate and be altruistic.

A 50-year-young construction worker and Navy veteran gave a splendid example of empathy and altruism. When he saw a man have a seizure and stumble off the platform onto the tracks in front of an oncoming train, Wesley Autrey leapt. He lay on top of the other man as five cars of the train passed over them before it could stop.

"We're O.K. down here," he yelled, "but I've got two daughters up there. Let them know their father's O.K."

"I don't feel like I did something spectacular; I just saw someone who needed help," Mr. Autrey said. "I did what I felt was right."

As reported in the New York Times, January 3, 2007

Mr. Autrey developed his social intelligence to be empathic and altruistic beyond what many others manage. To his credit, he provided a model for which all others might aspire.

We are strongly encouraged by Goleman's theory of social intelligence to hang out with individuals who are positive and upbeat. With our mirror neurons we will both see and feel the happiness that is expressed on another's face. These mirror neurons create a super-high-speed highway between brains causing powerful exchanges of information.

Can you get too much positive reinforcement? It's conceivable. But that's not what I've seen clinically. I'm happy to go on record stating that this might be the most healthy overdose. Catching yourself in the act of doing something well and thinking congratulatory thoughts can strengthen that behavior. Doing mindful meditation on a regular basis has been associated with an increase of the left PFC. This is the part of the brain activated by happiness.

Robert Sapolsky, PhD:
Stanford Professor and McArthur Fellow.

The most informative, entertaining, engaging,
brilliant science-writer of our time!

If erupting like a volcano with raucous laughter is
your idea of bedtime reading,
Why Zebras Don't Get Ulcers is your book.

If laughing is one of your favorite aerobics … same book.

If mastering the nuances of stress is your priority (as it should be)
… you guessed it …Why Zebras …
(as well as his other incomparable books.)

I have this dual scientific life in that I divide my time between being your basic laboratory scientist, studying neurons—in rats, in Petri dishes, manipulating genes in them—and being a field primatologist in Africa. When I started both branches of this work (around 1979), they were very close to each other. I was interested in issues of stress and individual differences—in effect asking, "Why do some organisms handle stress better than others?" The lab rat provided a model where I could understand what was happening in the brain, while the baboons in the Serengeti of East Africa provided a way to see if some of the things I was seeing actually were relevant to real organisms in the real world.

Since then, the lab work has gotten more reductive, heading in the direction of individual cells, individual molecules, while the baboon work has become more integrated, now resembling something like baboon sociology and health psychology.

In Harvard as an undergrad I focused jointly on doing biology and anthropology. I earned a PhD in neuroscience from Rockefeller, did post-doctoral work at the Salk Institute and am on the faculty now at Stanford where I have been for 20 years, which is a mind-boggling length of time.

Ideal Aging™ requires maintaining a lot of resiliency in responding to challenge. This typically translates into successfully making the transition from a younger person's world of stress management by trying to make stressors go away to stress management consisting of learning to accommodate stressors.

It includes a taste and capacity for ongoing stimulation (cognitive, physical, etc.) and a continued openness to novelty. You must have an ability to retain close friends amid greatly decreasing the size of your social community. That is, you distinguish between true friendship and acquaintances and recognize that there's little reason for the latter anymore. Ideal Aging™ would avoid depression and anxiety disorders. You have an ability to retain enough independence to still feel a sense of efficacy. There are enough circumstances of being able to help others so that you still have a sense of efficacy and purpose. It's a funny combination of a sort of pointillist ability to live for the present, but with the present having elements of anticipation of the future. That last one sounds impossible or Zen-ish.

I'm enhancing my aging via sociality, love of family, work, lots of exercise. If you want to be a healthy and long-lived male baboon, your social rank is far less important than your patterns of social affiliation and your capacity to roll with punches. And this is highly relevant to humans as well.

From email exchanges across early 2007 with a primatologist and scientist who is as informative and funny in person as he is in print. And whose works are "must" reads.

3. ENERGY ELEVATOR—THE VIGOROUS LONGEVITY YOU EARN FOR YOURSELF

Aerobic exercise can increase energy at the same time that it increases neurogenesis. Rats created more new brain cells whether they ran voluntarily or were forced to be aerobic. In a landmark study researchers found evidence of exercise-induced neurogenesis in humans. This evidence of new brain cells in the dentate gyrus of the hippocampus was related to better cardiovascular function and improved cognitive functions. This is the area of the hippocampus that is critical for memory. The so-called "normal changes of aging" have been associated with this part of the hippocampus.

In an informal survey every person who learned these facts vowed to be aerobic on a regular basis. Will you?

Inactive adults gradually become weaker. They lose muscle mass and strength. Aerobic capacity also decreases unless you continue to build it across your lifespan.

> Seikichi Uehara welcomed the new millennium in a match with a "thirty-something former World Boxing Association Flyweight champion for Okinawa." As a martial arts master, he was able to avoid all blows from the ex-boxer for more than twenty minutes. When the younger man finally tired and dropped his guard, Uehara took the thirty-something young man out with one quick blow.
>
> Uehara was ninety-six years young when he delivered the felling blow.
>
> As reported by Willcox, Willcox and Suzuki in
> *The Okinawa Program.*

Does that help you dispel some of the myths of aging?

Martial arts can keep you young and fit as it concentrates on maintaining a high level of physical and mental fitness. Benefits from this training are real even without attaining the level of a master.

Tai Chi may be the most well know form of martial arts. Research has shown its many benefits including increased energy as well as better bone mineral density.

A critical component of having the energy to enjoy vigorous longevity is to Exercise Right. As always that starts with measuring what you are doing now and adding one little baby step at a time ... then repetitively raising the bar of your own level of physical and mental fitness.

Equally important is Eating Smart Deliciously. Measure what you're doing now. Compare that to the wisdom of the Okinawan Centenarians.

Do not diet. However, do remember that calorie restriction has been a survival mechanism for diverse species from yeasts to mammals. Calorie restriction of up to 50% has lengthened the lifespan and reduced age-related diseases in rats and other animals. Even an 8% reduction in calories improves lab measures of inflammation.

It is plausible that dietary restriction with high quality food intake has already contributed to human longevity as demonstrated in certain populations. The centenarians in Okinawa may be one example. *Hara hachi-bu* as spoken by Okinawan grandmothers across the ages may still be sound advice: Eat only until you are 80% full. And **Eat Smart Deliciously** so that you enjoy getting all your essential nutrients.

Chris Crowley
Attorney and co-author of *Younger Next Year* and *Younger Next Year for Women*

I'm 72 years old, but it's not my fault. As Harry **(Henry Lodge, MD, co-author)** will tell you I had to get a note from my doctor. I live in New York. I was a Wall Street trial lawyer for 25 years, quit, moved to Aspen, but moved back to New York ten years ago. We wrote these Younger Next Year books. I'd had the idea of writing a book for baby boomers because I was 12 years older than the oldest baby boomer. I thought it might be interesting to them to see what's gonna happen next. Then I bumped into a guy in Aspen who talked about the revolution in aging mostly caused by changes in cranking up exercise an awful lot. Then I went to New York and met Harry who was way, way ahead of me intellectually on this stuff. I mean he really knows it cold. He's the brains of the outfit. I persuaded him to write a book with me.

Chris, how would you define ideal aging?

You want to be as healthy as you can for as long as you can. You want to make the best use of yourself that you can. I think a successful life at any age is using your gifts to the top of your ability. You can do that for a long, long time. The hardest part of aging is retirement. Once you give up that great responsibility of a career it's easy to just kind of fall apart. You have to keep yourself interested to do stuff, to use your gifts after retirement.

Other than writing these phenomenal books that everybody should buy and read, what else do you do to make sure you're making the best use of yourself?

I'm a good kid about all the exercise stuff that we write about. I really do practice all that stuff, and it's interesting, it really does work. I'm out here in Aspen. We had more than a foot of new powder snow last night. We were out there skiing with kids of 40 who've been skiing all their lives and we were the same people. We weren't the same age, but we were able to do this stuff just as hard and fast. It's just a joy that makes you feel different. If you're in decent physical shape there's a whole different attitude towards aging. There's a whole different mood level that is much better. You're more optimistic. You're willing to try stuff. I forget the question, but there's the answer.

Everyone has hardships, how do you cope with those?

Keep your spirits up and keep going. One of the interesting things about aging is you know you're gonna get smacked. You're gonna get sick, you're gonna bust something or other, there are things that just go south. You're not gonna be able to keep up doing something or other. We urge people to bear in mind is that while that stuff is inevitable, your chances of coming out the other side in decent shape are enormously influenced by what kind of shape you are going in. The greatest predictor of who does well coming out of the emergency room is what kind of physical shape they are going in. We also urge that, if you've had a physical setback, you get back on your pins as fast as possible and start doing stuff. It's enormously important.

When you look at the future, what are your dreams?

I'd like to have a larger success with this basic program that we're pushing! We think it's nuts to have American aging be so awful! I mean it's crazy that people are basically sick so much in old age in this country. If we are right—and I'm sure that Harry is—he says 70 percent of aging is voluntary and you don't have to go there. Fifty percent of all serious illness and accidents from 50 till the day you die you can skip. It's gaga to have those kinds of sicknesses and accidents in a country which is choking to death on medical costs! Everybody should be doing this stuff. I'd like to try to work on that. I want to keep doing what I'm doing. I want to be able to ski and run and jump and play.

If you had every resource you needed, how would you improve the world if at all?

I'd focus on the stuff that we're already working on. You have to focus. I would beat the drum on this topic. I would be promoting this model that Harry and I are talking about. Trying to get more people to have a better life—not just older people, but everybody.

What important life lessons do you appreciate now that you didn't when you were 20 or 40?

I realize family and friends are more important. You treasure them more as you get older. I wish I'd been a bit more of a hound intellectually. I wish I'd been a better scholar. I was a decent student but college is utterly wasted on kids. I wish that I'd been a better student then. I learned a lot of stuff but what fun it would be right now to just go and wallow in a great university for four years. What a treat!

What advice would you give my readers?

I'd beg them to go out and read these books that we've been pushing, not just to sell books but people should change the way they age. You can do so much for yourself. It's all in your control. Not all, but an awful lot, a surprising amount of the quality of life after 50 can be so much better than almost anybody can imagine in this country. We're just such dopes about it. My advice is jump in, find out a little bit about it and make it as terrific as you can. I've got the world's best job in a way. My job is to have a terrific time in my 70s and hopefully my 80s, and then tell everybody else about it and try to keep their spirits up. What could be more fun that that? I go and write my blog every day. Give them our website **www.YoungerNextYear.com**. That's where they can get to the blog I write every day. There are many thousands of people who come. It's great fun. It's a little community. I get these lovely responses from people. But basically my job is just to have a great time and tell them about it. What could be nicer than that?

From an energetic phone interview on February 14, 2007

EXERCISE RIGHT

"That exercise—the physical work of hunting and foraging in the spring—has always been the single most powerful signal we can send that life is good; that it's spring and time to live and grow."
Henry (Harry) Lodge, MD, in *Younger Next Year*

Goals

- Do aerobic exercises forty-five minutes every day at minimum … because exercise can signal your brain to produce its own best natural brain food and create new brain cells

- Balance minor mechanical stress and repair … because this can promote optimal growth:

$$(\text{minor stress} \rightarrow \text{rest and nutrition} \rightarrow \text{repair}) \infty$$

- Build bone mineral density (BMD)…because the same exercises that build better bones also improve how your brain works

- Plan for vigorous longevity … because the upper limits of positive health are not yet known

- Prevent falls … because that reduces injury to your brain and bones

- Reduce insulin resistance … because exercise is twice as effective as the prescribed medication metformin

- Enhance sense of well-being … because that improves overall performance

- Improve your immune response … because you stay healthy thru an occasional stress overdose

- Encourage growth … because aging is natural but decay from stress OD is optional

You'll note in reading this section that exercise clearly is critical to boosting brain function. Human and other animal studies have shown its influence on neuroplasticity. Aerobic exercise is one of the most powerful enhancers of neurogenesis. Both aerobics and neurobics keep your brain fit in more ways than one.

Science behind your plan

Legions of rats have run ragged to provide guidelines for your fitness. The volunteers among them became more efficient learners after choosing to run on a running wheel. This was thought to be related to the effect of exercise in creating more brain food. If that sounds like a contradiction in terms, this is how that works.

Shortly after beginning the spontaneous running on the wheel, brain-derived neurotrophic factor (BDNF) and nerve growth factor (NGF) increased in the brains of those rats that spontaneously ran. A neurotrophic factor, or neurotrophin, is the specific nutrition that encourages your brain cells to grow more complex on and between cells. BDNF and NGF are natural brain food.

This is a type of alphabet soup warrants developing a craving for it. When sending as well as receiving signals, certain brain cells produce neurotrophins to promote health of the cell itself, of the neighboring cells and of the synapses between these brain cells. So stimulating your brain with novel combinations of sensory information and actions turns those same brain cells into a sort of "self fertilizing garden" in which they create the very nourishment that is required for their growth.

That's huge! And transient in some respects.

After eating a high-fat, high-refined-carbohydrate diet those rats that ran had reduced BDNF. That's equally huge. Take it seriously in writing the choreography for your Ideal Aging™.

> *"To keep allostasis functioning on the protective end of the spectrum, the most effective steps you can take are the simplest: Exercise, a healthy diet, regular sleep, moderate-to-minimal alcohol intake, and no smoking."*
> Bruce McEwen in *The End of Stress as We Know It*

The good news is that voluntary running raised the BDNF again. So an occasional rich snack might not be the end of your new brain growth. But it is clear that an aerobic exercise would be your smarter choice (pun intended).

Also, after twenty minutes of forced exercise, rats showed an even greater increase in BDNF. Since protection of aging brain cells is one of the benefits of BDNF that makes aerobic exercise the much wiser choice for turning stress into power for vigorous longevity.

As Bruce McEwen aptly points out, shrinkage of your hippocampus in response to stress OD "isn't just a matter of cortisol corroding the neurons like battery acid; the reduction is a long time in making and scientists hope it can be prevented."

After an episode of elevated cortisol and stress OD which may have blocked your neurogenesis, consider this. Increasing your BDNF with aerobic exercise could restart the birth of new brain cells and protect the newborn neurons while you are restoring your health.

Gage and his colleagues found evidence of neurogenesis in eleven humans who were below-average in aerobic fitness prior to their participation. They did aerobic exercise four times a week for twelve weeks. After five minutes of warming up, then five minutes of stretching, they maintained an aerobic activity for forty minutes. This was followed by ten minutes for cooling down and stretching.

In his 2001 report the US Surgeon General recommended that children get at least sixty minutes of moderate exercise four or five days each week. Just by jumping off an object about 20 inches high kids increased their bone mineral density significantly.

Encourage adolescents to maximize their "window of opportunity." This is when maximum lifetime value of exercises for building Bone Mineral Density occurs. Adolescents do have a leg up on their parents and grandparents for building better bones. They may also have a neuron up on us for building better brains since memory in storage probably cannot be too excessive. We now know that some of our original brain cells can stay active and high functioning throughout our life. You use them to build them. If you build them they can stay.

Remember: It's never too early and never too late to enhance Ideal Aging™.

After exercise, even the frail elderly have shown increased bone size and density, birth of new brain cells, improved brain "horsepower," reduced risk of diabetes and heart disease and improved sense of well-being. Marian Diamond found a unique potential for brain cells to grow in complex branching even in very old rats. Her findings provide hope that an active lifestyle of continually stimulating brain cells to transmit messages can earn us "healthy mental activity throughout a lifetime."

Prolactin is generally discussed in terms of lactation in breastfeeding women. It has recently been discovered to have other roles. Prolactin given to rats while in stress OD reduced signs of anxiety. The more prolactin they were given, the greater the relief of their anxiety. Researchers suggest that prolactin might be a novel way of regulating emotions. Exercise increases prolactin circulating to your brain.

Endorphins. Increase of these with exercise affords the "runner's high" as well as reduced pain sensitivity. For many people, that makes exercise more attractive. Although that can be good, a word of caution is in order.

Pain is your body's way of bringing your attention to the inflammatory response to injury.

Therefore, the pain "should be considered an attempt by the brain to deal with emergency and not a sign of resilience," and "Exercise is seen as a stressor when taken to an extreme" according to Bruce McEwen,

For example, excessive exercise can change the level of sex hormones to the extent of interfering with reproduction and of decalcifying bones. This could leave you at risk for fracture and damage to other organs.

The positive here is the growth message in the small amounts of damage done early in exercise. A muscle contracting creates the beginning of inflammation and demolition with an increase of interleukin-6 (IL-6). After about thirty minutes of exercise, the IL-6 signals repair and the release of the anti-inflammatory interleukin-10 (IL-10). That's why a minimum of thirty minutes of exercise is likely to have the best effect in reducing inflammation in your body. That's why daily exercise for the rest of your life is essential for vigorous longevity. That's how you give your body the message that you choose to perform longer and better as you age better while holding decay at bay. Too little or too much inflammation defeats growth. So, in either instance only decay occurs.

As quoted earlier, Harry's (Henry Lodge, MD, co-author of *Younger Next Year*) words are worth repeating: "*That exercise—the physical work of hunting and foraging in the spring —has always been the single most powerful signal we can send that life is good; that it's spring and time to live and grow.*" Done daily, your brain and physical body continue the repair and growth process.

Refurbishing Is Constant... Give Your Body the Best

Marian Diamond was an early researcher in the realm of building on existing brain cells. She is one of my heroes. I had the pleasure of watching this remarkable woman present to a cavernous room full of professionals. She had complete control of her topic, data and equipment as she kept her audience on the edge of their seats eager to hear each word… about rat brains! She had shown that, when the brain received proper stimulation through all senses, the brain's neurons grew more complex branches on the dendrites, developed more spines that store memory and formed sites for connections in the synapses between the vast numbers of interconnected brain cells.

This neuroplasticity, the capacity of your brain to stretch and grow, is a major focus of this book because a growing body of research affords unprecedented hope. New biological data have expanded what is known in this realm.

Merzenich and colleagues describe the development of a "brain-plasticity-based training program." They believe evolving research indicates that declines in adult functioning can be reversed, stopped or reduced. In essence that could be beneficial to all adults. Their research aim is "to restore sensory, cognitive, memory, motor, and affect systems in aging." Their random controlled trial included 182 participants with age-related cognitive decline. Eight to ten weeks of training resulted in significant improvement in brain function. Memory improvements generalized to other tasks. Some of these gains were still apparent after three months without further training.

That's huge. It's exhilarating. And it's empowering because new scientific findings are identifying what enhances and suppresses neurogenesis as well as the survival of these neurons. New brain cells have also been found in the cortex of monkeys, the newer part of the brain that is responsible for such higher level thinking as spatial reasoning, short-term memory, executive decision making, and recognition of what you see.

The list of neurogenesis enhancers will grow with this expanding area of research. Some things are known now—Exercise Right.

After forty days of the mice's running on a wheel, newborn brain cells were found in mouse brains. In depressed experimental animals neurogenesis was decreased. It was induced after long term treatment with antidepressants. This treatment could reverse shrinkage of the hippocampus and/or prevent shrinkage by adequately treating strong emotions such as depression and anxiety.

The same exercises that could improve your brain can also cause remodeling of your bones. The physical strain that exercise causes on your bones can cause micro-damage to them. When this happens, a demolition crew dissolves the damaged portion of your bones so developers can rebuild them stronger. Your muscles send out the chemical messages for this repair process throughout your whole body.

These are some of the reasons that there's a move afoot … because we're increasingly aware of what we need to do to reap the benefits. You'll need your own baseline before you start. Then begin gradually.

A pedometer will keep you on track. Some experts are advocating 10,000 steps per day. How else will you count the number of times your heels strike pay dirt?

A heart rate monitor is essential and can be inexpensive. It's the easiest way to determine if your activity level is in the low end of the aerobic range to achieve your goal. According to Philip Maffetone, the 180-formula is the best way to determine your optimal heart rate in aerobic training. If you are under 16 years old, replace 180 with 165 in the formula below.

The 180-formula

1. Subtract your age from 180 (180 – age).

2. From these categories select the best modification of this number:
   a. Use this number if you have had no medical or surgical issues during the recent two years while exercising at least four times each week;
   b. Add 5 if you are a competitive athlete still in training and no medical or surgical issues have occurred during the past two years;
   c. Subtract an additional 5 for two minor illness in the past year – or for not being on an exercise routine as described above (180 – age – 5); AND
   d. If you take regular medication or are recovering from major medical or surgical events, subtract an additional 10 (180 – age – 10).
   e. Over the age of 65 you may have to add another 10 points if your healthcare professional believes your fitness and health are sufficient.

According to Maffetone, this formula gives you your *"maximum aerobic heart rate."* By subtracting another 10, you set your *"aerobic training zone."* A heart monitor will help you develop aerobic fitness by staying within this range of maximum minus 10.

For example, if you are 45 years old and have not exercised before:

180 - 45 - 5 = 130. Then your aerobic training zone is 120 to 130.

If your are 66 years old, healthy, physically fit and have had no medical or surgical events within the past two years during which you have exercised at least four times each week:

180 – 66 + 10 = 124. So your aerobic training zone is 114 to 124.

Phil Maffetone trains for endurance to increase aerobic functioning such that his clients have "nearly unlimited energy." After training with Maffetone, Stu Mittleman ran 1000 miles in 11 days and 20 hours setting a new world record in 1986!

Most readers will not have such ultra supreme fitness as a goal. However, learn from the wisdom of the trainer and monitor your heart rate to get the most fitness out of every step. If there is a magic pill of prolonging youth, surely aerobic exercise is it.

As is often repeated in this workbook, consult with your healthcare provider. This is particularly true in exercise. Individuals with a family history of health problems, suspected heart problems or blood pressure issues certainly need to consult with a physician before engaging in strenuous exercises. There may be a need to have a specialist do a stress test. A sub-maximal test could calculate a personal "safe" exercise zone.

Similarly, an elite athlete could benefit from an evaluation by a specialist. **CooperInstitute.org** is a valuable source of further information on exercise and fitness.

Litmus paper is another way to measure whether or not your pace is aerobic. If used after about thirty minutes of putting nothing in your mouth, it is accurate enough to measure your saliva. For example, if you refrain from brushing your teeth, swallowing anything or even rinsing your mouth for a half hour prior to wetting the litmus paper with your saliva, the average pH at 6 AM is expected to be acidic at about 6.5. Then check your saliva pH the same way during and immediately after your training session.

If the litmus paper indicates that your saliva is less acidic after exercising than before, you have been in your target zone for fat-burning aerobic training. On the other hand, if the litmus paper doesn't show your saliva as *less* acidic with your exercise session, you have not been in a fat-burning aerobic range. When your saliva measures as *more* acidic after exercise, you have been exercising too hard. You are burning sugar.

One final point – dress for success. Exercise increases your body temperature. If the result is too much warmth, you will not do as well. So wear layers that you can remove as your temperature rises.

The benefits of exercise are huge. The following tables make that clear.

What YOU do – EQUALS – What YOU Can Earn!

Aerobic weight-bearing with rapidly **rising force** such as jumping

Create new brain cells

Increased complex branching of existing brain cells

More efficient learning

Better executive functioning

Enhanced memory

Improved attention

Protection against brain damage

Faster reaction time

Improved self-esteem

Improved well-being

Save $$$$$ on medical bills

Higher energy

Outlet for frustration

Stabilized blood pressure

Lowered resting pulse

Increased lung capacity

Aerobic muscle fibers resist injury

Aerobic muscle fibers burn fat providing endurance and weight loss

Have antioxidant activity

Increase prolactin (cuddle factor & lower anxiety)

May reduce insulin resistance

Raises healthy cholesterol; lowers LDL

Improved immune response

Triggers inflammation via IL-6 which signals anti-inflammatory IL-10

Increases Bone Mineral Density (BMD)

Jumping & skipping increased BMD up to 4%

Master runners have maintained BMD for 5 years

Aerobically fit people have more FUN!

As you can see, there are so many benefits of being aerobic that a separate table is warranted. Surely you can identify at least one benefit of aerobic exercise that makes you be aerobic every day, every day, every day.

If that means you dance the night away for the fun of planning how you will use your new brain cells you might be nourishing into being, this could be good! Now for the rest of the choreography of Ideal Aging™.

Walk briskly 1 hour a day	Higher BMD
> 7.5 miles per week	Greater whole body BMD
30 minutes 5 times a week	Twice as effective in reducing diabetes risk as metformin, a prescription medication
3+ hours each week	½ the risk of heart disease as 1/4th mile/week
Stand more than 4 hours each day while being active	Higher BMD – not found in paraplegics because mechanical stress on the bone of muscular tension is essential to stimulate bone growth

Exercise Right • 143

Warm up	Increases blood flow to muscles Improves your use of oxygen Muscles move more effectively Less risk of injury
Strengthen specific muscles	Agility Increasing muscle mass and BMD in attached bones Trains muscle cells to burn more energy
Balance training Backward tandem walking	Improves dynamic balance Quicker response Can reduce falls by 17%
Stretch	Flexibility to avoid falls Increases pleasure in other activities Reduce stiffness & soreness
Cool down	Increases oxygen to muscles Prevents blood pooling in leg muscles –> dizziness

How to do it

Start with the BARE BONERS process (See Introduction). Your own baseline physical activity at this point sets the standard for how to begin, what to do, how to do it and how to measure as well as reinforce progress. This includes getting medical clearance for any changes.

Then pick one thing to add today. As your track your progress, you and your healthcare provider will the best judges of essential, safe and beneficial changes.

Walk

This seemed to be the exercise of choice in the nuns of Mankato, Minnesota, referenced earlier. Those who walked regularly aged with grace.

Remember that a simple 150 minutes per week in individuals at risk for diabetes was almost twice as effective as the standard medical intervention, prescribing metformin. This can be as easy as getting off the bus a thirty minute walk away from your place of work.

Some people are so fortunate that they can simply walk to the grocery store and carry their groceries home. Just remember to maintain a brisk pace. That means you will be moving out but not necessarily be short of breath.

Stand

And be active. There was a time when a special table was built that would stabilize paraplegics in a standing position. This was done in hopes of avoiding the osteoporosis of inactivity. The missing element was the lack of muscular activity pulling on the bones. Osteoporosis developed in paraplegics in spite of this effort.

So move about. Paint a painting; clean the house; mow the lawn; knead the dough and bake your own bread; create a culinary masterpiece; take a tour of the downtown park to see which flowers bloomed today; or some such.

Only if you have good peripheral vision and can be entirely safe while doing it, you might try what my physician colleague does: she "must have something to read while walking" from the emergency room to the cafeteria. Can you relate to that?

Warm Up & Cool Down

This is essential prior to your regular exercise program. This increases the blood supply and temperature of your muscles. Walk gently toward a goal or simply walk in place while moving your arms naturally at your sides. With a heart monitor you can proceed at a pace that keeps your pulse gradually increasing for about 10 minutes before entering your aerobic training zone.

Strengthen

Bone mineral density is related to the mass of the muscles attached to a bone. Resistance exercises have the most effect on muscle mass but only on the body parts exercised. The size of your muscles will only increase by using them.

For example, you might notice a difference in your arms because you use one more than the other. The arm you use most in day-to-day activities might show as much as 5% greater muscle mass and BMD. Researchers in Finland measured arms of women who played tennis or squash. With this increased use of the playing arm the difference was as high as 16%.

Remember the adolescent "window of opportunity." Research from Finland showed that women who started training before adolescence got twice as much benefit as the women who began the sport after puberty! So, encourage the kids and grandkids to take advantage of that. By the same token, there's an important caveat.

> It is never too early
> And never too late
> To enhance the growth of
> bones, brains and muscles
> for Ideal Aging™.

In preventing and treating osteoporosis focus on strengthening the muscles attached to your spine, wrists and hips. These are the most vulnerable to fracture.

As always you will begin by establishing your baseline and conferring with your healthcare provider. Then you will start with weights that are relatively easy to lift with your arms or legs. Gradually increase the weight of the weights you are lifting rather than the number of repetitions of lifting them. It is the gradual increase in the weights lifted that enhances the growth of your muscles.

Some specialists recommend raising the weight slowly to the count of ten seconds and lowering them at this same slow pace with a brief rest period between each lift.

The estimated muscle mass loss is five percent per decade after the age of thirty with the assumption that this may be more rapid after age sixty-five. However, these standards are usually set by what prevails in the "normal" population. That usually includes people who have grown increasingly obese and sedentary in our fast food nation.

The beauty and wonder of recent demands for optimal health on into the sunset may influence that statistic. Time will tell.

Mitochondria are the little energy factories in your muscle cells. They burn fat when you are in your aerobic target zone. The good news is that you can send a message to your mitochondria to increase their enzyme activity. How? Increase your physical activity.

Increasing your physical activity can also increase the number of these mitochondria in your muscle cells. Even frail nursing home residents have increased their strength and muscle performance with exercises and activities aimed at muscle strengthening.

Balance

The better your balance the less likely you will fall. You will respond more quickly to a sense of being out of balance. This can reduce falls by as much as seventeen percent. This is a major reduction in risk for injuries.

You can start by <u>holding onto something *sturdy* while doing any of the following</u>:
- standing on one foot
- swing one foot forward and backward while standing on the other foot
- stand with one foot directly in front of the other touching heel to toe
- walking with one foot directly in front of the other instead of side by side
- raise up on your toes
- walk on your toes
- standing on one leg, lean forward while raising the other foot behind you
- standing on one leg while leaning and lifting your other leg behind you until you are in the position of the famous portrait of the father balancing the babe on the arm extended before him (but leave the babe out of this one)

As your balance increases, you decrease your reliance on holding on to the sturdy support – but do so very judiciously. Your goal is to improve your balance to reduce your fall risk.

A nurse practitioner colleague of mine does her paperwork at a special low desk so she can sit on a large green balance ball. Every time you add exercise to your normal daily activities as this brilliant nurse does, you have multiplied your accomplishments.

Stretch

This is probably the most neglected skill in exercise routines. Even when it is prescribed by clinicians, people will fail to do it.

That should change as more people realize how easily stretching can be fit into your normal routine without a massive expenditure of time. Remember the woman who did her quad stretch with her right hand and leg while her left hand held the nozzle firmly as she filled her gasoline tank. Think safety first while creatively stretching.

I choose to do my stretches lying on a hard surface with a small pillow under the small of my back to protect it. Also, you may want to place a small pillow under your neck for support.

Begin by stretching the muscles you have just exercised. At first, hold each stretch for 10 seconds with gradual increases over several weeks until you can hold the stretch for 30 seconds. Up to 10 repetitions can be additionally helpful.

Pelvic Tilt

This stretches your back muscles while strengthening your stomach muscles.

Tighten your abdomen and buttocks to move the front of your pelvis up toward your chin pressing your lower back into the floor. This is a small and subtle movement.

This improves posture. It lessens the effort necessary for your back muscles to support your trunk. It protects the vertebrae of your spine by bringing it into better alignment.

For safe and effective exercises in other parts of your body this pelvic tilt is essential. It's easy to do even while sitting on a crowded bus. Just pull your stomach muscles tight to press the small of your back against the seat while your pelvis tilts upward. It might also be done on the balance ball at your low desk while doing paperwork – achieving three goals in one sit. Don't try this until you are comfortable and confident on a balance ball. Remember: Safety first.

Lower Back Rotation

This will stretch and strengthen the muscles used in rotating your back. Lying down as above, *gently* swing both knees to one side while rotating your head and shoulders to the opposite side. Repeat in the opposite direction.

Double Leg Pull

Stretch your lower back and buttocks with this move. With the pillows and lying on your back as before, gently pull both knees to your chest.

Neck Turn and Tilt

Gentle neck stretches can also be done lying down. These gently stretch the muscles where many people store tension.

Turn your head slowly until you are looking over one shoulder, hold that for 10 seconds, return to center and rest for a few seconds. Then turn your head slowly in the opposite direction to look over the other shoulder.

Also beneficial is tilting your head in one direction so your ear gradually approaches your shoulder. Hold in that position briefly. Return your head to an upright position for a brief rest. Then tilt you head in the other direction so that your ear gradually approaches your other shoulder. Again hold this gentle stretch briefly before returning your head to the upright position.

Tent Stretch

A brilliant fitness expert improved our sleep while we were bicycling around the world for the entire year 2000, spending half of the year in a tent. By teaching us how to stretch our hips, thighs and calves in a tiny tent, we were relieved of the nagging ache from miles and miles of pedaling.

Lying on our meager mat, we bent our left leg by positioning our left foot firmly on mother earth about 15 inches from our left hip. Then we placed our right ankle on our left knee. Grabbing the left knee just below where the right ankle was propped, we pulled those limbs toward our chest and held for up to 30 seconds. This stretched multiple muscles in the right hip, thigh and calf. After a brief rest, this was repeated on the other leg.

I am making no claim that this will help you … or even be safe for your use. But I use this stretch regularly. I will be grateful to the end of my days for one stroke of compassionate brilliance which eased my year-long bicycle trek AND continues to help me to this day. A case study, nonetheless.

Calf Stretch

This is often witnessed in the Downtown Park. With feet slightly apart, the front leg bent and the heel of the back foot kept on the ground you find fit folk leaning on a sturdy Douglas Fir (it's the sturdy part that's critical).

Hamstring Stretch

Also seen in Central Park is the one foot up on the park bench, the elevated leg and back straight, the runner bending forward slowly as if trying to touch her head to her knee. Lying on your floor, your heel on a sturdy wall will work just as well.

Quads

On a meager mat on a tent floor or plush carpeting, lie on your stomach. Bend one knee, grasp that ankle with one hand and pull it towards your buttocks. Standing, this exercise is also seen in Heathrow Airport while travelers are awaiting departure after a jog between gates. That's not only proper at Heathrow.

Shoulder Shrugs

With *proper* posture roll your shoulders up, back and down. Also, roll your shoulders up forward and down.

Stretching topics could fill a small textbook on their own. These are just some samples of how you can increase your flexibility, improve your posture and increase your fitness to keep up with the crowd courageously committed to vigorous longevity.

Now let the fun begin. The type of fun, that is, which tells your body you choose to hold decay at bay, to build better Bones, Brains & Beauty® for the health of it … the ultimate directive.

> "High-impact exercises that load bones with a rapidly rising force profile in versatile movements improve skeletal integrity, muscular performance, and dynamic balance in premenopausal women."   A. Heinonen and colleagues in *Lancet*.

Aerobic weight-bearing exercise with rapidly rising force profile

Using the 180-formula described by Maffetone, you have established your aerobic training range. Your heart monitor will make it easy and fun to watch how little effort it takes to get into that range. The pH of your saliva will verify that you have done so.

To make it more delicious, if you stay in this training range for about 40 minutes while dancing with your mate at your favorite social club while exploring interesting topics – how many neurobic interventions can you count while being aerobic to the beat of energizing music?

Doesn't that absolutely birth your new brain cells just thinking about these possibilities?

- Dancing
- Hiking
- Stair-climbing (upstairs & down)
- Running
- Skipping
- Jumping
- Skiing
- Playing tennis or squash
- Playing ball
- Walking briskly
- Bicycling (not shown to increase BMD)
- Water aerobics (not shown to increase BMD)
- Swimming (not shown to increase BMD)

So! There you have it. Multiple choices in many categories of how to **Exercise Right** for Ideal Aging™ of your Bones, Brains & Beauty®. By fitting these into your activities of daily living and socializing, you have a leg up on Ideal Aging™.

Measuring Goals

Pick ONE Baseline	Mon	Tues	Wed	Thu	Fri	Sat	Sun	Total
Walk briskly 1 hour a day								
> 7.5 miles per week								
30 minutes 5 times a week								
3+ hours each week								
Stand more than 4 hours each day <u>while being active</u>								
Warm up								
Strengthen								
Balance training								
Stretch								
Aerobic weight-bearing with rapidly **rising force** such as jumping _____ skipping _____ other _____								
Cool down								
<u>**Positive Reinforcement**</u> <u>Before</u> <u>During</u> After								

Exercise Right • 151

Summary

Decay is optional.

Refurbishing is constant when you make the choice to Exercise Right.

Since you've read this far, I am assuming that you are choosing vigorous longevity and sending that message loudly and clearly to your body on a daily basis ... not as a guarantee, but as a serious intent. At the very least, you can be happier and more fit unless (and even if) some tragedy befalls.

Life happens. Stress visits.

No guilt.

OK. Fleeting guilt for research, repairs and resuming differently. Evanescent.

Because stress OD needn't persist beyond those few blinding moments when tragedy must be faced for what it is, or might be. At best you'll bicycle, jump about with joy, dance, build the best possible Bones, Brains & Beauty®️ and have vigorous longevity to the moment of your last elegant, quiet sigh.

One of the exciting findings in this new research is that the same exercises that can help you build strong bones also have the potential to improve your brain and natural beauty. That's how the title of my first book, *Secrets inside Bones, Brains & Beauty*®️, came to be. As is made clear in that book and in other chapters here, our brains are very plastic—they change remarkably over time in response to what we think and do. That's extraordinarily good news! Exercise is one of the most powerful ways to influence how your brain grows. Just running on a wheel for forty minutes increased neurogenesis in rats. Being aerobic for forty minutes four times a week induced neurogenesis in humans! Is that enough to keep you being aerobic daily?

And your exercise routine, tailored to your unique being through consultation with your healthcare provider, will be guided by the BARE BONERS process to help you guide and reinforce your progress.

There's an extraordinary man who pedaled with the best of the riders on the O2K bicycle trek that went around the world during the entire year 2000 averaging 80 miles per day biking into and out of 45 countries on 6 continents in that one year! Half of that year was spent in tents. Long since retirement and with some physical limitations, he chose to go.

Did he manage 80 miles per day on his bike? No. But neither did most of the rest of that group of elite pedalers.

But 80 is how young he became that year. After which he returned to his "retired" full time position at the University of Washington where he continues to contribute with a passion. He usually bicycles there and back. He is a story in his own right. But that's another book.

So are you. Just remember to apply the concepts in **Create Conditioned Responses, Eat Smart Deliciously, Connect** and any other tool that will enliven your dance to Ideal Aging™ with the best of health into vigorous longevity.

> "My friend, you were right about aerobic exercise!
>
> At first, I had to force myself past grief and low energy to even get on the trainer. Then the saddle chafed so much I thought I just couldn't stay there no matter what. By force of will alone, I began to pedal.
>
> But ... around ten minutes, it was like—I could see clearly now that the sun was gonna come up.
>
> THEN ... around twenty-two minutes the sun did come up. I felt so much better that I knew I could make it to the goal of thirty minutes.
>
> *AND THEN ... as I was finishing the thirty minutes, I remembered that you said staying to forty was sometimes even better. So I stayed. At forty minutes it was like the SUN was **GLORIOUS!!***"
>
> A verbatim quote from a recent convert to the value of aerobic activity in changing the chemistry of grief.

When you capture a quote like that, you know you've really done it! You've improved the health of the nation, one soul at a time.

This report reveals that the friend has captured on a personal level the cognitive and emotional boosts afforded by aerobic exercise. And the friend has strengthened his long-term potentiation (LTP) with Positive Reinforcement of those benefits before, during and after the aerobic workout. That is critical in helping leverage yourself back into an aerobic pace—no matter what.

The next scheduled time for your exercise will be easier because the memory of the gains of this episode made it fun and beneficial. You will feel deprived if you miss it.

That's how habits are born. That's how you make exercise self-maintaining because it becomes something you enjoy, demand and treasure.

Lionel Wilridge approaches 72 focused on fitness.

I was active in sports just about all of my life. My last fifteen years at Boeing I was a manager in production control. I started running. I enjoy doing just about everything I do. I don't look at it as aging. I look at it as being experienced with my body. I'll be 72 years old next month. Fitness is part of my lifestyle now. I really enjoy working out in the gym. Ninety percent of my friends are people in the gym.

Ideal aging for me is doing the things that I want to do for my body. That is, staying fit, not only for my body but for my mind. If your mind is not fit then you can't control your body. I do a lot of reading. So that is exercising my brain. Ideal Aging™ from the top to the bottom. A lot of people in the gym say I am a role model for them.

Books and just training my body serve as my mentors. There are certain things in the gym that I should do to have the shape, the fitness, the muscle tone in certain areas of my body that I want. I eat healthy. I am more fit now than I was at age 28 to 34.

Actually, to be honest with you, I haven't really had any real hardships. My mother's still living. She'll be 95 in July. She gets up every morning and does her exercise. Probably one reason why I do what I do is that I think of her and I want to be doing what I'm doing now when I get her age.

Being happy, being able to do the things that I want to do for myself and for other people are the highlights of my life. Just being a good citizen.

To improve the world I would try to make it a better place for all of us to live—all people being friendly to everyone. Not only to the people in America. The entire world needs to become one group, not separated people. We should all be God's children and understand what He is doing for us.

We all need to get a good night's sleep. Eat healthy. Do not sit around at your home and watch TV. Get up in the morning, do things, get out of the house. Be happy. Be friendly.

From an inspiring interview February 23, 2007.

EAT SMART DELICIOUSLY

"... genes play an increasingly minor role in promotion of *single* risk factors, such as hypertension and high blood fats, with advancing age."

"By harnessing the power of proper diet, exercise, smoking cessation, and so on, we can prevent or defuse a potential genetic time bomb."
Both by John Rowe and Robert Kahn of the MacArthur Foundation Study in Successful Aging

Goals

- Learn to love your fruits, legumes, whole grains and veggies ... because they provide clean burning carbohydrates as fuel for your brain, add fiber, have antioxidants and have plant sterols as well as other hormonal compounds

- Eat 1 to 1.55 grams of dietary protein per 2.2 pounds of your body weight each day ... because it may increase some bone growth factors

- Get 30% or less of your calories from healthy fats such as fish, nuts and olive oil ... because the right fats are essential to your brain, skin, cell membranes and overall health

- Reduce your calorie intake 10% to 40% ... because it might reprogram your metabolism, improve your immune response, have an anti-inflammatory effect and prolong your life

- Count your micronutrients ... because vitamins and minerals are essential

- Add spices to your meals ... because they add antioxidants while increasing pleasure for the health of it

His Holiness the Dalai Lama believes that all animals want to be happy. Some of us also want to live long lives. Most of us want Ideal Aging™ which includes mental, emotional, social, intellectual, sexual and physical health. None of us want to be the one in our circle of friends who is suffering the indignity of aging the least gracefully. Most of us probably also want our friends to age gracefully with as much vigorous longevity as we plan for ourselves so we can continue to enjoy each other as we prosper.

This is not a one-diet-fits-all chapter. It will be especially delicious to use the BARE BONERS approach here. First, the American Medical Association responded to research out of Harvard by recommending that you take supplements. Second, several of the essential nutrients can only be gotten from food or supplements. And last, some of these nutritional components have upper limits.

The good news is that these are exciting times. The focus in preventive medicine is on diet for the health of it. Genes do not dictate. You can eat deliciously to influence how you age.

Consider antioxidants. The power of protection against free radicals is measured as the oxygen radical absorbance capacity (ORAC) scale. It is often recommended that you get about 3,000 to 5,000 ORAC units each day. For example 3.5 ounces of prunes contain 5,770 ORAC units. Unfortunately, they're pretty high in sugar.

The good news is that a half cup of blueberries have 2,400 ORAC units. We like to leave blueberries in the freezer and eat them as a frozen snack. They are more refreshing and healthful than sherbet because the carbohydrates in the berries have a gradual effect on blood sugar.

While writing my book *Secrets Inside Bones, Brains & Beauty*™ about osteoporosis, it was enlightening to learn several things. For example, by the time you do everything you can to Build Better Bones, you probably have also improved how your brain works AND enhanced your natural beauty with the radiance of health and some weight loss. This chapter shows you how to **Eat Smart Deliciously** for your *Bones, Brains & Beauty*® to enhance Ideal Aging™.

In 1987 the journal *Science* broke out of the disease model and started to redefine successful aging. The MacArthur Foundation Study emphasized the *"positive aspects of aging"* in dozens of research projects in America. This consortium of brilliant minds found that the way you live, more than your genes, determines your health and vitality. At the top of the list of healthy life choices is diet.

This chapter celebrates ways to **Eat Smart Deliciously** based on science. Knowledge is power … when you use it. People tend to find time and ways to do what they enjoy. Join me in combining the power of knowledge through science. There are many delights inherent in novel combinations of foods. A multinational approach can include the best food habits and culinary treats from many nations. These can bring maximum happiness in Ideal Aging™ for the health of it.

Science behind your plan

The high concentration of centenarians in Okinawa is an excellent example of successful aging. They have the lowest frequency in the world of heart disease, stroke and cancer according to the 1996 report of the World Health Organization. A twenty-five year research study examined more than six hundred Okinawan centenarians plus some "youngsters" who were in their seventies, eighties and nineties. They found the secrets to "everlasting health" as reported by Dr. Suzuki, the principal investigator of a study began in 1976. These included:

- Young arteries;
- Low-risk for hormone-dependent cancers;
- Strong bones;
- Sharp minds;
- Lean and fit bodies;
- Natural menopause,
- Youthful sex hormones,
- Reduced free-radical damage;
- Excellent psycho-spiritual health; AND
- Integrative health care.

Diet was a key lifestyle factor in the first eight of these ten secrets to the elders' vigorous longevity with everlasting health. These researchers report that one way Okinawans stay lean is by "practicing *hara hachi bu* – only eating until they are 80 percent full."

It is estimated that Okinawans consume about 40% fewer calories than Americans do.

It is well accepted that both eating fewer calories and getting adequate nutrients do delay aging and extend the life span in many animals. That's been shown in rats, protozoans, water fleas, worms, guppies and flies.

All cells in your body require total nutrition even though their functions are different. That's true of the cells in your bones, brains, gut, skin and everywhere. For example, bone cells mineralize, maintain, and repair your bones. They require a wide variety of fuel for energy and raw materials for building in order to work properly. They rely on adequate protein to build the pliable structure of collagen that is hardened with minerals such as calcium, magnesium and phosphorus. The cells of your brain require adequate healthy fats to build and protect it.

And so it goes for all cells. The needs are vast, complex and varied. That's delicious because it means your diet can be equally varied.

As long as adequate nutrition included all essential nutrients, the fewer calories eaten, the longer the life. In mice, the restricted calories with adequate nutrients also reduced the incidence of lifestyle diseases such as heart disease, cancer, hypertension, kidney disease, diabetes, cataracts and hyperlipidemia (high cholesterol).

That's empowering truth from the records of mice and Okinawans!

> "Now is clearly the time for a shift in thinking, a new approach to life, a new paradigm for healing, one that provides us with the tools to learn from the past, navigate the future, and seek health and fulfillment in the present."
> Bradley Willcox, MD, Craig Willcox, PhD and
> Makoto Suzuki, MD, in
> *The Okinawa Program*

Why this disease protection happens is not yet known. Richard Weindruch suggests that calorie restriction might reset how an animal metabolizes food. Current research also does not tell us what that means for humans. However, younger Okinawans who have adapted to the Western diet suffer "the highest level of obesity in Japan, the worst cardiovascular risk factor profile, and the highest risk of premature death."

Learning from benefits observed in Okinawan elders and putting this knowledge to use in our own lives can increase our chances for sustained success. So, if living well longer is more important to you than staying full, it might be worth reducing your calories by ten to forty percent ... depending on how much you would prefer to increase your physical activity. The MacArthur Foundation Study suggests burning about 150 extra calories each day in your choice of exercise. That is conservative in comparison to other suggested changes. More on that in the chapter **Exercise Right**.

Macronutrients

Carbohydrates.

Build to your strengths by eating smart. Carbohydrates are the primary source of fuel for the body. They are the clean burning fuel–unlike proteins which require sufficient water to wash the waste products out of your system. Certainly an adequate intake of carbohydrates is essential. The energy to build, repair and maintain all body cells for their peak performance comes primarily from carbohydrates.

For example, your brain uses glucose for fuel. It is one of the highest users of energy in your body. Giving it refined sugars can put it into an energy crisis similar to flooding. It creates a destructive cascade of events throughout your body.

Spikes in blood sugar elevate insulin and inflammation. Sugar molecules attach to proteins such as collagen. The sugar-protein bone, glycation, is a form of cross-linking that makes your collagen stiff and less flexible. The changes are most visible in skin which appears aged and wrinkled.

Other body proteins are also affected. This includes the collagen that holds the minerals which make your bones strong and hard. Whether or not glycation can be reversed is still being researched.

At the same time, with too few carbohydrates your brain does not have the type of energy it requires to do its best work. An amazing amount of energy in the form of glucose is essential for clear, cogent, convincing brain work. Balance is another focus in this book. The recommended way of achieving the right availability of glucose for best brain power is to consume carbohydrates as they come packaged for nature—encased in fiber. That delays gastric emptying and slows the digestion of complex carbohydrates so that blood sugars remain stable.

The Nurses' Health Study included 82,802 female registered nurses. During the twenty-year follow up, 1994 cases of coronary heart disease occurred. The nurses' daily carbohydrate intake ranged from 116 to 234 grams during the course of the study. The lower carbohydrate intake was associated with less heart disease when they ate vegetable sources of fat and protein as compared to when animal sources of fat and protein were eaten.

Whole Grains

There are many choices in grains that are great sources of carbohydrates. Making smart choices in the grain family, however, is probably more difficult than any other group of foods. Your local grocery store is probably stocked with thousands of products that would constitute a 'bad' grain choice because the primary ingredient is often processed white flours with a lot of additives such as sugars and unhealthy fats.

Fortunately, there are a few grain products in your grocery store that would be a wise choice. Old fashioned rolled oats is one of those. Oat bran is the gold standard for improving your cholesterol measures. Although they get less research, be sure to include barley and buckwheat on your list. Buckwheat is actually a seed. It has a high content of soluble fiber and other nutrients that can improve cholesterol levels, stabilize blood sugar levels and enhance colon health.

Read the package label closely. Make sure that you are purchasing whole grain foods if you want to make the best nutritional choice possible. Since the term "whole grain" is often used a bit haphazardly, it might be wise to purchase the product with the highest fiber content.

The fiber content in the whole grains causes them to be digested more slowly. Digesting white breads versus whole grains is sort of comparable to digesting marbles versus a whole freight train. The marbles pretty readily roll right over the boundary of your gut and into your blood stream. The freight train, on the other hand, must first be disassembled.

Since high fiber content will keep your blood sugar level more even, you will have a more steady supply of energy, feel satisfied longer, and tend to eat less. Again, it's the fiber content keeping your blood sugar even that avoids insulin spikes and feeling famished. Simple carbohydrates like white bread and the average pasta cause instability of insulin because they lack fiber. Avoiding this spiking effect by getting adequate fiber in the whole grains will allow you to maintain an even, constant level of energy and keep your metabolism working at its highest potential. You'll feel better and have more enthusiasm for your daily exercises as suggested in the **Exercise Right** chapter. And you will enhance Ideal Aging™.

Whole grains, vegetables and fruits are a great source of soluble and insoluble fibers. Fiber is not absorbed or digested. As it travels through the body in its original form, it can aid digestion, help prevent constipation, improve colon health, lower cholesterol, stabilize blood glucose and reduce risk of colon cancer. At least 25 to 38 grams of fiber per day are recommended. The average American diet only contains about 12 grams of fiber a day.

Water-soluble soybean fiber is one of the fibers that aids in calcium absorption. Getting a wide source of fibers from grains, vegetable and fruits is the wisest protection of your *Bones, Brains & Beauty*® which can only come from the radiance associated with overall health. The OKinawan diet includes seven to thirteen servings of rice, noodles, breads and other whole grains.

<u>Fruits and Vegetables.</u>

The Framingham Osteoporosis Study found that **a high fruit and vegetable intake** appeared to be protective in men. Diets high in candy were the unhealthiest for bones in both sexes. It seems that carbohydrates that come naturally packaged in fiber are critical to our health—especially when very little processing has been done to them before we eat them.

Standard fare for Okinawans is seven to thirteen servings of vegetables plus two to four servings of fruits. Then they include two to four servings of foods rich in flavonoids such as soy.

A government study into the dietary habits of the average American discovered that only 55% of Americans eat any vegetables or fruits *at all* on a daily basis. The other 45% eat none. Not an apple, not even a baby carrot or a single stalk of celery! Zip!

The low intake of vegetables and fruits by Americans may be as bad as being a couch potato!

There's little wonder that health problems and chronic disease caused by dietary deficiencies are on the rise. Vegetables and fruits are a great source of dietary fiber and a source of low calorie carbohydrates to be used for energy. The vitamins, minerals and antioxidants they provide are also vital to achieving good health and enabling proper calcium absorption.

Benefits of Eating Fruits and Vegetables

- Increases availability of important **vitamins and minerals**
- Promotes **eye health**
- **Builds better bones**
- Helps maintain **good blood pressure**
- Aids in digestion and overall **digestive health**
- Reduces cholesterol
- Helps body to utilize **glucose for energy**
- Provides **phytonutrients such as flavonoids** (plant derived substances that are the subject of intense recent research for their ability to protect against disease and prevent forms of cancer)
- Provides **antioxidants**

Proteins.

Amino acids are the initial building blocks of proteins. When two or more amino acids are linked together, a peptide is created. Those created in the brain are called neuropeptides. A polypeptide is the linkage of about 100 amino acids. When two hundred or more amino acids are linked together they are called proteins.

Neuropeptides in the brain act as neurotransmitters, the messengers between synapses at the end of your brain cells. They communicate about emotions (with serotonin for example), hunger (with leptin), pain and euphoria (for example with endorphins), and sleep (with melatonin, for example). Neuropeptides are discussed more in the chapter on Smarter This Year where you learn how to turn your brain into a "self-fertilizing garden."

Protein is essential in all cells. Collagen, a special kind of protein, warehouses the minerals that harden and strengthen your bones. When you Exercise Right, it is necessary in maintaining muscle mass and muscle strength. Proteins connect DNA to the cell and affect all cell functions. They are the framework that holds billions of cells in place. They carry supplies, like the helper protein in your gut that carries vitamin D across into your blood stream and oxygen from your lungs to your organs. They dance throughout your body telling the story line of your life. They are the power in your muscles and the antibodies that make your immune system strong. Your body is continually using and making new proteins. Your skin is renewed in about seven days. Some other tissues take longer.

To maintain this obligatory and intense rate of protein synthesis, the body needs a dedicated supply of amino acids.

The MacArthur Foundation Study suggests that about twelve percent of your total calories should come from protein. If you are consuming 2100 calories, 12% (252 calories) would be about 63 grams of protein at 4 calories per gram of protein. If your weight is 139 pounds, that would be about one gram of protein per 2.2 pounds of body weight.

In preventing or treating osteoporosis the recommendations for protein are somewhat higher. **When calcium intake is high enough**, adding protein to the diet can increase bone mineral density. Research recently published suggests that increasing protein intake to 1 or 1.55 grams per 2.2 pounds of body weight may increase some bone growth factors. This is true whether the source of protein is animal or plant. In the example above, that could mean getting about 97 grams of protein per day if your weight is 139 pounds. **Your calcium intake must be adequate so the added protein can be helpful**.

Proteins are complex molecules. How you get them and how you use them can be a complex topic. No consensus exists on the impact of the protein you eat on your overall use of calcium and on your bone health.

However, studies have found remarkable improvements in the recovery from hip fractures in hospitalized elderly individuals who were given protein supplements. Fewer deaths occurred. Medical complications and length of stay in rehabilitation units have been decreased. One study with individuals about 80 years old found increases in insulin-like growth factor-1 (IGF-1), a marker of bone formation. The individuals in this study who were given the protein supplement lost about half as much bone mass after the fracture in comparison to the elderly who were not given the protein supplement.

Another study looked at healthy men and women over the age of 50. Again, the individuals in the high protein group (1.6 grams per 2.2 pounds of body weight per day) had significantly higher measures of IGF-1 than the comparison group (0.78 grams per 2.2 pounds of body weight per day). It is noteworthy that this amount is greater than the Recommended Daily Allowance (RDA.)

It is also significant that the high protein group had lower measures on urine tests for bone breakdown. These researchers concluded that this increase above the RDA may have a good impact on the bones of healthy older men and women when calcium intake is adequate.

Remember that we need proteins to build all healthy tissues in our bodies. This includes our bones. It's no surprise that protein is critical to rebuild the structure of our bones after a fracture and to keep our immune response healthy.

Proteins are necessary during building, repairing, and replacing body tissues at any age.

One of the bad effects of a low protein diet may be related to the significant reduction in calcium being absorbed in the intestines. There is a helper protein involved in transporting calcium out of the gut and into the blood.

Isoflavones are a specific kind of soy protein that may protect your bone health. The authors of *The Okinawa Program* believe that the high amount of soy and soy products in their diet contributed to the bone health, heart health, mental alertness and relative freedom from cancer in the Okinawan elders. Soy is rich in phytoestrogens and flavonoids (hormone blockers from plants). These can protect from the damaging effects of estrogen while having all the beneficial effects.

The typical Asian intake is about 10 grams of soy per day. This can be considered safe. If you prefer to buy soy protein powder, 80 milligrams of actual soy Isoflavones has been shown to address postmenopausal issues as well as bone mineral density. Long term use of soy as a source of protein has been associated with healthy bones in the elderly. As previously stated, water-soluble soy fiber aids in calcium absorption.

Protein can also be harmful to bones. Balance it with calcium and vitamin D intake.

By the same token, eating **too much protein** has clearly been shown to **increase the amount of calcium lost in the urine**. It has been estimated that every gram of protein intake may be associated with the loss of 1.5 mg of calcium in the urine. Thus it is important to balance the amount of protein eaten with the amount of calcium and vitamin D consumed.

Also, protein is not a clean burning fuel. When your body digests it, large molecules need to be rinsed out of your body. Otherwise, these remnants of protein digestion do not dance through your kidneys well. Therefore, it is important to drink eight to ten glasses of water a day when you eat higher amounts of protein to help keep your kidneys healthy.

For your bones, brains and general health, consider getting much of your protein from salmon, sardines and mackerel. They are rich sources of calcium as well as healthy fats and proteins.

A positive impact on bone health is generally found in studies in which the calcium source was dairy products. This suggests no bad effect of the protein in dairy products. However, dairy foods vary widely in their content of nutrients. Some research suggests that milk and yogurt could be beneficial while cottage cheese, which has higher protein content and lower calcium content, may decrease calcium absorption.

Fats.

The walls of the cells in your body contain fats. Fat is necessary for repair and healing of your cells. It helps you absorb the fat-soluble vitamins A, D, E and K. Cholesterol is a fat that is used to form testosterone, estrogen and other hormones.

Fatty acids are the building blocks of fats. There are two essential fatty acids (EFA) which your body cannot make. Linoleic acid is an omega-6 EFA found in corn oil, safflower oil, and soybean oil. Linolenic acid is an omega-3 EFA found in soybean oil, walnuts, canola oil and flaxseed.

The omega-6 EFA group is necessary in the fight or flight process to protect you from any injury. They promote blood clotting so you won't bleed excessively with injury, raise your blood pressure and create inflammation at the site of injury. The omega-3 EFA are growth and repair oriented. They have anti-inflammatory effects and reduce blood clotting. The recommended ratio of omega-6 EFAs to omega-3 EFAs is between three to one and five to one. Human cells have about that ratio.

Monounsaturated fat might also help reduce your risk for diabetes and cancer. The best sources include olive oil, flaxseed oil, canola oil and avocados.

Micronutrients

Vitamins – the Importance of vitamins D, A, B, C and K…

As mentioned earlier, fruits and vegetables are great dietary sources of many essential vitamins that are needed for good health and proper calcium absorption. Because the diets of many Americans are very low in these important foods (and because of possible nutrient loss in food due to environmental pollutants, count your intake of these nutrients closely.

You will want to make up for any inadequate dietary intake. As has been suggested by the American Medical Association's response to research, most people will need to take vitamin supplements. Through dietary and supplemental sources, make sure that you get the following vitamins.

<u>Vitamin D</u> might be one of the most exciting areas of new research. It serves your health

in several ways. Each of these affects your bone health and your safety. And the intake recommended by the experts has eased higher across years of research aimed at identifying what is optimal.

For starters, vitamin D is required to form the helper protein that carries calcium across the wall of your intestines into your blood stream. Without vitamin D the calcium you've swallowed just does a fluid dance out of your body in your urine. With adequate vitamin D you have a better chance of getting the most out of the calcium you swallow. Studies that increased calcium intake without adequate vitamin D showed less improvement in bone density than when vitamin D was added along with the calcium.

Additionally, the reduced risk of fractures found with vitamin D supplements might be related to the ability of vitamin D to decrease the risk of falls. The activity of vitamin D in the muscles could explain this. It may be responsible for helping your muscles be stronger so that you are more stable in your dance of life. Since falls account for most of the fractures in osteoporosis, this role of vitamin D is critical in your overall bone health.

Depression is another risk factor for falls. A fascinating study on reported levels of wellbeing compared the effects of vitamin D at an adequate intake of 600 International Units (IU) per day versus 4000 IU per day. IU has been used to indicate the number of International Units of vitamin D. To put that in the language of the newer Dietary Reference Intakes (DRIs), no RDA has been established. However, the "Adequate Intake" (AI) of vitamin D is expressed as micrograms. One microgram of cholecalciferol is equal to 40 IU of vitamin D. Cholecalciferol, the form of vitamin D in most supplements, 25(OH)D is the form of vitamin D measured in your blood serum. The adequate intake of vitamin D starts at 5 micrograms (200 IU) for people from birth through age 50 years including pregnancy and lactation. It advances to a high of 15 micrograms (600 IU) for women older than 70 years.

So, the fascinating depression study gave either 15 micrograms (600 IU) or 100 (4000 IU) micrograms of vitamin D to patients. Since all subjects were below the recommended level of serum vitamin D, it was not appropriate to give the control group none. Both doses improved their wellbeing. Patients taking the higher amount of vitamin D, however, improved more on this measure of wellbeing. Since depression increases the risk of falling, vitamin D may be reducing fall risk by lessening depression as well as strengthening muscles. What an improvement that could make in your dance!

CAUTION: There are upper limits to vitamin D!
Confer with your healthcare provider AND get a blood level of vitamin D before changing anything.

The best health results with a blood level between 90 and 100 nanomols of 25(OH)D per liter of serum.

With regard to bone density, the addition of 700 IU of vitamin D supplementation along with calcium citrate malate up to a daily intake of 1300 mg calcium resulted in a significant gain of about 1% in bone density in the spine. This combination of supplements also reduced fractures by 50% in healthy men and women aged 65 or older.

Sunlight supplies most of our vitamin D requirement. Even elderly individuals with adequate sun exposure can achieve increased blood concentrations of vitamin D. Good food sources include cod liver oil and oily fish such as salmon, mackerel and sardines. Eating oily fish 3 to 4 times a week will help satisfy the requirement for adequate intake. Many fortified cereals and fortified milk are also good sources of Vitamin D.

Some recent research findings will help you and your healthcare provider determine your personal optimal intake of vitamin D. Former recommendations were that **5 micrograms (200 IU)** to **15 micrograms (600 IU)** per day would be adequate. That deserves a closer look.

Recent research suggests these amounts are inadequate. A consensus evolved among experts who analyzed the data. They found that **700 to 800 IU per day appear to reduce fracture risk. Thus 800 to 1000 IU of cholecalciferol (vitamin D3) or more per day for adults may be necessary.**

To get a picture of how much vitamin D that really is, there are about 100 IU of vitamin D in a glass of milk or fortified orange juice and about 360 IU in a 3 ounce serving of salmon. Supplements containing vitamin D3, cholecalciferol, could be a realistic way to increase your intake.

So, how will the adequate intake of vitamin D for you be determined? A team of scientists say that you need to keep your blood level of 25(OH)D, one form of vitamin D, above 80 nanomols per liter to prevent osteoporosis. The most recent review indicated that the best health results with your blood level between 90 and 100 nanomols per liter of serum 25(OH)D. This review of the literature included strength and function in leg muscles; avoiding falls; dental health and avoiding cancer of the colon and rectum.

Your healthcare provider can help you determine what your blood level of this form of vitamin D is. Use that information to determine how much you may need to consume to keep it above this level. This is one of your baseline measures that will assure that your efforts in consultation with your healthcare provider are tailored specifically to your body's unique needs.

Vitamin A can be obtained from the foods you eat. Too much vitamin A through supplements can be harmful to your bones. Taken in the form of retinol, it may contribute to hip fractures in women with osteoporosis. However, beta carotene in higher doses has not been shown to increase the risk of hip fractures. Further research is needed on the role of vitamin A and on the preferred amount to get in your diet. If you are taking fish oil supplements as well as getting vitamin A in a multivitamin, be sure to count both sources.

The B vitamins, especially folic acid, can improve your chances of avoiding such serious conditions as birth defects, heart disease and cancer. Folate, or folic acid, plays important roles in repair of damaged cells and in healthy cell division. Also, Vitamin B6, vitamin B12 and folic acid are part of the chemical reactions that change homocysteine into other amino acids, the building blocks of proteins. The main protein in your bones and skin is collagen. Keeping homocysteine levels low is important to building collagen and to your heart health.

Vitamin C is needed to form the protein structure of your bones. Collagen is the most abundant protein forming that structure. It is special protein that forms the framework that minerals will harden. Vitamin C is needed to allow the collagen to create the right kind of structure. Then adequate calcium helps to harden the bones around that structure. The combination of vitamin C and calcium in adequate doses increases bone density.

Vitamin K plays a role in production of osteocalcin, the second most abundant protein in your bones. Vitamin K also influences the functioning of osteocalcin. In these ways it helps your enzymes make the structure of your bones stronger. Because vitamin K does not seem to influence bone mass, it is not clear why vitamin K reduces fractures of the spine and hip in women. However, recent studies suggest that 375 micrograms might be needed for optimal bone health. Since this is higher than the RDA, your healthcare provider can help you decide what is best for you. It's especially important to monitor this vitamin intake if you are taking anticoagulants or blood thinners.

Recommendations for Vitamins

Vitamin D (discussed in an earlier section)–base your intake on your blood levels of 25(OH)D with the best health results being between 90 and 100 nanomols per liter.

The only research showing reduction in fractures combined Vitamin D with calcium supplements.

700 to 800 IU per day reduced risk of falling by 22%.
1000 IU OR MORE of Vitamin D per day may be required in the elderly.

Low blood levels of 25-hydroxy vitamin D may be associated with periodontal disease regardless of BMD.

4000 IU of vitamin D per day increased wellbeing—this antidepressant effect might reduce falls.

Beta carotene

8,400 micrograms for females and 10,800 micrograms for males

Vitamin B

Vitamin B6   1.3 mg

Vitamin B12   2.4 µg

Folate as Folic Acid   400 mcg

Vitamin C

75 mg for females and 90 mg for males is the RDA.

However, taking more than 600 mg of Vitamin C per day has been recommended to improve the collagen essential for strong bone.

Vitamin K (medications may influence this dose)

The RDA is 90 micrograms for women and 120 micrograms for men. However, research suggests that even 375 micrograms may be too low to prevent osteoporosis.

Minerals.

There are several reasons to start with calcium. Calcium is essential in cell membrane functioning, conducting messages along nerve cells, contracting a muscle, clotting blood, regulating inflammation, and influencing some enzyme activity. It is so critical to so many body functions that measured blood levels tend to stay within the critical range—even if this results in taking calcium out of your bones to the point of leaving them fragile.

> You might want to double your calcium intake immediately.

Almost 100 percent of the US population is consuming *half* the amount of calcium that is recommended as the minimum daily requirement. However, almost everyone believes they are getting enough of this essential mineral. For that reason, we need to focus on calcium before we explore other necessary vitamins and minerals.

Start by getting calcium in what you drink and eat. An eight ounce glass of milk would supply about 300 mg of calcium.

<u>*Calcium*</u>.

Recommended daily intake of calcium are within the following ranges:

Adults	1000 mg
Men & women ages 50 or older	1000 to 1500 mg

In many nations the main sources of dietary calcium are milk products and green, leafy vegetables. The value of milk products as a source of calcium for some people is evident. Both Croatia and China give us good examples.

In Croatia, District A consumed more dairy products than was natural to District B. District A had about twice as much calcium intake as District B. Hip fractures were less frequent in the elderly of District A than in District B.

In China, women aged 35 to 75 years living in five rural counties were investigated. These women in pastoral counties had higher dairy calcium and total calcium intake than the women living in non-pastoral counties. Women with the higher dairy sources of dietary calcium had increased bone mineral density by facilitating optimal peak bone mass earlier in life.

We know that other things also influence our bone mineral density, but inadequate calcium intake in the foods we eat is one of the most important. Doctors and nutritionists recommend getting about 500 mg of calcium at every meal since the body can only properly absorb a fairly small amount of calcium at a time.

The dairy group is currently experiencing some resurgence in popularity. Recent scientific studies have shown that getting three servings of calcium rich nonfat dairy foods a day can actually help facilitate weight loss in women who eat a sensible diet. Hence the "get three a day" ad campaign you may see in the media.

If you could possibly lose a few pounds (which many of us could afford to do) and build strong bones at the same time, there's even more reason to make sure you get an adequate intake from the dairy group.

It's worth repeating that almost no one gets an adequate intake of this all-important mineral. This doesn't have to be the case. The choices of foods that are calcium rich are a gourmet's delight. Even the non-gourmet has plenty of options. Whether you're making a calzone packed with calcium rich ricotta cheese and broccoli, or simply packing raisins in a sack lunch, you can pick delicious foods that will introduce more calcium into your diet.

A little tofu or black strap molasses in your fruit smoothie or yogurt on your oatmeal can add interest as well as calcium to some of your favorite recipes. Other tips for increasing calcium are substituting canned salmon with bones for tuna fish in making sandwiches, salads, fillings, or on a bagel. Chop tofu or tempeh into salads or stir fry dishes. Use broccoli, kale, okra, turnip greens, collards, and beet greens regularly in soups, salads, or other recipes. Add powdered milk to recipes. Mix nonfat yogurt instead of sour cream or mayonnaise in recipes. For more inspiration and information on calcium in several categories of foods, consult Appendix E in my book on osteoporosis entitled **Secrets Inside Bones, Brains & Beauty®**.

Also, many foods are now fortified with calcium. Read labels to check for this. One example is the addition of calcium citrate malate to some brands of orange juice.

Take calcium supplements if indicated. The Harvard review of a large body of research objectively demonstrates the value of adding nutritional supplements to your daily regimen. They can aid in the prevention and/or treatment of diseases or specific risk factors for diseases, including osteoporosis. The American Medical Association has recommended nutritional supplements subsequent to that review.

No matter how nutritious your diet, chances are you won't be able to get an adequate supply of calcium simply through the food you eat alone. There are a wide variety of factors that contribute to dietary deficiency of calcium.

Some people find it difficult to get adequate calcium because of lactose intolerance or a busy schedule with little time to devote to preparing proper foods. Too many others have opted to drink things other than milk – such as cola drinks or other beverages that have high amounts of sugar and no calcium.

Even those people who strive to prepare healthy meals rich in calcium, however, may still have difficulty achieving proper levels of calcium and other nutrients. Genetically engineered food and pollution can compromise the nutritional value of the food that we eat. Therefore, supplementation can be essential to get adequate calcium.

Consult your doctor for calcium supplement recommendations and empower yourself by doing your own research.

The more you educate yourself prior to the office visit, the better your questions will be. Being an informed consumer is more critical today than it ever has been. Studying up on the health of your Bones, Brains & Beauty® may be one of your best educational investments ever. Since more than one form of calcium supplement is available, you will want to learn about several of them. You can get detailed information from my book **Secrets Inside Bones, Brains & Beauty®**.

One important requirement for a calcium supplement is that it must be easily absorbed by the body. Before it can be absorbed, it has to be dissolved. To test your calcium supplement, put it in a small glass of warm water or vinegar. If it has not dissolved within 30 minutes, it probably will not dissolve in your stomach either. You might want to look for another source of calcium.

Calcium Citrate Malate

- Has approximately 40% more absorption than other forms of calcium.

- Reduced bone loss in the spine of postmenopausal women by 60% compared to those taking a placebo or to individuals taking calcium carbonate.

- Increased bone mineral density in the hip and wrist of men and women 65 years old and older.

- Reduced fractures when taken with Vitamin D.

- Increased bone mineral density when taken with protein supplements.

Also, read the label to determine the actual amount of calcium in the supplement. This is usually referred to as elemental calcium. This will determine how many tablets you need to take to get enough calcium.

The absorption rate of calcium carbonate, calcium citrate, calcium lactate and calcium gluconate are similar to the rate that calcium is absorbed from milk products. Calcium citrate malate has shown approximately 40% more absorption than calcium carbonate.

For example, a supplement of 300 mg of calcium in the form of calcium citrate malate would yield absorption of 105 to 126 mg of calcium delivered into your blood stream as compared to approximately 75 to 90 mg that actually makes it into your system from milk or many of the more common calcium supplements such as calcium carbonate or calcium gluconate. Bone mineral density actually increased at the hip and wrist for those women taking calcium citrate malate.

A later study looked at men and women who were 65 years of age or older and living in their community. The treated group added 500 mg of calcium citrate malate plus 700 IU of vitamin D3 (cholecalciferol) per day for three years. This combination moderately reduced bone loss in the hip, spine, and total body in these men and women.

Since this improvement was still evident after three years, this suggests long-term effectiveness of supplementation in terms of the skeleton as a whole. Also, a reduced incidence of non-vertebral (non-spine) fractures was noted.

Another study found reduced risk of fractures in elderly women treated with 1200 mg of calcium plus 800 IU of vitamin D. This reduction in fractures was not found when vitamin D was given without calcium. Vitamin D is essential for proper calcium absorption, which will be discussed in greater depth later in this section.

What else is important about the calcium you take?

You should space your calcium intake out across the day. For one thing, by consuming part of your calcium at bedtime and another part first thing in the morning, you can compensate for the bone loss that can occur during sleep at night. Also, your body can only absorb a certain amount of calcium at one time.

Take no more than 500 mg of calcium at any one time.

That will maximize the amount that your body will absorb. With certain supplements, eating a meal just before you take your calcium can also be beneficial. Many supplements will break down more quickly with the presence of stomach acids that increase during times when food is introduced to the body.

Calcium citrate malate and calcium citrate avoid the problem of having to take your calcium supplement at mealtime. That's because stomach acid is not required to dissolve these molecules so they can be absorbed.

Calcium and Prescription Medication for Osteoporosis

High calcium intake is especially important when taking prescription medications for osteoporosis. It is calcium and phosphorus that harden the bone structure. All medications work best with adequate calcium intake.

For example, bisphosphonates (brand names such as Fosamax or Actonel) have been approved by the FDA for use in both prevention and treatment of osteoporosis. They decrease the action of the osteoclasts, the bone cells that break down bone. This drug family is more effective when combined with calcium supplement treatments.

Though side effects are relatively uncommon with these medications, some patients have reported abdominal and musculoskeletal pain after taking them. Others cite increased instance of heartburn and irritation of the esophagus. Appendix C of **Secrets Inside Bones, Brains & Beauty**™ provides more information on the various medication options available.

Why all the fuss about calcium?

Fracture protection. This may be the most critical reason for doing everything possible to keep your bones healthy. Adding 500 mg per day of calcium citrate malate plus 700 IU vitamin D yielded a 54% to 64% reduction in fractures in humans 65 or older living freely in their community.

The Secret Life of Bones Nearly everyone is consuming **half** the amount of calcium that is the minimum daily requirement. Most people do not realize that they are not getting enough calcium. The secret life of bones includes drastic decline in bone health with no symptoms.

Waiting until you have a fracture to find out about your bone health is like waiting until you have a heart attack before checking your cholesterol.

Too many people do both. Count your calcium—you probably need to double your intake of it.

Other Important Minerals.

RESEARCH FINDINGS

Other minerals your bones need each day:

Phosphorus   1,741 (Plus or Minus 535) mg

Sodium   2,400 mg or less per day

Copper   900 micrograms

Zinc   8 mg for females & 11 mg for males

Manganese   1.8 mg for females & 2.3 mg for males

Magnesium 320 mg for women & 400-420 mg for men
(Magnesium should be ½ of the amount of calcium)

Boron   No more than 20 mg

Magnesium. We need about half as much magnesium as calcium for our bodies to process the calcium. They help control inflammation. The quality of bone structure is improved by magnesium. Both minerals along with phosphorus contribute to increasing bone mineral density. They are involved in the formation of hydroxyapatite (bone mineral) that hardens your bones.

In the Framingham Osteoporosis Study magnesium intake was associated with better hip bone density in both men and women. Females, particularly teenagers, may be more at risk for inadequate intake of this mineral.

The **RDA of magnesium for adult women is 320 mg** a day and for **men is 400-420 mg** a day. Selected food sources of magnesium include green leafy vegetables, unpolished grains, nuts, meat, starches, and milk.

Phosphorus. This mineral is as important as calcium in making your bones hard. It is needed in every cell of your body. About 85% of the phosphorus in your body is in your bones. It is less of a focus for concern because it is so available in foods commonly eaten.

Approximately 1741 ± 535 mg each day was beneficial for maintaining bone mineral density in adult men when calcium intake was adequate (1200 ± 515 mg). The **RDA ranges from 700 a day for adults to 1250 mg a day during adolescence.** These numbers do not change during pregnancy and lactation. Dietary sources include milk, yoghurt, ice cream, cheese, peas, meat, eggs, some cereals, and breads.

Copper. Copper is also not a large focus of concern because we tend to get enough in our diets. However, it does play a critical role in making the proper structure of the collagen in our bones. It is part of the enzyme that helps knit the strands of collagen together for the best mechanical strength. For **copper** the daily **RDA is 700 micrograms for pre-adolescents, 890 micrograms for adolescents, 900 micrograms for adults, 1000 micrograms during pregnancy and 1300 micrograms during lactation.** For adults the Upper Limit is 10,000 micrograms per day. Dietary sources include seafood, nuts, seeds, wheat bran cereals, whole grain products, and cocoa products.

Zinc. This element also has a role in several enzymes. Some of these influence how various minerals make your bones hard. Others are essential in how your collagen forms the structure of your bones. It is an important part of how our body uses protein. The daily **RDA of zinc for adults is 8 mg for females** and **11 mg a day for males.** For pregnant females this increases to 13 mg during adolescence and 11 mg for adults. During lactation this increases to 14 mg during adolescence and 12 mg for adults. The Upper Limit for daily intake of zinc is 40 mg. Dietary sources include fortified cereals, red meats, and certain seafood.

Manganese. Manganese is another element that helps enzymes work properly to form the protein framework of your bones. It helps regulate the protein for stronger bones. **Manganese has a daily Adequate Intake of 1.8 mg for women and 2.3 mg a day for men. This increases to 2.0 mg during pregnancy and 2.6 mg during lactation.** The Upper Limit is 11 mg per day. Dietary sources are nuts, legumes, tea, and whole grains.

Sodium. Sodium intake should be carefully monitored. About 1500 grams per day is considered an Adequate Intake. However, the average person in the USA swallows a great deal more than that. This is, in part, due to the increasing reliance on fast foods.

Keep this in mind. The sodium and calcium that gets into your blood stream follow similar paths through your kidneys. This is part of the reason that your sodium intake influences how much calcium you lose. For each fifty-seven mg of sodium you eat you lose about one mg of calcium in your urine. The American Heart Association set an upper limit of recommended sodium intake for adults at 2,400 mg per day. <u>Count yours</u>. That may help you get the most value out of the calcium you swallow.

Boron. Calcium absorption may be improved by boron. Boron might also increase the effect of estrogen. **Boron has no RDA** but its daily Adequate Intake is 11 mg during preadolescence, 17 mg during adolescence and 20 mg throughout adulthood. These numbers do not shift with pregnancy and lactation. The **Upper Limit** for adults is **20 mg** a day. Selected food sources include fruit-based beverages and products, potatoes, legumes, milk, avocado, peanut butter, and peanuts.

Fluoride. New bone formation might be stimulated by fluoride. This may explain why habitual tea drinking of more than 10 years had a good effect on bone density of the total body, spine and hip in adults. Teas are a source of fluoride. Adequate Intake is 10 mg daily from preadolescence throughout life.

For extensive information on nutrition, go to the US Department of Agriculture site at www.nal.usda.gov/fnic/foodcomp/Data/SR17/wtrank/wt_rank.html. It is full of information about the nutritional benefits of food.

Other Delicious Options

> "—food is not just 'fuel' for the body, but is one of the joys of life, for all its associated tastes, textures, sights and scents, and for the pleasures it brings in allowing shared time with family and friends."
> Bess Dawson Hughes, MD in *Invest in Your Bones* for
> World Osteoporosis Day 2006
> which celebrated the theme of food and nutrition.

Spices. This is where the dietary fun accelerates for me. The focus will be on "spicing up life" rather than trying to discriminate between a spice and an herb.

For example, it's delicious to share why I own so many of the books written by Nathan Pritikin. The science behind his recommendations has stood the test of time … except that he ruled out all kinds of fats and insisted that only ten percent of daily calories come from fat. Rather than let that part discourage you, it clearly is worthwhile to modify the fat percentage in his recipes while including only healthy fats such as extra virgin olive oil.

A major asset is that Pritikin hired a gourmet cook to write the recipes for his books. I almost had my lunch stolen right off my desk—mid-spoonful—in front of me by colleagues at work who were so enticed by the aroma of seasonings. At potlucks when I don't identify the author of the recipe, people gobble up any Pritikin recipe I've ever taken and ask that I bring it again.

Well, that is, except for his coleslaw recipe that I made with purple cabbage—because

I cherish the unique delicate lavender color of it as it matures over a few days in the refrigerator. Lavender coleslaw is so unexpected that people hesitate even though it's a bowl of health, zesty flavors and beauty.

<u>Curcumin</u>. Tumeric is a spice used in Indian curries. While with the Peace Corps in Borneo, I learned to make my own curry powder. Ever since I've suspected that the tumeric was added primarily to give the distinctive yellow color as I don't detect much of a taste. However, that yellow pigment in tumeric contains curcumin, a substance that is showing a great deal of promise in recent research.

Curcumin has both anticancer and anti-inflammatory effects. Lower rates of colon cancer are found in individuals with diets high in curcumin. It remains a mystery how it protects normal cells while making cancer cells more vulnerable to chemotherapy and radiation. Research suggests curcumin may be effective in treating pancreatic cancer. prostate cancer and melanomas as well as effectively treating and reducing the risk of Alzheimer's disease. It could reduce the sclerotic plaque that clogs and inflames arteries.

Researchers at the University of Texas developed a safe method of giving curcumin intravenously to make it more bioavailable. Their laboratory results indicated that curcumin had anti-tumor effects. They believe that curcumin could be an effective, nontoxic treatment for pancreatic cancer.

Bengmark reviewed 1500 studies of curcumin, most of them recent. He concluded that animal research found preventive and treatment value of curcumin for several diseases. These included "arteriosclerosis, cancer, diabetes, respiratory, hepatic, pancreatic, intestinal and gastric diseases, neurodegenerative and eye diseases." Bring on the curry.

<u>Ginger</u>. This is another spicy ingredient. It is one of the most highly consumed dietary substances in the world. In many parts of Asia ginger is used in curries and other delicious dishes. China and Malaysia have used it as a medicinal herb to treat such ailments as the common cold, digestive problems, pain and motion sickness.

My Mom was a registered nurse. She gave ginger ale to the seven of us to settle our upset stomachs. Back then real ginger extract was used to create it. Current ginger ale may be made with a synthetic. Cooking with ginger and without sugar is preferred.

Gingerol, a phenolic substance, is one of ginger ale's ingredients that is exciting the scientific community. It has been shown to have anti-tumor, anti-oxidant AND anti-inflammatory properties. It is unknown why normal cells stay hardy while cancer cells die during exposure to gingerol. It reduces nausea. By dilating blood vessels, it lowers blood pressure. Gingerol is the part of gingerroot that has the strongest aroma. It adds depth of character to the flavoring of curries and many other dishes.

<u>Oregano</u>. Mexican oregano has an oxygen radical absorbance capacity (ORAC) rating of 92 while Greek mountain oregano rates 65 on the ORAC scale. The ORAC scale indicates the power of the antioxidants in food. Foods that score high on this scale can reduce the oxidative

damage to your cells. This could slow the aging processes in your body and your brain. The ratings of Mexican and Greek mountain oregano makes both of them powerful antioxidants for absorbing and neutralizing free radicals. They rate higher than ORAC ratings for berries, fruits and vegetables according to Zheng and Wang. Spice up your salad or soup with a sprinkling of low-calorie, high-antioxidant oregano. Just make sure it's Mexican or Greek. The Cuban oregano only rated an ORAC of 5.

Cinnamon and Cloves. Just reading the word cinnamon activates the part of your brain that smells. Keep that in mind when enjoying the chapter **Smarter This Year**.

Also, there is beginning research with rats showing benefits in stabilizing blood sugar and insulin resistance. Cinnamon extract seems to have a moderate effect in reducing fasting plasma glucose in Type II diabetic patients who had poor control of their blood sugar and were given 3 grams of cinnamon per day. That's about 2 ½ teaspoons of cinnamon powder. It also can help reduce inflammation. Cloves have similar good effects for Type II Diabetes management of blood glucose.

Chocolate. In the USA chocolate is eaten primarily as a snack. It's estimated that chocolate provides twenty percent as much antioxidant in the American diet as is obtained in both fruits and vegetables. Cocoa butter is a pro-oxidant, meaning that LDL and VLDL (very low density lipid) cholesterol are more vulnerable to oxidation even four hours after cocoa butter is consumed. The good news is that, even four hours after consumption of cocoa powder, a powerful antioxidant effect was measured. It made LDL and VLDL more resistant to oxidation according to Vinson et al. Their subjects had been given 22 grams, or about 3 ½ tablespoons, of cocoa powder. That would suggest that the best overall nutritional value can be realized by consuming cocoa powder and avoiding the cocoa butter, any other added fats and sugar typically found in chocolate products.

In a review of the literature, Ding and colleagues found that the flavonoids in chocolate may protect against death from heart disease. Cocoa has been shown to reduce blood pressure, reduce inflammation, enhance platelet activities so blood flows more fluidly, raise HDL and decrease oxidation of LDL.

> If the readers of this book look extraordinarily healthy, they may be consuming cocoa.

Stevia. This natural sweetener was used in many countries globally prior to its becoming available in the USA in 1995. In therapeutic doses it was shown to lower blood pressure in people with hypertension. That was in amounts exceeding normal use as a sugar substitute. Advantages to stevia include that it lacks calories, it is many times sweeter than table sugar, it has good shelf life, it helps with dental health because it does not cause tooth decay and it can be used by individuals struggling with diabetes, obesity and phenylketonuria.

Remember...
It is never too early And never too late To Build Better Bones, Brains & Beauty® For Ideal Aging™.

How to do it

We learn from new research how important a wide variety of nutrients are to your vigorous longevity in Ideal Aging™. The trend of research in recent years has been to consider what defines optimal health.

In order to achieve an adequate daily intake of these important nutrients, you get to enjoy eating a complete and varied diet. This isn't a book on proper nutrition, but what you eat has a tremendous effect on your overall health. Therefore, a quick overview of what would constitute a healthy diet is definitely worth our time.

One size does not fit all.

As one option, you can go to mypyramid.gov to get YOUR personal guidelines from the USDA. With the incredible amount of diet and nutrition information available today, it's hard to believe that the updated good old-fashioned food pyramid would retain any relevance, but it remains a useful tool for creating a healthier and more complete diet. At this site you can personalize your Food Guide Pyramid for Ideal Aging™.

The United States Department of Agriculture (USDA) created the food pyramid to help people understand the different varieties and quantities of food they should try to include from each food group in their daily diet. By choosing wisely from these groups, you can boost your intake of all nutrients that can Build Better Bones, Brains & Beauty™ for Ideal Aging™. In addition to the USDA food pyramid, you have another option.

Take seriously the lessons of rats and Okinawans.

Remember that Okinawa has some of the longest living people. Even their centenarians enjoy vigorous longevity without the lifestyle diseases that threaten to bankrupt much of the rest of the world. It is worth comparing the USDA Food Pyramid with the ordinary Okinawa intake. Confer with your healthcare provider to determine what fits your needs most closely. Then Eat Smart Deliciously

Serving Recommendations in the USA and in Okinawa:

Categories	USDA Food Guide Pyramid	Okinawa Foods
Grains	6 to 11 servings whole grains	7 to 13 servings of whole grains
Vegetables	3 to 5 servings, eating a variety	7 to 13 servings, eating a variety
Fruits	2 to 4 servings	2 to 4 servings
Flavonoid Foods		2 to 4 servings
Milk & Dairy	2 to 3 servings	
Calcium Foods		2 to 4 servings
Omega-3 Foods	2 to 3 servings	1 to 3 servings
Meat, Poultry, Fish, Beans, Eggs & Nuts		**Meat, Fish, Poultry & Eggs** 0 to 7 servings
Oils	Aim for 5 teaspoons of oils a day	1 to 2 tablespoons
Sweets	Limit extra fats & sugars to 195 calories	0 to 3 servings

Please note that the chart above does not comment on adding spice to your life. I believe you have to have it! And you get to use your wildest imagination in creating novel combinations for the health of it.

Eat Smart Deliciously • 183

On the one hand, it was profoundly sobering to learn recently that another of my siblings has cancer. I am number seven of seven children. Four of my siblings have had six kinds of cancer. That is pause for thought! It finally occurred to me that, by probability theory alone, I couldn't possible get cancer. Rates of cancer that high in one family would surely be unheard of. The amount of curcumin I've consumed over the years is added cause for optimism. Research on curcumin, a component of tumeric, is increasingly encouraging.

As described above, spices can contribute to your overall nutrition. They can go beyond simply "spicing up your life."

The poster that follows is based on research on bone health. It lists some of the important micronutrients. At BonesBrainsAndBeauty.com you can download this poster free to post it on your wall. It will be updated as new science dictates.

To D or not to D?

You have to ask that serious question!
First, because most people are NOT getting enough vitamin D.
Second, because vitamin D has an upper limit.
A blood study is the only way to tell whether you need more.

Nutrition	Daily	Sources
Protein	1 to 1.55 grams for every 2.2 pounds of your body weight	10 grams isoflavone-rich soy protein each day (typical Asian intake). Fish.
Vitamins *Beta carotene*	8,400 µg for females 10,800 µg for males	Liver, dairy products, fish, darkly colored fruits, orange vegetables, tomatoes, dark green leafy vegetables
Vitamin C	Taking more than 500 mg of Vitamin C per day improves collagen	Citrus fruits, kiwi, strawberries, cantaloupe, tomatoes, broccoli, peppers, potatoes, Brussels sprouts, cabbage, leafy greens
Vitamin D	Blood 25(OH)D 90 to 100 nmol/L, which may require up to 2200 IU a day.	Sunlight, cod liver oil and oily fish such as salmon, mackerel and sardines 3 to 4 times a week.
Vitamin K	375 micrograms or more if indicated	Deep green vegetables, soybean oil, and some cheeses.
Minerals *Calcium*	Children 800 to 1200 mg Adolescents & young adults 1200 to 1500 mg Adults 1000 mg Adults ages 50+ 1000 to 1500 mg or more as indicated	Milk, milk products, corn tortillas, calcium-set tofu, Chinese cabbage, kale, broccoli, juices and milk fortified with Calcium Citrate Malate. Take supplements containing Calcium Citrate or Calcium Citrate Malate.
Phosphorus	1206 to 2276 mg	Milk, yogurt, ice cream, cheese, peas, meat, eggs, some cereals, breads
Copper	90 µg	Seafood, nuts, seeds, wheat bran cereals, whole grain products, cocoa
Zinc	8 mg for females & 11 mg for males	Fortified cereals, red meats, and certain seafood
Manganese	1.8 mg for females & 2.3 mg for males	Green leafy vegetables, unpolished grains, nuts, meat, starches, milk
Boron	No RDA but the Upper Limit is 20 mg	Fruit, potatoes, legumes, milk, avocado, peanut putter, peanuts
Fiber	25 to 40 grams a day – read labels for fiber content	Whole grains such as buckwheat, rye and oats; raw whole vegetables; raw whole fruits; beans; legumes; seeds; sprouts

Also, count your protein intake. I was amazed to find that my intake was lower than this chart indicates is necessary to bone health. Protein is essential for building, maintaining and repairing all of your body's cells.

Definitely count your grams of fiber. The average American diet only includes about ten or twelve grams of fiber per day. As you see above, that's far less than half of what is recommended.

Measuring Goals

First, review the BARE BONERS process in the Introduction. It's too easy to assume you are getting what you need. Know where you're starting so you can be realistic about making changes. Begin A Realistic Effort: Baseline-Options-Now-Evaluate-Reinforce-Start over is the Dance of Ideal Aging™ ... and added spice is nice.

Pick one of the categories of food choices on which you want to focus for a few weeks. Measure your intake of that before changing anything. Then confer with your healthcare provider about changes that will enhance Ideal Aging™. Although medical counsel is an important step in any change, it's particularly important in Eating Smart Deliciously. Some of the nutrients have upper limits which should not be exceeded. Some nutrients can be measured in your body fluids prior to your making any changes in dietary intake to determine if any change is needed.

Also, it's particularly interesting how positive reinforcement works here. It is well known that many people use food as a reward. That's an unhealthy habit!

So why is positive reinforcement included at the base of the Your Delicious Choices from 2 Food Guides measurement form found on subsequent pages? It's there because how you talk to yourself will have a huge impact on your eating behavior. If you savor a meal while thinking, "What a gift to be eating the most delicious salad on the planet while building better Bones, Brains & Beauty®," you are more likely to repeat **Eating Smart Deliciously**.

Let's consider another scenario. Imagine for a moment that what you really want is some comfort food such as a root beer float. Moments like that have driven me to think creatively. As I researched osteoporosis for my book, **Secrets Inside Bones, Brains & Beauty**™, I was amazed that I wasn't getting enough protein! Research suggested that ten grams of isoflavone-rich soy per day, the typical Asian intake, might improve bone health and be safe. Be sure to review this recommendation with your healthcare provider. The phytoestrogens in soy can be beneficial to bone health but the jury is still out on their role for certain forms of cancer.

What do protein and soy isoflavones have to do with a root beer float? By creating a fat-free, sugar-free root beer shake with added soy isoflavones, I had come up with a delicious flavor that was brimming over with health – AND that kept me feeling satisfied for hours. Why? There was no sugar in it to cause a sugar rush and crash. Stevia was the sweetener. Also, protein tends to digest more slowly and prolongs your feeling satisfied.

A few quick reminders: With increased protein in your diet you may need to adjust your calcium intake. Also, proteins are the building blocks and workhorses of your body but they are not a clean burning fuel. So you need to get the amount of protein that your body needs while also getting enough water to wash out the "stuff" of the protein metabolism that your body does not use.

It has to be delicious when you create it to your own personal standards.

But a protein drink I invented only addressed my yearning for some immediate pleasure. The most important part of change is those little words we think so quickly and silently that we often are not aware that we have been thinking. But our emotions dance to the rhythm of that thought drummer. And positive thoughts beget positive emotions that enhance Ideal Aging™.

So I learned a new script. It went something like this: "What I really want right now is a root beer float. Good for me. I know how to have the flavor I want while making it brim over with health. This is delicious! I am creating and enjoying pleasure AND health. Tastes like Ideal Aging™ to me!"

It is frequently suggested that these shakes be made in a blender. I'm philosophically opposed to extra work. By shaking this in the container I can easily carry about, I only have one item to clean. More importantly, I can sip on the shake throughout several hours. That makes it easy to drink extra water throughout the day.

These are a few of the flavors I've enjoyed. For additional nutritional value, fiber and texture, I have also added a tablespoon of crushed flax seed meal.

Deliciously Smart Root Beer Shake

Combine in a shaker:
- 8 ounces nonfat milk
- 1 serving of your favorite protein powder (with soy isoflavones or whey proteins)
- Root Beer flavoring
- Stevia (optional)

Shake until frothy. Enjoy leisurely throughout the day.

Deliciously Smart Cinnamon-Roll Shake

Combine in a shaker:
- 4 ounces nonfat milk
- 4 ounces buttermilk
- 1 serving of your favorite protein powder (with soy isoflavones or whey proteins)
- ½ to 1 teaspoon cinnamon
- Stevia (optional)
- (1 tablespoon flaxseed meal—optional)

or
(1 tablespoon wheat germ—optional)

Shake until frothy. Enjoy leisurely throughout the day. Adding flaxseed meal increases your omega-3 intake. Either the flaxseed meal or the wheat germ also add a hint of chew factor.

Deliciously Smart Eggnog Shake

Combine in a shaker:
8 ounces nonfat milk
1 serving of your favorite protein powder (with soy isoflavones or whey proteins)
½ teaspoon nutmeg
1/4 to 1/2 teaspoon rum flavoring
Stevia to taste

Shake until frothy. Enjoy leisurely throughout the day.

With each of these recipes, remember to tell yourself at every step—from deciding to make them, through enjoying the flavors and through noticing how much more energy and brain power you have—that you are enhancing Ideal Aging™. Label the benefits you are giving yourself with this stable supply of proteins, carbohydrates and healthy fats without the sugar spikes and crashes. These words become the rewards that create new habits of health. These reinforcing words put you in complete control of making new food habits permanent for the health of it.

> Education alone will
> not make a new you.
> It's after you've learned,
> what you think and what you do .

Labeling the benefits as you enjoy them, novelty and deliciously smart foods are your most powerful tools for changing your eating habits! Do not diet. **Eat Smart Deliciously**.

I've created about 15 flavors of protein shakes. Gradually I'll make these recipes available at IdealAging.com as more testing is done to see which ones are favorites of other people. Suggestions are welcome. If you would like your idea of a terrific flavor considered, just email it to Recipes@StressPower.com.

And remember: educate yourself, measure your baseline, have a sense of what you want to change AND confer with your healthcare provider before modifying what you're doing. Then design changes so you will enjoy Ideal Aging™.

The form on the following page measures food choices represented in the USA pyramid and in the Okinawan diet described earlier. I've added a row so you can keep track of your daily fiber to emphasize the importance of that to Ideal Aging™. The other form measures macronutrients and micronutrients.

Have fun! Choose one little baby change at a time. For example, starting with calcium could be a good beginning because most people think they get enough when they don't. The emphasis is on Eating Smart Deliciously for the health of it.

Your Delicious Choices from 2 Food Guides

Food Choices	Mon	Tues	Wed	Thu	Fri	Sat	Sun	Total
Whole Grains								
Vegetables								
Fruits								
Flavonoid Foods								
Milk								
Calcium Foods								
Omega-3 Foods								
Meat, Poultry, Fish, Beans, Eggs & Nuts								
Oils								
Sweets								
Spices (add name)								
Fibers Soluble Insoluble								
Positive Reinforcement Before During After								

Your Nutrient Choices

Nutrient Choices	Mon	Tue	Wed	Thu	Fri	Sat	Sun	Total
Macronutrients								
Proteins								
Fats								
Omega-3								
Omega-6								
Saturated								
Trans fatty acids								
Carbohydrates								
Complex								
(Lightly processed)								
Sugars								
(Highly processed								
Micronutrients								
Vitamins								
Beta Carotene								
Vitamin C								
Vitamin D								
(cholecalciferol)								
Vitamin E								
Vitamin K								
Thiamin B-1								
Riboflavin B-2								
Niacin B-3								
Pantothenic Acid B-5								
Pyridoxine B-6								
Cyanocobalamin B-12								
Folate								
Biotin								
Choline								

Positive Reinforcement

Before _____

During _____

After _____

Your Nutrient Choices (Continued)

Nutrient Choices	Mon	Tue	Wed	Thu	Fri	Sat	Sun	Total
Micronutrients								
Elements								
Boron								
Calcium								
Chromium								
Copper								
Fluoride								
Iodine								
Iron								
Magnesium								
Manganese								
Molybdenum								
Phosphorus								
Selenium								
Zinc								
Potassium								
Sodium								
Chloride								
Positive Reinforcement Before _____ During _____ After								

Eat Smart Deliciously • 193

Summary

The benefits of studying the many nutrients required for Ideal Aging™ are huge! The more you know about them, the more you can decide what to measure in yourself. The more you learn about your current state of health, the better equipped you are to ask good questions of your healthcare provider. As an informed consumer, you can work with your healthcare provider to develop the choreography in this intricate dance of the many nutrients required for Ideal Aging™.

When you start with one small change at a time, stick with it for at least two weeks. Write your own script of celebration of each change. Remember to reward your changes with positive words. That's how you empower yourself to make these new food habits permanent for the health of it. What that means to you is that you have a lot of complex but easy, fun and delicious ways to influence your food habits to enhance Ideal Aging™.

> "Let food be thy medicine and medicine be thy food."
> Hippocrates

Education alone is insufficient. Changing your choices deliciously and telling yourself rewarding thoughts for these changes are essential to permanent change.

I've lost count of how many people have told me that they have chosen to regain their health after getting "a diagnosis of diabetes (or whatever lifestyle disease)." That means at least two things. It's never too late to enhance Ideal Aging™. It's never early!

The good news is that you get to choose the timing. Then remember to use words to reward every step of your changes so you can make these new habits permanent for the health of it. In fact, you could master this so well that people you love might feel compelled to follow your example just to keep up with you. Wouldn't it be wonderful to know that your example helped prolong the life of someone you love and want to hang out with in vigorous longevity?

John Rumberger, MD, PhD, Cardiologist
And world-renowned expert in preventive medicine with nearly twenty years experience in EBT technology, the gold standard for early detection of heart disease and guiding clinical care.
Author of *The Way Diet*.

I started out as an aeronautical engineering doing biomedical research. I decided to pursue medical training rather than to become an astronaut. I loved cardiology. After attending Ohio State University for Internal Medicine, I went to the University of Iowa for Cardiology. I was at the Mayo Clinic for a dozen years. After trying to develop methods for prevention and early detection of heart disease, I moved on to Columbus, Ohio to found Healthwise Prevention Center. I'm continuing my efforts at the Princeton Longevity Center in Princeton, New Jersey.

For me ideal aging would be to continue development of your mind, continued wellbeing, doing everything you can to try to stay healthy and to continue to learn. Perhaps get older but never grow up. If we continue to learn, continue to be healthy, remain a good friend and remain a loyal family member, I don't think you could ask for anything more.

I continue to be as physically fit as I can. I realize I'm not 20 years old but I can do a fair amount of physical activity. I try to relate that largely to continuing mental activity, continuing to try to find new things to learn, being willing to admit that I was wrong and reinventing myself. That is what I've done every five to ten years. I've just continued to hone in on what I feel good about and I think is reasonable. I've now moved on from working with patients with advanced heart disease onto the area of early detection and early prevention. I just look forward to learning something new every day.

We were fortunate to develop applications when I was a fellow with the University of Iowa and at the Mayo Clinic where we could use a CT scanner to define the presence of early plaque or hardening of the arteries. Using that information we could make some sense about how the patient should be treated or whether they need additional medication or testing. So it's been a continued challenge to look at early detection of heart disease much the same way that we now accept early detection of breast cancer with mammography and early detection of colon cancer with colonoscopy. This is just the next move to look at heart disease.

I'm medical director at Healthwise Wellness Diagnostic Center in Columbus, Ohio. The web site is healthwisecenter.com. I'm also a director of cardiac imaging at the Princeton Longevity Center in Princeton, New Jersey. That website is ThePLC.net. In my ideal world, people would be talking to each other. I see a lot of strife, confusion and hatred based on ignorance. The gift of education, of understanding would be the most important thing.

I've had a number of mentors. In college I was lucky to have an engineering mentor who really had vision of teaching me to try to understand data. I had an outstanding mentor in cardiology who was really committed to excellence in training and teaching and made you feel proud and knew how to guide you. I've had my family and my friends whom I continue to learn from. Luckily I have the support of my family. It's been support of family and friends that have sustained me.

My advice: Stay young. Continue to stimulate yourself. Read good books. Learn a new language. Learn new words. Learn how things are put together. Experience other cultures.

From an invigorating phone interview February 12, 2007

4. SEXUAL SAUNTER—THE BRAIN WORKOUT THAT'S DELICIOUS AT ANY AGE

"To think that a good sexual encounter also helps keep the brain alive is almost too good to be true. But it is; more than most 'routine activities,' sex uses every one of our senses and, of course, engages our emotional brain circuits as well."
by Lawrence Katz and Manning Rubin in
Keep Your Brain Alive.

In the middle of a scientific lecture at the university on a hazy Friday afternoon the scientist from the East with credentials up the Ying Yang informed us that the brain chemistry of healthy emotions drop off with aging "unless you make the right lifestyle choices."

The posture of the audience improved. At the first sign that questions were permissible, hands shot into the air. "What lifestyle choices?"

"Exercise, sleep and sex … but not in that order," was the learned reply.

As soon as he put these choices in proper order for greatest purchase of enduring healthy emotions, politely suppressed chuckles revealed that he had made everyone's day.

Sex came first from his view.

For Starters – by Janice Katz Gargen, MD

Some things are just right.
- The spilling of summer into fall and winter into spring
- The puffy vibrations which inflate a balloon
- The WHAPF of a great golf swing
- Barbecuing with friends
- Lying skin-to-skin
- Pendulums
- Feathers
- Stars

Sex on Sunday.

MEAT EATERS

Perhaps you are one of those people who likes to skip **introductions** and go straight for the meat of a book. I hope not, but if this is your usual habit, just this once, give the **Starters** a try.

ALL THE WORLD'S A TUBE

All of human life is a tube. The eye, ear, nose, throat, spinal canal, heart, lung, trachea, esophagus, intestine, kidney, biliary system, muscle spindle, bone marrow, gland … all tubes. But just what does it mean to be a tube?

This turns out to be an intriguing query. Physically, tubes can expand, contract and stretch without breaking. They can maneuver wicked turns, squiggle through the most miserly spaces and provide a conduit for almost anything, from blood to electricity to air to information to heat to water to waste. Tubes are simple yet rugged, dynamic yet fixed, accommodating yet supportive. In short, tubes are incredibly versatile. But tubes have a literally fatal short coming–they must remain open, meaning hollow in the middle. It is within this hollow space, this tiny world of open versus closed, where our journey involving human stress must begin.

GO WITH THE FLOW

Look back at the **Starters** for a quick minute. Within the **Starters** is a specific, intentional flow of words which should strike you as a gradual slowing of speed—not because of masterful writing—but because of a consciously planned diminishing of syllables: 15-12-7-6-5-3-2-1.

Moreover, if you tune your ear correctly, you should detect the lowering of pitch with the slowing of tempo, from the rat-a-tat-tat of the first words to the more yawning legato of the last. This slowing of tempo and lowering of pitch is a *literary* stress reduction.

Significantly, it is not simply a metaphor for stress reduction, it is the reduction itself. Slower tempo, lower pitch. Accomplishing this task with words is a cinch: mastering the same task within one's own body takes a bit more skill and training, but it is no less doable. Slow the tempo, lower the pitch. To make this happen, all of your physical being must be "hollow in the middle." In other words, your tubes must be open.

HUMANS REVEALED

The human world is sexual. It has always been so.

In the beginning, when humankind existed in a hunter/gatherer society, sexuality was a necessity for species survival. The hunters (the males) reflexively sought to procreate with the healthiest, most-likely-to-produce-healthy-offspring gatherers (the females.) The healthiest females were most prized. How did the earliest males identify the healthiest females? Very simply: open tubes.

The result of open tubes is **viewable** sexual health. A few examples:

	LIPS	PUPIL SIZE	VOICE PITCH	SKIN TEXTURE
PERCEIVABLE CHARACTERISTIC	Deeper crimson	Wider pupil	Lower range of female voice pitch	Shining glossy skin
VIEWED BY MALES AS	Increased attractiveness	Increased sensuality	Increased sexuality	Increased attractiveness
DEGREE OF DESIRABIITY	More desirable	More desirable	More desirable	More desirable
ORGAN SYSTEM EXHIBITING OPEN TUBES	Open arteries	Visual accommodation/ ciliary muscle	Wider larynx	Wider dermal capillaries
PHYSICAL RESULT OF OPEN TUBES	More blood	Better vision	Better air exchange	Increased blood flow
DEGREE OF HEALTH	Healthier mate	Healthier mate	Healthier mate	Healthier mate

During the sexual experience, lip color deepens, pupils widen, voice pitch lowers and skin exhibits a more intense sheen. All of these perceivable qualities are the end result of increased tube radius. They are automatic; thus, at least physically, engaging in sex results in decreased flow resistance for all organ systems and an enhanced state of physical health.

Now, let's ask this question … does engaging in sex and its resulting enhancement of physical health translate directly to a reduction in mental stress? The answer is both YES **and** NO. There is this one little complicating factor called your brain.

BRAIN SEX

Every emotional state, be it rage or bliss, comes about as the result of a chemical—called a *neurotransmitter*—directly communicating within your brain. At night, to induce sleep, the neurotransmitters which are calming and quieting typically are in charge of the communication process. In the morning, energizing neurotransmitters take control. During exercise, and sex is the most supreme form of exercise, the neurotransmitters allowing euphoria are handed the reins.

The truly remarkable consequence of this chemical-brain interaction is the cascade of <u>physical</u> changes which the interaction generates. Your BRAIN perceives only the emotional signal. In other words, your brain recognizes or names a particular feeling: happiness, contentment, anger, restlessness, and so forth, but your BODY physically reacts to that signal.

BRAIN::RECOGNITION				BODY::REACTION

This reaction remains true even if you mentally are unaware of, or voluntarily ignore a particular emotion. Men who are comatose continue to achieve erections. Little three-and-four-year-old children, both male and female, who have not yet learned to attach emotional names to the feelings of sexual pleasure, will nonetheless naturally, regularly engage in self-stimulation to achieve that pleasure. The common denominator between an adult comatose male and a three-year-old child is the elimination of the brain factor … the brain is simply out of the equation. But in non-comatose, adult human beings, the brain can rule the day.

This unfortunate condition is called being a grown up. This is not to say that we should all wait until we are in a coma prior to engaging in sex just so that we are sure of achieving the desired physical results (although it is arguable that this practice occurs in many environments on a daily basis). It is simply one illustration of our grown-up selves allowing our brain to take control inappropriately. And that, in a nutshell, is stress. Stress is NOT the result of a brain that is out of control; rather, stress comes from a brain that is IN control when it shouldn't be… when the brain is inappropriately pushing the override button … when it tries to make sense of the counterintuitive and organize that which is random.

Remember … your tubes must be open.

More Science

The vast literature on sexual difficulties is adequately covered elsewhere. This unique perspective for Ideal Aging™ will focus on health benefits whether you are in a monogamous relationship or home alone with your own resources. This will be a lovely complement to the medical model of disease and dysfunction.

Women were studied to compare orgasms from genital self-stimulation with those from imagery. In both cases significant increases in blood pressure, pulse, diameter of the pupil and pain tolerance and awareness were found. In young males sexual arousal and orgasm increased the immune response. Specifically, there was an increase in the leukocytes, the white blood cells that protect against infection. Both studies had small samples and further research is needed.

According to the US Census Bureau, 29 percent of 45 to 59 year young adults were single in 2003. They say that's up from 19 percent in 1980. The advantages of being in that crowd didn't used to get even a nod.

Newsweek (February 20, 2006) reported several interesting statistics from a study by AARP: twenty percent of older singles have sex once a week or more with an additional two percent having sex every day. Of the men in this group, twenty-two percent were looking for marriage or were living together with a significant other. Only fourteen percent of the women wanted that kind of commitment.

By "older" they were referring to adults age 45 to 59. Good grief, AARP! How restricting! Helen Gurley Brown, author of *Sex and the Single Girl*, asks in the Newsweek article: "Sex is such an enjoyable activity at any age. Why delegate it only to the young?" Touché.

Given the clinician's vignette below, it is a major concern that unprotected sex is reported by sixty-one percent of older sexually active singles.

> "I'm 82 years old but I look a lot younger than I am. So there are these guys trying to … (delicious giggle which continues throughout the conversation) … you know?"
> "Coming after you?"
> "Yeah!"
> "Sounds good."
> "Yeah, but they're so young!"
> "That's OK! I was talking with a couple today–she's 82 and he's 63."
> "Yeah, but one of 'em, he's 39!!"
> "Sounds terrific!"
> Her chuckle softens as she says in a hushed voice, "Yeah, but I think they're after my money!"
> "Oh, I get it! If they're after your money, that's not acceptable. BUT, if they're after you're body, that's OK?"
> "Yeah!" she laughed uproariously from the core of her elegant, eighty-two years young self!
>
> 2007 telephone consult verbatim with a lovely 82 years young woman.

Sex, attachment and nurturance in an elegant and balanced dance continue the species. Sex is the usual beginning of life. We feel attached to the people who nurture us and these are the people we tend to miss when they are not with us. We often become caregivers for the people who give us the most cause for concern..

Aerobic exercise can increase desire for sexual activity in women. Men who exercised four days a week increased the frequency and enjoyment of sexual activity. Running three hours a week was more effective than medications for correcting erectile dysfunction in men. Sexual intimacy in a loving relationship improves quality of life and emotions.

A survey was done with 27,500 men and women in 29 countries. The subjects were forty to eighty years young. Depression had reduced satisfaction with their relationship. However, it did not reduce the importance of sex or the satisfaction with sexual functioning. Sexual well-being was associated with greater happiness, physical and mental health and being in a satisfying relationship.

Edward Laumann and colleagues did a cross-national study of sexuality and aging in the Global Study of Sexual Attitudes and Behaviors. They suggest that healthy sexual expression is a wise socioeconomic investment. They believe it could reduce the development of Type II diabetes.

> "... the expression of sexuality at older ages enhances the beneficial effects and minimizes the detrimental effects of aging on the health of both individuals in the relationship, and also acts as a buffer against chronic illness, physical disability, medication use, cognitive decline, depression and social isolation at older ages."
> Edward Laumann and colleagues in
> *Archives of Sexual Behavior*

In 914 men between the ages of 45 and 59, sexual intercourse at least twice a week might have protected from them fatal coronary events. This was in comparison to men having sexual activity less than monthly. Testosterone, estrogen and progesterone dilate blood vessels. This may protect against chest pain and heart problems.

Sexual activity is associated with living longer. Women who enjoyed sex more lived longer than those who didn't.

Oxytocin, the "cuddle hormone," increases with orgasm in women and men. Handholding and other touch also increases this hormone which has a relaxing effect and increases sexual arousal. Elderly adults who masturbated had decreased risk of depression.

In their terrific book, *Keep Your Brain Alive*, Katz and Rubin have a unique perspective on sexual activity. In their view, lovemaking is the "ultimate neurobic workout." Review **Smarter This Year** to refresh your memory about neurobics. They say: "To think that a good sexual encounter also helps keep the brain alive is almost too good to be true. But it is; more than most 'routine activities,' sex uses every one of our senses and, of course, engages our emotional brain circuits as well." That's certainly worth remembering! I join them in recommending that you let your imagination go wild in every sense. "... wear silk, strew the bed with rose petals, burn lavender incense, have chilled champagne, massage with perfumed oils, put on a romantic CD ... and whatever else turns you on."

Lovely findings for science, yes?

From the clinician's office comes a perspective also worth sharing.

~~~~~

The lovely young woman rushed into my office short of breath and rather desperately distraught. Before she made it to the chair her words rushed and tumbled like a tidal wave to flood the very corners of the room and bounce back full of her outrage.

"I have never been so upset in my whole life! That jerk that lives across the hall from my apartment was waiting for me when I came home last week. He threatened to kill me for giving him herpes!

I told him he was out of his mind! I couldn't possibly give him herpes because I don't have it and just to prove it to him, I was going straight to the doctor's office, get the test done and have the results sent straight to his address. I ran out leaving him fuming in the hallway.

Fortunately my doctor was in. But she refused to send him a copy … and mine came back positive!"

~~~~~

Ladies and Gentlemen: If that was the one and only time I heard words like that in the privacy of confidential psychotherapy sessions, it certainly would never have made it into print and I probably would be less conservative than I have become over the many years of serving the walking wounded like you and me.

It was not. I am not.

The identity of the speaker will forever be concealed. It left its mark. With clients, friends and associates I have shared the gist of the story whenever appropriate. Then I ask them as I am asking you now: In the story above, who gave herpes to whom?

I rest my case.

When it has been appropriate to, I have shared my perspective on sexual activity. I include the vignette above as an example of why, in the age of HIV, my point of view is admittedly ultraconservative and decidedly protective of health.

- I recommend that you don't even think of being sexually active with another person until you have known them long enough to ensure that you trust them. Without trust there is no relationship.

- Still do not have sexual contact until you obtain a sexual history and clean lab results for both of you sufficiently after the last sexual encounter to assure

Sexual Saunter • 203

accuracy of the lab results. For example, if it is six months after exposure to HIV before the lab test would be accurate, wait until six or more months after the last individual sexual encounter, get the lab tests and have proof of health before sexual contact. If this seems too conservative, ask yourself: If the person you are considering pairing with doesn't care enough about you to assure your health, do you want to be with him? This is not about blame. It's about realities such as the quote above from the woman who was so irate when she was accused of spreading disease. Also ask yourself: If you had a sexually transmitted disease and didn't know it before you shared it with a partner, how would you feel about that?

- When you do choose a sexual partner, require monogamy. Define what that means to each of you. Know why and how you trust each other.

This is just one clinician's perspective. It's presented here to protect the innocent and those who may not know the extent of the risk. It evolved in response to stories like the Herpes one and crystallized with the first news of AIDS. In comparison, all other sexually transmitted diseases (STD) are small potatoes. And AIDS continues to spread to increasing numbers of innocent parties.

I describe my bias as one small effort to stem the tide of STD. I share the gist of clinical secrets because I am a practical person.

At the very least, use this confidential quote as a call to do your own research. Use to your best benefit the findings of science that can both protect and enhance your brain power. Celebrate the perspective of Katz and Rubin that sexual activities can be one of the best neurobics ever.

Include health and safety first in this component of your brain fitness program, too. There's more than one way to take matters into your own hands.

5. WORLD WORKS—PASS IT ON FOR THE HEALTH OF IT!

Could it be that every cell in your body wants to excel, or at least to be happy? When he spoke in Arizona in the Fall of 2005, His Holiness the Dalai Lama said that, on a global scale, all every animal wants is to be happy in ways that cause no other being any harm.

That's the unique approach of this chapter. It will include information on how to foster healthy growth from a cellular to a civic level. Only those associated with increased brain fitness will be considered.

With the research of Csikszentmihalyi (pronounced "Cheeks sent me high") we will explore finding flow. Then we'll look at how you can create happiness with the memory of those best moments.

A huge body of research describes the fruit of the labors of those who participate for the greater good of the community. Some profound examples of people fulfilling this role will be inspiring. They can be examples of how to participate in similar ways.

Financial security is one thing. But being rich can expand participation profoundly. The Bill & Melinda Gates Foundation and the efforts of Warren Buffet are my favorite examples. Being extraordinarily wealthy means you can afford to attend to the problems of the world that no other person, government or organization can adequately address.

To forgive may, or may not, be divine. In any case, it improves the chemistry of stress in ways that could enhance your brain fitness.

Another route to improve your stress chemistry is to Untwist Twisted Places where some of your thoughts sabotage you. You can learn how to drop the misplaced angst. The benefits of psychotherapy can be the best gift you ever give yourself. I've suggested to several family members that they stay in therapy episodically for the rest of their lives—not because they are "that bad" but because they were wise enough to start in the first place. I see no value whatever in trauma unless one has the guidance and wisdom to learn from it. An effective psychotherapist can afford you that.

Strategic goals enhance brain fitness when you set them. Achieving them can be the best bonus.

Celebrate randomly. The philosophers among my clients got furrowed brows when I described myself as an existential hedonist. Perhaps that's an awkward juxtaposition of terms. But it captures a skill that has served me so well that I present it here as my clinical bias for those who will find it useful.

Kemper Freeman

Third generation in a family that built Bellevue Square, added Lincoln Square and is bringing PACE (Performing Arts Center Eastside) to downtown Bellevue WA

In 1946 my grandfather and father first opened Bellevue Square. My grandfather had the original ten acres. My dad said that would be a great site for this shopping center. I've continued the business since then.

My grandfather, my father and I have all believed in not just working in a community. Each of us has spent about thirty percent of our available time building the community in which we get to live and do business. We work on everything from building water systems, sewer systems, transportation systems to helping Bellevue become a city. My grandfather was the original inspiration of the "first floating bridge", the Mercer Island floating bridge. My dad was probably the leading inspiration for the second one.

What makes us unusual is all of our work in real estate development has been in one place—in Bellevue. It started out with ten acres and now there are about 50 acres. Bellevue Art Museum evolved from a community fair, now called the Pacific Northwest Arts and Crafts Fair. It is the community's biggest festival; 340,000 people came over three days in July 2006. It helps the art community raise about $200 million a year. That makes it one of the largest injections of resources into the arts in the Northwest. The Performing Arts Center Eastside I've worked on for about 23 years. I offered to donate the land and to be the capital campaign fundraiser for it.

I think that getting older is a pretty nice thing. I'm 65 and I still feel like I have as much or more energy than I've ever had. I feel like I can do as much in a day as I ever could. I'm active in all the things I ever have been active in. I still ride motorcycles, ski, boat and water ski. I exercise every day.

I grew up on a farm so I have always enjoyed fruits and vegetables. I eat well. Most of my life I've eaten too much. In the last six months I've gone from 224 pounds down to 184, which puts me back to one pound less than I was in high school. Just before

I committed to lose the weight, I had a complete physical and the doctor said I had everything right where it should be: cholesterol, blood pressure and everything. When I came back three months later having lost forty pounds, he did a blood analysis again. He said he's never seen that much improvement. While everything was fine before, he said it's now incredibly fine! One thing he was really impressed with was an inflammation factor. Mine was well within the norm for my age before but, in three months time, it literally went to zero. He said the inflammation factor over time gets you in trouble. It can lead to hardening of the arteries, buildup of plaque. Alzheimer's and all that kind of stuff. He was impressed and that impressed me. It's sort of fun to have the doctor get excited in a nice way when he's going over your lab report!

I've tried all my life to not reinvent the wheel. I try to learn from other successes. If there was one thing I wish I could have done my whole life … most of my life I was running hard on adrenaline and caffeine and, a long time ago, nicotine. I've always driven myself hard so I've pumped a lot of adrenaline. You add adrenaline to caffeine and nicotine, those three puppies together can get you pretty wired. When you get used to doing that, you don't even think it's unusual. Once you learn to keep yourself calmer, you work better and you think better. I wish I could have learned and not done that, although I don't know if I could have done all the stuff I've done if I hadn't pushed myself to that degree.

Everybody just assumes that success is automatic but, I felt most of my life if I let up for five minutes nothing would have happened. The last 11 years since I stopped drinking coffee, I really enjoy literally being calm. It is nice just being able to be calm and enjoy what's going on. I think I've burnt the candle in several places most of my life. I'm lucky that that didn't result in a heart attack, stroke or something like that.

My mother and father were a big influence in my life. I worked with my dad for twenty years before he died, so that was amazing. Another person I call my second dad was the manager and owner of a farm that I worked on. When I was nine years old my parents rented a house which was right next to it. It was an active 540-acre dairy farm. I was almost a foot taller than anybody in my class at age 9 years old, so I could go next door and meet the guys that were running this farm. It was like being tossed into Disneyland! I mean there were all the animals, equipment, tractors, trucks and mechanical things and everything that went on. I had a job working from when I was 9 'til I was 23 on that farm. I would work most days after school and weekends. Then I worked there all summer. It would be seven days a week from the day school let out 'til the day school started again. I just felt like this is as close to heaven as you can get to be able to do that kind of work and be around that kind of lifestyle. I've always loved the equipment, animals and all the stuff that was going, so to get paid in addition was like a bonus. When I was nine I got $0.50 an hour. When I was 22 my salary had grown all the way to $2 an hour. That first summer when I was nine years old I saved up close to $400.

By the time I was 16, the guy I worked for needed another tractor. I'd saved up enough money and I could borrow some money to buy a tractor so I went in business with him.

A year later I had two tractors. We did custom farm work. It was $2 an hour for me but the tractor got $5. Later on I got a hay baler, which cost half as much as a tractor but the hay baler got $7 a ton, so that was $17.50 an hour and $175 in a 10-hour day.

Then we got a newer hay baler that mechanically tied the knot in the twine. If the machine couldn't tie the knots, the whole operation came to a stop. There was only one mechanic that knew how to fix the knotter. I asked if I could watch him. I became the second to know how to fix it. That was another learning curve. Farmers would come get me during the noon hour, take me over to their farms, and I'd fix their knotters. I could only earn $2 an hour but a farmer would give me $25 or $30 just for fixing the knotter during my lunch hour. I learned a lot of important lessons on the farm and loved every minute of it.

That whole time we lived on the farm we had a big vegetable garden. Every day whoever came in for lunch first would get things out of the garden and start boiling new potatoes, swiss chard or whatever. I learned the taste difference between fresh beets right out of the garden versus after they've been picked and the sugars all turn to starch and completely taste different … just to have an appreciation for all that stuff! To this day I have a garden, raise tomatoes, raise artichokes and always have fresh fruit trees.

God, just being alive every day is like a dream. I wake up optimistic every morning. I'm enthused in the worst of times and the best of times. I feel good about what I'm doing and feel lucky that I get to do it. I get a big kick out of my motivation for building things, to see how much money I can make or whatever. That all of my efforts have turned out well is sort of a byproduct. What I enjoy is building things that customers react to, appreciate and use. I enjoy watching restaurants become successful. The movie theater has come into the Top 10 of over 60,000 theaters in America in terms of average tickets sold every day. The shopping center is 1 of 63,000 shopping centers. It's in the Top 10 in America in terms of sales per square foot. So it's fun! I guess the most fun is to see the stuff working. I just get a lot of satisfaction out of that. When it's working, it's a good business decision, too. All these things roll together.

It's just ridiculous that there's something in human nature that gets people fighting with each other. I watch what's been going on for thousands of years. It's going on to this day that people have learned almost by instinct that they hate their neighbor or hate their neighboring country. You just wonder how that can even be, but they do and that hatred is real. I don't know how to solve that one. I mean it's just crazy.

I've been lucky that I've lived a fairly health lifestyle with exceptions of just putting myself in self-induced pressure. When you're young you think you're bulletproof, but the sooner somebody develops healthy lifestyles, both physically and mentally—and I think the two are interlinked—the better. I guess it's never too late but start sooner. It's a lot harder to figure out how to keep your heart healthy if you've already had the first heart attack than it is to keep it healthy before.

From an engaging phone chat on February 27, 2007

FLOW

"... what we feel, what we wish, and what we think are in harmony. These exceptional moments are what I have called flow experiences."
Mihaly Csikszentmihalyi in *Finding Flow*

Goals

- Have clear goals and immediate feedback in complex tasks that match your complex skills ... to increase your time in flow, growth and creativity

- Engineer daily activities for high challenge that stretches your high skills ... to improve the quality of your life

- Spend time with positive friends ... to elevate your mood

- Know how elements of the environment are related to your emotions ... to choose what helps you be in flow

- Be aware of how you do what must be done ... to assure you are in flow

Science behind your plan

Csikszentmihalyi values the wisdom of the ages as expressed by prophets, poets and philosophers. He also believes that science clarifies information that is essential to humankind. His work integrates the messages of the ages with scientific findings that accumulate slowly. He believes that the only way to make sense of our life is a "patient, slow attempt to make sense of the realities of the past and the possibilities of the future as they can be understood in the present."

What we think, how our thoughts effect our emotions and what we do—these things determine the quality of our life. People who believe they can make a real difference through their choices and initiative are most likely to rise above fate.

"Flow" is that wonderful impression that what you are doing is effortless, timeless and focused on a clear goal where what needs to be done is known and steps toward that goal is given immediate and relevant feedback. It involves a delicate balance between the complex challenges and your skills such that complete focus—as you are being stretched to the fullest—is associated with increased confidence. Sound delicious?

Csikszentmihalyi's research shows that it is immersion in flow that improves the quality of life. The experience of flow "acts as a magnet for learning—that is, for developing new levels of challenges and skills." Therefore, flow increases complexity and growth of consciousness.

Periods of flow are remembered as the best moments in life. However, the happiness comes from what we think of those moments. Happiness is not inherent in flow. But we are encouraged by Csikszentmihalyi to be in flow as much as possible for enhanced quality of life. As is often stated in this book, the increased happiness we create as we review these highlights could have a positive effect on many components of our health.

The most common sentiment expressed by extreme achievers interviewed by Csikszentmihalyi was a sense of melding of work and play. They didn't view themselves as workaholics. They said, "You could say that I worked every minute of my life, or you could say with equal justice that I never worked a day."

It's essential to recall that being in flow is not a function of what you do but of how you do it. This is made so clear by the example Csikszentmihalyi gives of a factory worker, Rico. While the workers in that setting tended to persist in a negative view of their situation, Rico chose to be in competition with himself. On a task that allotted just forty-three seconds in the assembly line, he experimented and refined his approach to the task. After some years, his average was twenty-eight seconds. Nothing else changed except his "exhilaration of using his skills fully." He was also taking courses toward a career in electronic engineering. It's interesting to remember his choices when reading the chapter **Smarter Next Year**.

How to do it

Keeping a journal can help clarify the quality of your life and what accounted for it. It is a common way of identifying what you might want to change. It has the limitation of self report after the fact.

Csikszentmihalyi developed the Experience Sampling Method to increase the accuracy of data collection. To follow the same scenario, set signals to go off at random times within a two-hour time span from awakening to bedtime. This can be done on your programmable pager, watch or PDA. Carry a small notebook with you. At the sound of the alarm, record your location, actions, thoughts and the people you are with. Then rate your happiness, your ability to concentrate, your level of motivation and your self esteem. The SUFI Report© would be useful for this activity.

The value of this process is finding the little surprises about which activities, environments, experiences and people contribute to your being in flow. Then you can experiment with adding a few positives. A coworker spent the weekend in the office painting, hanging pictures and putting new drapes at the windows. Another covered the office floor with a beautiful carpet around which she placed a plush sofa and armchair. Both had long term positive effects on everyone sharing the space.

Once you've identified the small things that can make a big difference, your goals become more realistic. Some of your goals will change the environment in ways that are under your control. Others will change how you do what must be done. Above all else, remember that you're in total control of the view you take of doing the work—which has far more influence than the task itself to help you be in flow.

> *"Without a consistent set of goals, it is difficult to develop a coherent self. It is through the patterned investment of psychic energy provided by goals that one creates order in experience. This order, which manifests itself in predictable actions, emotions, and choices, in time becomes recognizable as a more or less unique 'self.'"*
> Mihaly Csikszentmihalyi in *Finding Flow*

Measuring goals

Keep a journal at the end of the day. Journaling is referenced several places in this book because of its multiples benefits. For this chapter just focus on your journal entries at the end of the week to see how frequently you were in flow. Also, these notes create the rich data needed to add life to your memoirs when you are ready to write them.

Then program your PDA, watch or cell phone to send random signals that average out to every two hours between awakening and going to bed. Make a copy of the recording system found on the next page. Filing it in a notebook can add data to your memoirs. Carry this form with you everywhere. Record observations on it each time the alarm sounds. For example, if your cell phone awakens you at 6 AM with a gentle sound that could be far preferable to the standard alarm clock. Program that same sound at something like: 6:48 AM; 10:02 AM; 11:21 AM; 2:09 PM; 4 PM; 5:11 PM; 7:55 PM and 9:11 PM. The concept of this timing is that it averages out to every two hours while you are awake between, say, 6 AM and 10 PM. Accept yourself AS IS when writing your comments. We credit Csikszentmihalyi for this Experience Sampling Method for finding flow. Do it a minimum of one week to establish the flavor of your life and frequency of flow.

Your Name _____ **Today's Date** _____

Your SUFI© -10 to +10	What you are doing	What you are thinking	How happy you are	How high your self Esteem is	How well you can concentrate	How motivated you are	Where you are	Who you are with

Summary

"We are not disturbed by things, but by the view we take of things" is the wise counsel attributed to Epictetus in the 4th Century in dealing with distress. Csikszentmihalyi restates that in the positive in Finding Flow: it isn't the task, it's how you do the task that can result in your finding flow. By integrating the wisdom of the ages with the richness of scientific data you can reclaim ownership of your life and transform the mundane into an exhilarating activity. His poignant example of Rico on an assembly line brings this to life.

Flow involves using your high level skills in a complex challenge that involves so much focus that time evaporates, your confidence and motivation stay high and you are afforded immediate feedback on your progress toward a clear goal. Happiness is not part of being in flow. As a result of the view you choose to take of these "best moments", happiness can be a long term benefit of being in flow.

"...it is how we choose what we do, and how we approach it, that will determine whether the sum of our days adds up to a formless blur, or to something resembling a work of art."
Mihaly Csikszentmihalyi in *Finding Flow*

Rheba de Tornyay

Dr. de Tornyay is Dean Emeritus of the School of Nursing at the University of Washington.

The de Tornyay Center for Healthy Aging at UW honors her for her lifelong contributions in gerontology

Please call me Rheba. I'm a nurse.

I fell into nursing by the luckiest accident in my life. During World War II you had to do something for the National Service. The Red Cross Nurse's Aide program was appealing. I really wanted to be a veterinarian but women didn't become veterinarians. I was helping a nurse who said, "Rheba, have you ever thought of being a nurse?" I said, "They're so overworked and underpaid." She said, "That's very true but it's a very satisfying profession. I think you'd be a good nurse." As I followed her advice, I went to the wrong school of nursing. By wrong thing I mean it took me forever afterwards. I went to a diploma program in nursing. I really wanted to be a bedside nurse. My father wasn't happy when I quit college to go to nursing school, so I felt I had to go back.

I went to San Francisco State and got my bachelor's degree. I was invited back to my own diploma program—the merging of teaching and doing nursing was wonderful. I took a job in a long-term care facility. Other nurses looked down on me saying, "You're a good nurse why aren't you in a hospital working?" I said because this is real nursing to me. I love to help people age gracefully. I had no intention of being a dean. It just happened naturally. I've been a dean at two major universities, UCLA and the UW.

In fact, you were instrumental in creating a doctoral program in nursing.

I wouldn't say I that. I would say it was during my watch that that occurred. I think my greatest role was attracting the very best possible people. I think I did an awfully good job of that because many of them are still there. Then staying out of their way and letting them do their creative thing. So, I don't take credit for anything other than getting awfully good people there.

To me Ideal Aging™ Is going with the flow. I like being old because I'm more at peace with myself than I've ever been in my entire life psychologically.

I was born with very good resilience. My mother was a wonderful role model. I now have a husband who is quite ill. He's been in hospice care longer than usual. My mother cared for my father who had a series of strokes for a ten-year period. She managed cheerfully and was never a complainer. I think some of her qualities may be part of me. I keep active. I'm at the gym on Mondays, Wednesdays and Fridays. It's sacred time. I do not let anybody call me. I do strength training. Six days a week I walk a mile on a treadmill. I think there is nothing more important. Research is indicating that people who keep active physically are also better off mentally.

I cope with my husband's condition by being realistic. My husband is 95 years old. We've been very lucky. Until a year and a half ago, he was amazingly well. This is a man who took no prescription drugs, none! I'm 80 and my health is really quite good. I think we've done the right things. We've exercised. I've always been a nutrition nut. I grew up on a farm with a garden. It was a chicken ranch. My Dad fertilized his vegetables with chicken manure. It's rich in nitrogen. I did lots of exercise over the years. But I have to tell you, in spite of all of that, I still have osteoporosis—you know I read your book. Everything that you say one should do I've done. I exercise. I eat properly. I certainly take supplemental calcium. I know it's controversial but I've been on HRT for a long time because my physician feels that it's a matter of risk/benefit. I take calcitonin ….

But I haven't done some of the things you recommend like having my Vitamin D blood level measured. Or Counted my protein intake. I guess it's never too late to give those a try. I think it doesn't make any sense to live a long life unless you enjoy it. Rudy and I like living so that's the reason that we don't give up easily.

I worked terribly hard to have my successes look easy. Before I gave a report to the faculty, I rehearsed it more thoroughly than anything. I would predict what questions I would be asked from all sides. I think you need to prepare for everything you do like you were an attorney preparing for a case. I work very, very hard. I'm pretty much a workaholic. In retirement I'm still doing a lot of the things that normal people would not be doing. I love committees. So I got myself into the UW Retirement Association. It's filled with ex-deans and ex-people like me who are used to running things and still want to. I like lectures and meeting new people. It keeps my mind active.

I think my husband has been my biggest life mentor. My Dean mentor was a wonderful woman at UCSF. She was a marvelous example of being willing to trust her faculty. That's where I learned to get the best people you possibly can and then support them.

The two highlights in my life really were my choice of a life partner in Rudy and that lucky accident of finding nursing.

My philosophy that developed as I matured was *that* It's okay to accept yourself as you are. Because at 20 I didn't like myself. I wasn't sure of myself.

The very last class that I taught at the UW was a class on ethics. I did a really risky thing. I said, "I'm going to tell you a story." I have a friend who got hold of the last evaluation of me at Langley Porter. It was my very first job out of nursing. It was a really awful evaluation—they concluded the whole thing saying they wouldn't rehire me and I asked too many question and I this and I that. It was really terrible. I read it to the students, and said to them, "Now I want you to listen to this because I grew up and amounted to something and so will you."

When people ask if I have any regrets, now this will be sweet music to your ears, yes. My one regret is that I should have started strength training many years before. I've always walked but I waited 'til I was 75 to start weightlifting. The most amazing thing about it—I went down a whole size in clothes. I didn't lose weight but I firmed up. I feel so much better. I do strength training because it's a great antidepressant, also.

AARP's recruitment to get the 50-year-old's into their organization—they say "sex in later life" and they were talking about 60!

I think the idea that sexual behavior in the "elderly" refers to those in their 50s and 60s is just hysterical. I think the amount of sexual dysfunction that is occurring in males in their 40s and 50s probably has to do with all the tremendous stresses that they're under today.

My dream to improve the world is to stop wars. I mean that. I think is just immoral and terrible. In a society that has limited resources, I would focus on children. I also believe we could improve the quality of life and health for our older population. I would certainly have a decent universal health care system, for heaven sakes! I have great admiration for the Gates Foundation trying very hard to improve health globally.

From a wonderful telephone interview February 19, 2007

PARTICIPATE

"Jesus did not mean that there was something wrong with being rich. Jesus said these words to explain what God expects of a person in order to gain admission to heaven—and the special, even higher, obligation to help others that God expects of those who have achieved economic success."
Paul Zane Pilzer about Matthew 19:24 in
God Wants You to Be Rich

Goals

Volunteer … because staying socially active stimulates your brain to stay fit
Smile freely … because it can transform someone's entire day in a positive way
Be socially active … because relationships are pharmaceutical

Across time your history weaves the tapestry of your unique worldview. If yours is extraordinarily positive, celebrate being in one of the dances of Ideal Aging™ for brain fitness. If not, it is never too early and never too late to reweave your worldview with increasingly positive threads for the health of it.

My worldview keeps evolving. Traveling around the world reshaped many threads. My early efforts at giving service had seemed sufficient until observing how much need exists at home and abroad. After a brief immersion in depression over the futility of making a hint of a dent in all perceived needs, I set different goals. As a clinician, I resolved to empower the gifted who had a track record of service for civic welfare and knew how they wanted to make a positive difference. There is ample research showing the broad health benefits of providing service wisely.

Science behind your plan

There is ample research showing the broad health benefits of providing service wisely. Some of these studied survivors of the holocaust. Individuals who found ways to be of service in spite of trauma fared better. For example, Ellie Wiesel, author of *Night*, found strength in learning from the pain. A survivor of the holocaust, he decided to write on that experience and to encourage all people to live a life of moral responsibility that would reduce hate crimes in the world.

How to do it

Ryan Hreljac might an excellent example of this. As reported at RyansWell.ca, this remarkable young man had a unique combination of vision, mission, drive and other qualities.

At the age of six Ryan learned that some African people without access to clean water suffered many illnesses. He resolved to raise $70 to build a well for one small village to relieve their suffering. In four months he met that goal.

Word spread, his goals grew and the report at RyansWell.ca indicates that the latest figure raised is $1,500,000. Just one idea in an especially positive six years old boy has changed the lives of countless individuals. In Africa thousands of people who saw losing their lives at a young age as their future now have health, hope and a model of unusually effective proactive behavior! In many other countries the nameless have been moved to contribute to a small lad's view of what could and should be done. He is now fifteen years wise. Ryan's Well Foundation continues the work inspired by just one idea in the life of just one small boy. Learn more about that at RyansWell.ca.

If you were just six years of age when you first learned of Ryan Hreljac's impact on the lives of so many people, what effect would you guess that would have on the tapestry of your worldview and on your happiness? What effect does it have now?

I believe that bringing the movie of Ryan's story to youth around the world would be deliciously beneficial. I believe that it would also be beneficial to Celebrate Randomly the positive threads within the tapestry of your worldview. Very few people will identify anything in their own lives that compares to Ryan's story. Comparison is not your goal. Simply finding whatever is positive in your world up to this point and celebrating that is the suggested starting point.

Many people also have elements of their worldview that were woven in pain and trauma. Some have found strength is learning from pain. Elie Wiesel, author of *Night*, comes to mind. A survivor of the holocaust, he decided to write on that experience and to encourage all people to live a life of moral responsibility that would reduce hate crimes in the world.

Some respond to a felt need to improve the lot of a loved one and evolve into making huge civic contributions. Barbara Barger personifies this.

Her disabled daughter was cared for in a nursing home. In an effort to establish something different, Barbara approached the Helping Hands for the Disabled. It had been established in 1975 as a nonprofit organization. Barbara's influence helped it flourish.

Its mission now is to support people with developmental disabilities in achieving their potential, build their self-confidence and enhance their community involvement. To accomplish that, Helping Hands for the Disabled commits their energy and resources to developing and maintaining residences and a continuum of program services to meet their needs. They also provide advocacy and referral services to many families who need services for their handicapped family members.

Under Barbara's direction, Champion House opened April 8, 1983. That would be remarkable enough if her service to the community had extended no further. However, at the printing of this book she remains at the helm of the agency. At one point HUD invited her back to Washington DC to enlighten them on how she was able to provide such high quality care with such economy. Three more group homes have been established. These four homes accommodate a total of twenty-four disabled adults in homes nestled in communities. Barbara Barger and Eva Robinson have taken an additional four individuals into their own home on a long term basis. One still resides with them. They also provided episodic respite care for an additional five adults. I've heard legal and healthcare professionals express amazement at the capacity of these women to provide care in unbelievably extreme situations.

I had the honor and privilege of being an independent consultant at Champion House in its early days. All of the homes provide the level and quality of care that most people would cherish for their loved ones. Much more can be learned about this organization including how to donate to this worthy cause at HHFTD.org.

There are many therapeutic techniques which have shown significant value. Cognitive Behavioral Therapy is just one category. Rest assured that many people have recognized and healed themselves using these skills independently. The same has been true with pillars in the community. A business associate once asked me to explain what I do that is called psychotherapy. After hearing my explanation, he said, "Isn't it a shame that more people don't have good friends. It seems like some of what goes on in psychotherapy could be handled with healthy friendships." There is a grain of truth in his perspective. I gave a lecture recently on Loneliness to a standing-room-only crowd. It has often been part of my clinical practice to teach people how to develop healthier friendships.

An excellent psychotherapist can expedite and focus the healing of historical shadow dances. Keep it on your list of possibilities. Even if you enjoy some healing changes using the skills in this workbook on your own, psychotherapy could still be one of the best gifts you ever give yourself.

"As long as a man stands in his own way, everything seems to be in his way."
Ralph Waldo Emerson

Measuring goals

Start with measuring your participation now. That could be intellectual such as sharing your wisdom or teaching your skills. It could be civic in terms of contributing time, money or other resources to your favorite cause. A social participation might be spreading cheer, bonding relationships, or cozy time with family.

Look at frequency, intensity and duration of your participation. Note who is with you.

How many times was your participation intellectual? _____ Civic? _____ Social? _____

How long did you participate each time? Intellectual _____ Civic? _____ Social? _____

What effect did it have on you? _____
_____
_____

Who was with you? _____

What about the situation made you happy? _____
_____
_____

Also do an abbreviated SUFI measure at the end of the day. Refer to the description of this tool in the Introduction. In an overall sense of how you feel about the day, give yourself a score between -10 and +10.

Subjective Units of Feelings Index (SUFI Report™)
-10	0	+10

Your score at the end of the day _____

Look for the relationship between your SUFI score at the end of the day and the frequency, intensity and duration of your participation during the day. As the amount of time you spend in these activities increases, your SUFI Report should become more and more positive.

Summary

The effects of traumatic events may dance like a shadow on your path. For Ryan the suffering of others led to actions which inspired a multinational response to the needs of the waterless in Africa. Wiesel's losses influenced him to focus on reducing racism, genocide and hatred of others globally. Each of them used the energy of suffering to empower efforts for global welfare. Developing Stress Power is pivotal to this workbook because it is a crucial component of Ideal Aging™.

An important part of Stress Power includes several approaches to healing. Research has shown that service to others is one way to turn the energy of stress into jet fuel for growth. Various forms of expressing emotions associated with trauma have the potential to heal.

"Tree Angel", Tree Chic, CindyKatz of Plant a Tree USA:
The woman with the goal of planting 18 billion trees and educating millions.

I am the CEO and founder of Plant A Tree USA. I travel the world to take a look on the bright side. I've become a beacon of light for the environmental movement. I've moved the need for environmental responsibility, planting trees and re-educating people from a non-profit handout to a point of urgency, strength and power like Oprah or Bill Gates.

Ideal Aging™ will differ from person to person, from species to species, and from custom to custom. For me personally Ideal Aging™ will be when you can see that your choices today have consequence for your immediate future, your far future and the future of those around you. When you come to that maturity you look at yourself as not perfect and not lasting forever.

Spirituality has played a role in my life, absolutely! I think that people will probably benefit from thinking of spirituality not just in an organized religion but also in the sense that it's a personal choice. I believe everything you do will be a direct reflection of your personal belief system.

There will be hardships. Sometimes it's a stand-and-bear-it process to wait it out. Another is to realize that most hardship is in between your temples. It's in your mindset. When you see it as your way to grow, you can concentrate on the reason for what you're going through so you can actually find pleasure in knowing that you're gonna come out on the other side stronger and wiser.

Our children have learned that there is no such thing as black and white; we live in shades of gray; we have the ability to cope. One sense for me to get there is our mission of planting 18 billion trees swiftly and beautifully and ending up re-educated so that the "rape" of the planet through deforestation doesn't happen again. My dream is providing an environment of beauty and a healthy planet where we're taking care of our soil and atmosphere so we have clean air to breathe and reduce the illnesses we're causing to ourselves; the space where not only we but our children know that they _can do_. Their true purpose and passion are naturally found in them. They have the confidence to know as Nelson Mandela quotes, "We are powerful beyond measure."

If I had unlimited resources, we'd get together the greatest comedians and the author of the book *The Tipping Point*, and have an idea spread like wildfire, ('though I don't like to use wildfire since I'm into reforestation but there is a real natural need for the forest fire). Using the assistance of a comedian to make it palatable and fun for everyone, I'd set little forest fires where necessary to spur growth. It's called succession in ecological terms. In an old-growth forest you reach the climax community where all the old trees get to the point where there are so many of the tall trees with the large canopy, that there is no sunlight at the bottom of the forest floor. When a wild forest fire comes through, the ashes of the large trees are now the nutrients that are returned back to the soil. Slowly but surely the forest starts again, first with small seeds, little seedlings, grasses and shrubs. Years go on and it becomes a mature, growing forest. I think I would start forest fires (funny as it might sound from Tree Chick) around the world that could re-educate us.

A little bit of chaos is part of the natural system. Even the wildfire that spreads sometimes knocks out some of the old ideas from some of the old growth trees that have lived their purpose. I believe there are some things on earth that have gone beyond our need, be it reliance on oil, if it's getting rid of all kinds of bombs, if it's taking away some of our technology to getting us back in control of our lives. I think sometimes there's a need for a clearing and a restart, but in the restart there'd be a reprogramming so that the education that I spoke about before, what our children believe, know and have a responsibility towards themselves and to others, will be ingrained in us and your book Ideal Aging™ will become self-evident to kids. Maybe even become part of their genetic nature because, Dr. Joyce, what you're doing is taking something that people usually find out too late and you're bringing it earlier in life and the word aging is not connected to old. People think old is a negative term, and I think aging is a beautiful term; it's development. You age from the minute you're born. Trees age from the minute they sprout. Embracing the development and the aging process is something I'm so thankful to you for bringing out in public. I want to see Ideal Aging™ spread like wildfire.

One of my biggest influences when I was a teenager was an activist for the homeless. I heard him say, "Do you have more than one pair of shoes? If so, why do you have them when others don't have any?" Not that people should take away from what they have, but there was a perspective, and I worked with the homeless for a while.

Every day is a highlight in my life, honestly. It's really a process that every day I feel highlights of different sections of my life, learning, growing and being thankful for realizing what I have.

Some of the myths of aging are related to the garbage we put in our lives. I believe what we put in our bodies and what we eat is actually killing us. We want ease, packaging, all kinds of stuff—but it's really hurting us. I say garbage, not because it's not true that there are many ailments that are affecting our brain as we get older, but that we have the ability to do something about that. We have choices as to what we put in our mouths, what we put in our brains and what we think we're going to experience when we're older. What we tell ourselves is what will most probably occur, so if people have the mindset that we're going to get older and be decrepit, we're going to fulfill that. Mark Victor Hansen and Art Linkletter wrote a book called *How to Make the Rest of Your Life the Best of Your Life.* Mark talks about how to get a whole generation of retired people doing something. We could have enough people spend time in the Peace Corps to be active in society and the more active you are, the more you're needed. People, I think, die and their body gives up when they feel they're not needed any longer. Even the linguistics that we use, like "senior moment," probably is not helpful in terms of envisioning our aging process. How about a new dictionary, Dr. Joyce?

I learned that when you care about people, it's not enough to care. It's to know how the actions of your care affect others and to be able to morph; to change. 'Cause it's not black and white.

I would want your readers to know that there is good and bad within them. Appreciate their good, take some discipline to make changes in their bad, and move forward each day. Be able to accept when you make mistakes and move forward. Live long and prosper!

From an exciting interview with a brilliant Tree Chick on February 13, 2007.

BE RICH

"God does want each of us to be rich in every possible way—health, love, and peace of mind, as well as material possessions. God wants this, however, not just for our own sake, but for the sake of all humankind."
Paul Zane Pilzer in *God Wants You to Be Rich*

Goals

- Tithe … to support your favorite cause.

- Develop unlimited wealth … to fund worthy cause(s) into perpetuity.

- Teach others to prosper … to grow as everyone prospers everyone else.

The focus of this chapter will be to highlight resources available for increasing financial knowledge and security. Your brain fitness can improve simply by exploring these options. Complex and novel learning has that potential advantage if action is coupled with the new learning. New knowledge alone has not been shown to increase the complexity of dendritic branching, spines and synaptic connections in brains. Only the rats that took action with the new toys showed positive neuroplasticity. Rats who only observed in an adjacent cage did not show improved brains.

I laughed all the way to the bookstore to buy *God Wants You to Be Rich*. I thought it would be a comedy. Visions of a camel trying to get through the eye of a needle had dominated my childhood. Actually, recognition of how similar thoughts sabotaged my progress has come slowly. Changing them is still a work in progress.

What a relief it's been to entertain this different perspective. Pilzer is a must-read. His brilliant treatment of resources portrays a cornucopia of abundance balanced with social responsibility in prosperity. He gets money right. He makes the language of economics easily understandable. On stage he visibly bounces with the energy of wellness. And he is comedic.

The Bill & Melinda Gates Foundation could surely strengthen anyone's resolve to prosper for everyone's welfare. Their goals for global health alone are supreme. While aiming at equalizing availability of healthcare in impoverished populations, they highlight how gifted others really are. Warren Buffet also serves as an inspiring model for responsible accumulation and use of wealth. Enlightened wealth is having the resources and capabilities to address problems of the world that no other person, organization or government has the resources to manage.

My own struggles to endorse reasons to establish enlightened wealth have been a valuable series of neurobic exercises. It is delicious that it's never too early and never too late to be rich with enlightened goals for the welfare of our precious globe and its inhabitants. I will forever be grateful to so many mentors. That includes my privilege of being in the Inner Circle of Robert G. Allen and Mark Victor Hansen. Each of these men is a uniquely brilliant mentor. It is unlikely that this chapter (or even this book) would ever have been written without their influence and the combined impact of others in that setting.

The huge body of research on the benefits making a contribution the enlightened way can afford your brain, mood and general health need not be repeated here. Review **Smarter This Year** along with all references to the role of the chemistry of stress.

The machinations of how to achieve wealth can be learned from many mentors. That will also form guidelines to measure your progress.

Robert G. Allen wrote the best selling book of all time on real estate when he was thirty-one. It's entitled *Nothing Down*. Since then, more than a million people have learned how to become wealthy through real estate using none of their own money. The Enlightened Wealth Institute, **EnlightenedWealthInstitute.com**, which he co-founded with Mark Victor Hansen and Tom Painter, is an awesome resource. Bob also wrote *Multiple Streams of Income* and *Multiple Streams of Internet Income.* These are among the courses that are taught through the Enlightened Wealth Institute, many of them in teleseminars. That means you can pursue education to the full extent that time allows without leaving the comfort of home. The last time I counted there were over thirty classes available per week!

Eventually we learned to only take one teleseminar at a time. This is a message worth repeating: Taking action on new learning is essential to make your brain more fit. Taking one teleseminar at a time and doing ALL homework can maximize return on investment. That's especially been true because of the nature and complexity of the homework assignments that have been typical in the enlightened wealth program.

October 28—the day we first met him in Seattle—is Robert G. Allen Day in our home. It commemorates the paradigm shift that has evolved within each of us since that day as a result of benefiting from his brilliant mentoring, his Enlightened Wealth Institute and membership in Robert Allen's and Mark Victor Hansen's Inner Circle.

Another resource in real estate is Robert Kiyosaki, author of *Rich Dad, Poor Dad*. This is another must-read for awareness of differences in how the rich and the poor handle money issues, thoughts and behaviors. Groups of people meet in a variety of places to play his game, *Cash Flow*. My granddaughter, Morgan, loves the game as much as we do. In fact, she's only played it three times and she won every time!

Having good credit can increase options for being rich. Donna Fox became my mentor after we met in the Inner Circle. **Credit-Millionaire.com** introduces you to her system. An attorney by education she is also a highly successful entrepreneur. As a result of her wise counsel, I markedly increased the amount of money I could borrow with zero interest and raised my credit score so high that investment monies are easy to obtain.

If public speaking is the business you want to pursue, your best source for professional training is **speakingwithjohn.com/cmd.php?af=173630**.. The Million Dollar Speaker Training by John Childers can take your career to a whole new level in "The World's Highest Paid Skill". With decades of experience, he has the public speaking skill mastered. He's a supreme and entertaining trainer of professionals while he models integrity and deep respect.

The Small Business Administration (SBA) is another huge but under utilized resource. The website is **sba.gov**. The SBA offer tons of free materials and assistance in offices throughout the USA and online. For example, they produced a National Lender Guide. Keep in mind that the government wants new businesses to thrive. That's an essential part of a strong economy.

Service Corps of Retired Executives (SCORE) is a resource partner of the SBA. Their information is at **SCORE.org**. These volunteers are dedicated to educating entrepreneurs and helping them succeed in business. I am very grateful to Bruce Brown for his help through SCORE. He has mentored me and opened doors for valuable business connections. According to their website, "there are more than 10,500 SCORE volunteers in 374 chapters operating in over 800 locations who assist small businesses with business counseling and training. SCORE also operates an active online counseling initiative."

PaulZanePilzer.com is the source for more on Pilzer's perspective. As a world renowned economist, his view has influenced many administrations. He has been a frequent guest in the media because of his expertise. His new book, *The New Health Insurance Solution,* describes how to get cheaper, better health insurance from birth to old age without an employer plan.

Whatever road to wealth you trek, financial expertise will be critical leverage. **DatingYourMoney.com** will introduce you to Jennifer Wilkov. As a former Certified Financial Planner, she has over a decade of experience with money relationships—both corporate and individual. By the same token, plans that anyone makes and communicates effectively will be appreciated in the unfortunate time when an unexpected event derails one's life. The Loved Ones Kit (**TheLOK.com**) provides the resources to make, organize and communicate the best laid plans while realizing *Ideal Aging*™.

Napoleon Hill found in his research that the highly successful rich all had mentors, masterminds, many sources of continual education, etc. For the wide variety of travel needs that will result from adopting this perspective, consider **ytbtravel.com/jim53** with Jim Higbee. If there was one person on the Odyssey bicycle trek around the world whom everyone respected and considered to be a special friend, Jim Higbee probably was that one. He was so innovative, diligent and determined that he was the only one of about 250 Odyssey bicycle riders who pedaled the whole route through Japan. For various unique reasons we didn't have our bicycles in Japan. So Jim bought one and cycled while we bussed.

To be rich and enlightened is deliciously empowering. You have the privilege of choosing from the many worthwhile charities, causes and foundations already in existence. Some examples include: Helping Hands for the Disabled at **HHFTD.org** which empowers developmentally disabled adults in the community; **Heifer.org** which is an international effort to end hunger while caring for the earth; **PlantATreeUSA.com** which celebrates life one tree at a time with the goal of planting 18 billion trees; **www.Agros.org** which is committed to breaking the cycle of poverty for rural families in Central America and Mexico with a holistic and sustainable development model; or others too numerous to mention.

You also have the luxury of participating differently—you could develop one of your own philanthropies after the model of The Bill & Melinda Gates Foundation. Barbara Barger did such an excellent job with the nonprofit organization that she heads that government agencies are awed. Various media have focused on her accomplishments. Excitement is palpable about her presentations at *Ideal Aging*™ events where she shares her expertise.

Summary

Pilzer and others make a clear, cogent and convincing argument in favor of being rich. Multiple resources exist to assist your efforts to do so. The Bill & Melinda Gates Foundation and the added resources of Warren Buffet are stellar examples of how being wealthy makes it more likely that you can afford to attend to those worthy causes that others do not have adequate resources to address. Since I'm late in coming to this realization, this chapter focused on referring you to some who can assist you with components of your journey to enlightened wealth.

> "We make a living by what we get;
> we make a life by what we give."
> Sir Winston Churchill

Robert G. Allen,
Author of *Nothing Down,*
the best selling book on
Real Estate ever

I'm Robert Allen, who was a nobody before I wrote a book, and still am nobody to most people in the world. In 1980 I wrote my first book, *Nothing Down*, a proven program that shows you how to buy real estate with little or no money down, because the previous five years I bought a lot of real estate with little or no money down. I wrote *Creating Wealth* which is also a huge New York Times bestseller, *The Challenge, Multiple Streams of Income, Multiple Streams of Internet Income, The One-Minute Millionaire* with Mark Victor Hansen, *Cracking the Millionaire Code* with Mark Victor Hansen and recently *Nothing Down for Women* with Karen Nelson Bell. So eight books have come out of my little life and we've helped lots of people achieve financial freedom.

My definition of Ideal Aging™ is growing younger every day. You do what you love to do. Therefore, age never comes into it. It's based on four basic concepts. The purpose in life is to do what you love to do; that's what you're passionate about. What you're good at; that's what your talents are. What you feel is important to you; those are your values. And then finally what you feel you were born to do, which is part of your destiny. So destiny, values, talents and passions—when you mix those all together, the mix comes up with a person who's happy all the time. You're just getting younger and younger every day because you've found who you are. I've just been one of those lucky people who's found himself. I feel young and vibrant and although I might have a wrinkle or two, I wanna do what I love to do until they turn the lights out for me.

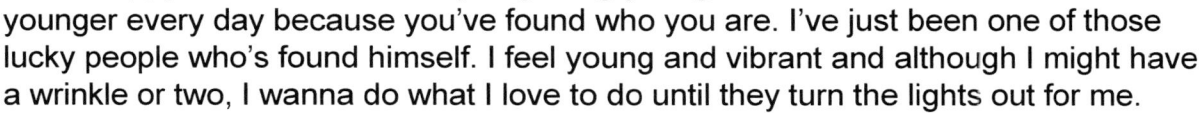

March 15, 2003, when I was driving home, I don't know what happened. All I know is I woke up in the hospital and life has been forever changed for me. I realize how fragile life is. I became so much more grateful for every single breath I take. Every day is special. I'm lucky I'm here frankly. So I feel like I'm ageless. I believe that I existed before I came here. That my spirit existed in a heavenly home and was trained and tutored like I believe all of us were to get ready to come to earth; to have a graduation experience in this very tough place where we get to test our faith. That's why I believe all of us are brothers and sisters. We are literally of the same divine DNA. We put on this uniform called a body and the body does age. It weakens and deteriorates but the spirit just gets stronger, more vibrant, more knowledgeable and wiser. The spirit is ageless. I just live my life as fast as I can, do as much as I can and feel wonderful about life.

I would've never done what I did this last year if it hadn't been for you and all the other members of my Inner Circle. We had a wonderful time together didn't we in our Inner Circle experience?

One of our members climbed six of the tallest seven mountains on all the seven continents. I said, if he can climb Mount Kilimanjaro, why can't I? This was just a year after my car accident where I blew my knee out and broke my back. He said: I'll take you to the top of Mount Kilimanjaro. We peaked Mount Kilimanjaro on the 3rd of August 2006 at about 10:00 in the morning. We started at 11:30 the previous night. We climbed all night almost 5,000 feet vertically; about a mile throughout the middle of the night. It was steep, hard and exhausting. Then we had to come all the way back down. We were on our feet 18 hours of very, very tough climbing. Before my car accident I never would've done anything like that. Afterwards it's, like, yeah, bring it on baby! Because you never can tell how long you're gonna live. So cram as much into life as you can. Take it with both fists. Just grab as much as you possibly can experience. I want to go to every country in the world.

The physical and mental repairs that you have achieved are phenomenal.

You can come back from everything. Your body is a magnificent tool, an unbelievable machine. We don't even know what's causing it or how it works, but what we do know is those seven to ten thoughts we think every day. So every minute, every second of every day, we have control of those seven to ten thoughts. We can choose whether we want to think positively or whether we want to think negatively. We can choose to get younger or we can choose to get older. If we choose older thinking, like, I'm getting older, I'm gonna die, everything hurts—whatever you think, you get.

If there was anything that could have expedited your success, what would that be?

I would've learned earlier how profoundly wise our own intuition is. I would've learned much more quickly how to listen to my true voice and how to follow it. It took me 40 to 45 years to finally trust myself enough that when I knew something was right I'd just do it. When I knew something was wrong, I wouldn't be tempted into it. This little intuitive flame that each of us has is so subtle, so profound. And on either side of that subtle flame are these two big bullies. One's the bully of greed and the other one's the bully of fear. The bully of greed is saying: "Go for it, no matter what the cost. Do it unethically, illegally or whatever, but go for the gusto." The bully of fear is saying: "Don't go for it, be careful, watch out, life is dangerous, be careful." The fear stops us from doing anything, and the greed encourages us to do the wrong things. The true intuitive voice basically doesn't listen to either one. It just does what's right for you. I just wish I'd listened earlier. As Oprah says, you gotta get it in the whisper. Because, if you don't get it in the whisper, you get it when the brick falls on your head. If you don't get it when the brick falls on your head, you get it when the wall of bricks falls on you. If you don't get it when the wall of bricks falls on you, you get it when the whole house collapses around you. But you're gonna get it. It's just cheaper, easier and faster to get it in the whisper.

Who was your mentor?

I've had about 40. Sometimes those mentors will last a minute, a day and sometimes they'll last years. I wouldn't say that any of them was my most important mentor because every one of them opened up a door that I would not have gotten to if it hadn't been for that mentor saying: "Open that door." I just believe in mentoring and how important it is to give credit to the people who opened your eyes, enlightened you to see the world in a different way. Do not believe in all the negative stuff, but see possibilities and opportunities. Steven Covey was a profound mentor for me at a very critical point. Mark Victor Hansen's been a very powerful mentor for me. Each one has a different reason. Mark's because he's such a giving person. He's a wildly giving giver. He's certainly taught me to be much more giving. Each one has their own claim to my fame.

When you look into the future, what are your dreams?

It starts off every morning in my own personal spiritual soul search. I read scriptures that are really important to me and seem to speak to me. Words of profound wisdom from the prophets, the sages kind of get me in the right frame of mind. It's a kneeling prayer, because I didn't do much before I had my car accident. Now I do it every day. Before, I just didn't get how grateful I was for every breath. In my prayer I'm going, hey, I've got all kinds of things I could do. I've got 20 projects I'm working on. I've got new books I want to write, new seminars I want to create, new businesses, new this's and that's. In my prayer I basically want to bring my burdens, cast them at the feet of Higher Power and say: Here are my burdens. Let me clear my mind and talk about what you want me to do. Who can I talk to today? How can I lift somebody today—smile with somebody in a special way. How can I be part of the team that makes the world a better place? So all I want to do is make the world a better place one person at a time.

If you had every resource that you needed, how would you improve the world?

I've always been teaching that there are six resources in our life: body, brain, being, time, people and money. We are all given those resources to use, the raw material of life. If I had the ability to help change the world, I would start inputting all of that kind of content into the educational system. They teach kids reading, writing and arithmetic, but they don't teach kids how to work on their inner wealth. If a kid has high self-esteem, they can learn from the worst teacher. But if a kid has low self-esteem, they can't learn from the best teacher. Inner wealth is what I would teach. How do you build confidence, strength, courage and persistence? These are easy words to say, but what are the physical or the material manifestations of inner wealth inside of a human being? How does a person create inner wealth so they can accomplish anything in the outer world? I would work on transforming kids from the earliest ages to the oldest of us to learn how unbelievably wealthy we really already are.

I always ask audiences, how many of you are millionaires? I'll have one or two percent of the people raise their hands. I say, let me ask one more time. How many of you are millionaires? Multi-millionaires? A few more hands go up. Wait a second. How many of you in this room, I mean, are you living in America? You're not a multi-millionaire? Finally I say: how many of you have a left kidney? People raise their hands. How many of you would sell your left kidney for a million dollars? And nobody raises their hands. Would somebody pay you a million dollars for your left kidney? There are people all over the world, very wealthy people who would pay you that kind of money. It's illegal for you to sell it, but the bottom line is, it's worth a million. But you won't sell it. So since you won't sell it, and you own it, aren't you a millionaire? What about your left eyeball? What about your left lung? What about all the physical resources that you have that you wouldn't sell? What about one of your children? Well, unless they're teenagers you probably wouldn't consider it. Will you sell your citizenship for a million? We go through a list of a hundred things that they already own but they won't sell. I say: you already have a hundred million dollar net worth; what are you complaining about? There are people who are banging the doors to get into this country and you're not appreciative? What's your citizenship worth? Your hidden assets are so valuable that if you really appreciated them, you'd be worth hundreds of millions. Start appreciating what you have. Stop harping about somebody's driving a better car than you are or somebody's living in a better apartment or their drapes are prettier. It's nothing! What you have is freedom to do what you want to do and manipulate those thoughts in your head every single minute.

Aging is mental, spiritual and physical. This human body we've been given is just so unbelievably magnificent that it has to be a temple. If we don't treat it like a temple, then we age quicker. I'm the greatest temple builder. I lost 50 pounds over the last couple of years and definitely feel dramatically better. Exercise is critical. You've got to take care of your body that way. And the nutrition. The way the foods we eat, are grown, the way they're prepared, the way they're frozen and the way they're delivered to us, is deteriorating the food supply unbelievably. The nutrients are degraded beyond recognition. Even fresh foods you get at the grocery store. In the 1950's there would be 50 milligrams of iron in a bowl of spinach. Today there's 2 milligrams of iron. The same fresh spinach still tastes just as bad, (at least to me) but the nutrients just aren't there anymore. I believe you need mega-doses of a lot of nutrients that are not found in our food supply any longer.

You're an amazing human being. Your book is awesome and everybody needs to go buy ten more copies of this book to hand out to people. I believe you're the person to tell the message because when they see how spry you are, so vibrant and funny. At one of our recent Inner Circle events you just cracked me up. You're amazing.

My best to all of your incredible readers and listeners.

From an enlightening phone chat with a stellar mentor on February 13, 2007.
Visit **www.RobertAllen.com** & **www.EnlightenedWealthInstitute.com**.

FORGIVE

"When I received the call from Mike, my brother, on New Year's morning, I was stunned. 'Something terrible has happened,' he said. 'Mama's been murdered. There was blood on the carpet, the walls...'"
Everett Worthington
in *Five Steps to Forgiveness*

Goals

- **R**ecall the hurt ... to transform the treasure into gold.

- **E**mpathize ... to achieve compassion for the transgressor.

- **A**chieve altruism ... to give the gift of forgiveness for the benefit of the other.

- **C**ommit publicly to forgive ... to release any doubt in your mind that you have forgiven.

- **H**old on to forgiveness ... by rehearsing to the point of mastery.

Brain fitness depends on reducing the amount of time you experience negative emotions and increasing the amount of positive emotions that populate your existence. That makes forgiveness an essential skill for Ideal Aging™. Most of us will avoid the level of trauma cited above. None of us will pass through this life free of insult. Any of us can capture the essence of the level of forgiveness that can enhance our brain power.

David Tinney suffered severe physical injuries when he was pushed off his bicycle onto the hard pavement by a carload of teenagers. Knowing the emotional and physical purchase of positive emotions, he gathered people in his hospital room the next morning before facing extensive surgery. In the crowd was his surgeon along with his family. He led them in a healing service. He forgave. He now rides a recumbent tricycle that flies the flag "Grace Happens!" In 2006 he led a 1,000 mile bike trip from Montana, through Idaho and across Washington ending near Portland, Oregon.

All of the research in this chapter is credited to Dr. Worthington. The quote above captures a real event in his life. His mother was murdered by a young burglar in 1995 in her home on New Years Eve.

It gives one pause for thought that he had made significant contributions to the psychological literature on the topic of forgiveness prior to this phone call—and has continued to do so. His poignant portrayal of pulling all his scientific expertise into the work of healing from such gross abuse and annihilation of a loved one is instructive.

If you are drawn to read his work, it will likely inspire you. Any and all of us can benefit from his wise counsel. The bullet points above highlight the REACH model of forgiveness developed by Worthington.

Science behind your plan

It is part of the human condition to occasionally be harmed. When this is the result of how we perceive an event, we are in complete control. We can choose a different view of it.

Whatever the circumstance of the perceived or real harm, anger and fear are likely to be part of the reaction. Trauma activates the part of your brain that processes and remembers emotional matters. The cost to your brain and general health of such emotions is covered in other chapters. Replacing these negative emotions with positive ones is key to achieving forgiveness and Ideal Aging™.

Without compassion or empathy for the transgressor forgiveness is unlikely. As discussed earlier, Goleman's research suggests that humans are hardwired for empathy.

After all of these efforts, why would you make the whole spiel public? Forgiving does not eliminate the memories. And the memories can serve as guidelines in future decisions. However, they can also sometimes raise a specter of doubt. It is not possible to anticipate when and where you will recall being hurt—and whether your altruistic forgiveness will persist. Therefore, Worthington advocates adopting the Boy Scout motto: "Be prepared." Making your forgiveness public makes it more real. Environmental involvement can make your forgiveness more permanent and pervasive.

How to do it

Tinney used his experience and the experiences of others to develop and teach healing through forgiveness. *Start* with an intentional plan to forgive. *Stop* any attempt to retaliate or get even and avoid revisiting the injustice. *Separate* the deed from the person. *Seek* to identify with the wrongdoer. Finally, Tinney recommends that you *surrender* to something greater than yourself.

Reviewing memories of trauma is painful. However, the goal in Worthington's REACH model is to create vivid images of the series of traumatic events while pairing these memories with empathy and compassion.

Establishing empathy for the transgressor can free up the energy that would have gone into controlling the rage within. Replacing the rage with a growing understanding of what might have contributed to the actions of the others does not mean forgetting what they did. It can mean empowering yourself to be more effective in dealing with the ills of society. For Worthington this was a powerful shift.

> *"When I felt unforgiveness toward the killer, I wanted to bash him. I wanted to add to society's violence. When I forgave, I wanted to stop the crime, stop the senseless murders."*
> Everett Worthington in *Five Steps to Forgiveness*.

Make a commitment to think, write and feel the emotions associated with the trauma. Remember that you are hardwired for empathy so make empathy an important next step.

Remember times when others have forgiven you for your errors—without taking a measure of how awful your errors were. Write down at least three of these events. The important point is that none of us is without errors. The sweet sense of being forgiven is a gift the other gave you. Your gratitude to the person who forgave you can help you do the same.

Altruism in this instance means giving the transgressor the gift of forgiveness simply for his benefit. Without even telling the transgressor, you can give the altruistic gift of forgiveness to the person who needs it by changing your actions to reflect your change.

Commitment can increase the probability of permanence. Create your own forgiveness certificate and decide whether you will post it somewhere or file it where you can pull it out as needed.

Write a letter of forgiveness that you do not mail to anyone—except, perhaps, to your therapist. Your nightly journal entry is another place to record your commitment to forgive.

Holding onto forgiveness is not simply a matter of willpower. When something brings these memories back, visit the emotions briefly before moving to the positive perspective you have cultivated. Review your certificate or notes to remember how you came to forgive. Social support can strengthen your hold on forgiveness.

Measuring goals

List at least three individuals you have not forgiven. Use the following form to track your progress through Worthington's REACH model.

Your Name _____ **Today's Date** _____

Your SUFI© -10 to +10 before	Recall the event	Empathize	Achieve Altruism	Commit to forgive	Hold onto forgiveness	Your SUFI© -10 to +10 after

236 • Ideal Aging

Summary

Most of us have heard "To err is human, to forgive divine." Worthington goes beyond this. In a poignant portrayal of how he struggled to apply what his own research has shown to be essential, he shares a model of hope even while recovering from extreme trauma. At each step through the REACH model of forgiveness he acknowledges the work involved in the actions that are essential.

Forgiveness may or may not be divine. In any case, it replaces the toxins of unforgiveness with the positive emotions required for Ideal Aging™. As such, it is an essential skill for your brain fitness.

And Tinney is right: "Grace happens!"

UNTWIST TWISTED PLACES

"Oh, the twisted places we will take ourselves!"
Personal communication of Julia Singer, PhD, in response to irrational guilt.

Goals

- Learn what "that little voice inside you" is saying to make sure "you maintain that certain level of misery throughout your life … " so you can learn how to create the level of happiness which can keep your brain fit

- Change what you say to yourself … so happiness persists

- Achieve unconditional self acceptance … so you enjoy yourself even when you fail

- Have unconditional acceptance of others … so you can remain calm even when their behavior is ugly

- Accept life with all it includes … so tragedy offers opportunity for growth

- Develop a high tolerance for frustration … so stress and regression build character

- Learn optimism … because it is a contagion that can improve brain architecture

This chapter eagerly acknowledges that tragedies happen. In the face of catastrophe, strong emotions are usually part of the picture. Sometimes the most humane and effective way of dealing with the painful emotions of tragedy is with psychotherapy. In no way is any part of this book meant to take the place of psychotherapy which can be many times more effective than any self help book.

Still, there's a potential for growth in looking at the few individuals who face tragedy with little apparent emotional burden. For example, when asked what it was like being married to the comedian Steve Allen, his wife reportedly said it was terrible … because even when they were pacing the sidewalk watching their mansion burn to the ground he was issuing one-liners. Apparently, his brilliance with humor was also one of his forms of healing.

You might counter, "Yes, but, he only faced the loss of material goods. What about all of the lives lost in the attack of 9/11?" Lisa Beamer showed the world how faith gave her extraordinary strength in the face of loss. The media portray her as bewildered by their attention and celebration of how she has grown through the tragic death of her husband.

The capacity of the few to thrive in the face of unimaginable horror does not reduce in any way the validity of the strong feelings felt by others. Emotions are. Individuals differ. Emotions have their value or purchase as well as their cost. The purpose of this chapter is to find those thoughts that lead to the painful emotions, to examine the thoughts, to change the thoughts that are adding excessive pain, to reduce the length of time spent in real emotions of real trauma, to learn to think differently whenever it is wise to do so and to do so in the interest of minimizing the damage done by painful emotions.

Albert Ellis was one of the founders of Cognitive Behavioral Therapy. At ninety-one years young he wrote that he (really) became a therapist to heal himself. Troubled by anxiety throughout much of his life, he forced himself to do the things he most feared—dating and public performance. He was a miserable failure, having only gotten one date in a succession of 130 invitations—and she didn't show up. However, he noted that he suffered no physical harm, "no one called a cop and none of the women ran away vomiting." This cured his social phobia.

From the age of 5 he had feared public performance. Philosophers who wrote on happiness helped him with this. Epictetus encouraged him to look at things differently. Ellis saw that he could fail miserably while stubbornly refusing to look down on himself. Thus he avoided anxiety. The clinician healed himself.

> "We are not disturbed by things, but by the view we take of things."
> Epictetus in the 4th Century

Lisa Beamer's reaction to tragedy took the additional step of celebration. She saw and spoke of the power, beauty, integrity and magnitude of the gift her husband gave to the world in organizing the failed flight plan of that third jet on 9/11.

Both tragedy and celebration are the focus of this chapter. You will learn how to change "that little voice inside you that makes sure you maintain that certain level of misery throughout your life." You will also learn how to give "that little voice inside you" the words of celebration of life. You can use these tools to empower yourself for greater health and longevity. This learned optimism can increase your immune response and your brain power. As Goleman describes, it could also be contagious and have a positive effect on the immune response and brain architecture of the people you link and loop with.

Science behind your plan

The World Health Organization has reported that depression is the number one cause of disability in the world. Seventeen percent of adults in the USA have at least one major depression episode during their lives. Anxiety also takes it toll.

Other chapters of this book comment on the importance of adequately treating depression.

For example, depressed rats given long term antidepressants showed increased neurogenesis and better nurturance of new brain cells. Applying science on rats to humans is usually quite reasonable since the similarities are greater than easily meets the eye. However, this may be one finding worth looking at more closely.

First, consider the comparison in humans of Cognitive Behavioral Therapy versus commonly prescribed antidepressants. The rats are of little use here.

Simply stated, Cognitive Behavioral Therapy focuses on your thoughts and your behaviors with the goal of challenging beliefs and activities that you use to sabotage yourself. That's not a put down. It just means that you learned a way of thinking and acting that worked well when you learned it in the first place … or seemed to. That means that you can learn. Great! That's the good news. That's important.

That also means you can discover your current styles of self-sabotaging thoughts (SST) and self-sabotaging actions (SSA). You can measure what you get and what you lose with each one of them. That is similar to the costs-benefits analysis commonly used in business. In this instance you are using Cognitive Behavioral techniques and doing the costs-benefits analysis to help you choose which thoughts and behaviors to change for mental, emotional, physical, financial, social and career health.

AND you can learn to change. Your SST can be changed to self-empowering thoughts (SET). You can learn how to change your SSA to self-empowering actions (SEA). Sometimes you will make these changes on your own using the tools of Cognitive Behavioral Therapy. There can also be extreme value in seeing a Cognitive Behavioral Therapist to hasten and fine tune your learning of these skills. Generally speaking, growth is more profound and persistent with an effective therapist just as academic pursuits are hastened with an erudite mentor.

Research is clear that Cognitive Behavioral Therapy is as effective as medication in treating depression, anxiety and other distresses. Cognitive Behavioral Therapy is superior to commonly prescribed medications in preventing relapse.

There are several theories about how some people end up more depressed than others do in similar circumstances. Negative thoughts are pivotal to all of them.

Seligman noted in humans, rats and others that depressed behaviors were associated with learning to feel helpless. He also studied the way people explain bad outcomes. Pessimistic people were more miserable and helpless. They saw the cause of bad outcomes as permanent, pervasive and beyond their control. In comparison optimists had a better sense of wellbeing. They saw the bad outcome as temporary, related to a specific cause that they could influence (such as studying more before a test) and not pervasive.

Beck also described styles of thinking that increased the likelihood of one's becoming depressed. He believed that negative thinking *is* the disease of depression. He was one of the first psychiatrists to teach that depression was a disease of disordered thought rather than being due to bad brain chemistry or anger turned against the self.

Albert Ellis and Robert Harper believed there are ten ideas which were illogical and irrational. These ideas are powerful in creating anxiety, depression and hostility. These ideas have been abstracted from their book.

1. The idea that you must have love and approval from all significant people.

2. The idea that you must be thoroughly competent, adequate and achieving.

3. The idea that people acting obnoxiously and unfairly should be blamed, condemned and seen as bad, wicked or rotten people.

4. The idea that you have to see things as awful, terrible, horrible and catastrophic when you are frustrated, treated unfairly or rejected.

5. The idea that emotional misery is a result of environmental pressures and you have little ability or control to change your misery.

6. The idea that if something seems dangerous or fearsome, you must preoccupy yourself with and make yourself anxious about it.

7. The idea that it is easier to avoid facing many life difficulties and responsibilities than to use more self-discipline.

8. The idea that your past remains all-important and that because something once strongly influenced your life, it has to keep determining your feelings and behavior today.

9. The idea that people and things should turn out better than they do and that you must view it as awful and horrible if you do not find good solutions to life's grim realities.

10. The idea that you can achieve maximum human happiness by inactivity or by passively enjoying yourself.

"People, in order to make themselves minimally disturbed, had better achieve unconditional self-acceptance (USA), unconditional other-acceptance (UOA), unconditional life-acceptance (ULA), and a philosophy of high frustration tolerance (HFT)."
Albert Ellis, PhD,
founder of Rational Emotive Behavior Therapy
in *Why I (Really) Became a Therapist*, 2005.

It's timely to share a personal communication form Albert Ellis. In the midst of a series of long and severe traumatic experiences, I only envisioned two alternatives in reaction to the teachings of Ellis. Either his perspective was a crock of stuff or I was a miserable failure at being rational. I wasn't comfortable with either.

At one of his workshops I gave him a thumbnail sketch with no identifying data so he could not have guessed I was talking about myself. He was quick to be much more compassionate with "the case" than I had been with myself. "There are some outcomes in life that are truly tragic. They warrant strong emotions."

The use of Cognitive Behavioral Therapy is never meant to deny real pain resulting from real tragedy. It is meant to decrease the intensity, duration and frequency of these emotions to help until the storm passes. Go gently through the dark clouds of tragedy knowing that there is light at the end of each tragedy. And bring light into the tunnel where you can. The kindness and compassion of Albert Ellis in that evanescent moment has often helped me turn lemons into lemonade. I am still grateful.

David Burns is the author of *Feeling Good: The New Mood Therapy. The Clinically Proven Drug-Free Treatment for Depression.* First published in 1980, this book as sold over four million copies. That's a lot of help for a large number of people.

Burns has identified twenty-three self-defeating beliefs. He lists them in the seven categories of achievement, love, submissiveness, demandingness, depression, anxiety and other.

Achievement

1. Perfectionism
2. Perceived Perfectionism
3. Achievement Addiction

Love

4. Approval Addiction
5. Love Addiction
6. Fear of Rejection

Submissiveness

7. Pleasing Others
8. Conflict Phobia
9. Self-Blame

Demandingness

10. Other-Blame
11. Entitlement
12. Truth

Depression

13. Hopelessness
14. Worthlessness/Inferiority

Anxiety

15. Emotional Perfectionism
16. Anger Phobia
17. Emotophobia
18. Perceived Narcissism
19. Brushfire Fallacy
20. Spotlight Fallacy
21. Magical Thinking

Other

22. Low Frustration Tolerance
23. Superman/Superwoman

Sometimes it is difficult to catch yourself thinking in any of these ways. So much of what we think is as rapid as an auto-responder. It is in the nature of humans to put as much as possible into the form of a conditioned response. Saves time for creativity and socialization.

Psychotherapy may be necessary to help find such self-defeating thoughts. If any self-defeating beliefs do relate to your discomfort psychotherapy is ideal for personal empowerment. It puts you in the Thinker's seat. You and you alone have the full twenty-four hours to tinker with your Thinker. Some details of change follow in the "How to" section.

Many studies have shown that Cognitive Behavioral Therapy is at least as effective as prescribed antidepressants (Antonuccio, 1999). This has been found by patient report. It is particularly true for long term benefits. Avoiding the side effects of prescription medications is a strong argument in favor of changing your thoughts rather than resorting to prescription drugs.

Seligman studied college students who reported mild to moderate symptoms of depression. The workshop group was taught several Cognitive Behavioral techniques while the control group received no treatment. Increased optimism accounted for fewer symptoms of depression and anxiety as well as a better sense of wellbeing in the students in the workshop compared to the control group.

By learning to explain situations with more optimism you could prevent some depression and anxiety. Pessimism results in less achievement, less effective immune function, and ill health. It is associated with depression and even suicide. Of course, some measure of pessimism can be essential. In its healthy form it urges caution with adequate attention to grim reality. Balancing these two perspectives with more optimism than pessimism will be your work of art.

How to do it

For relief from the angst caused by irrational ideas posed by Ellis and Harper, restate them with hope and personal empowerment.

1. Wanting the love and approval from all significant people is healthy when you can be understanding when it is withheld

2. Planning to be thoroughly competent, adequate and achieving is deliciously empowering as long as you also love yourself when you fail miserably.

3. Recognizing that people sometimes act obnoxiously and unfairly is realistic when couched in the wisdom of learning to live with and adapt to human error.

4. Realizing that frustration builds character brings the healing power of hope to situations when you are frustrated, treated unfairly or rejected.

5. Appreciating the wisdom of Epictetus that we are disturbed not by events but by the view we take of them reduces the impact of environmental pressures.

6. Studying something that seems dangerous or fearsome for enough time to plan your way out of danger is empowering.

7. Facing many life difficulties and responsibilities increases your skills and flexibility.

8. Exploring your past to see how it influences you now can help you rewrite some the rules you held sacred and change some of your conditioned responses that worked when you learned them but cost you a lot now.

9. Preferring that people and things turn out better than they have could help you identify what to change to get a better result in the future.

10. Searching for maximum human happiness can lead to more involvement in activities and in your community.

Ellis believes that all emotional disturbances stem from "musterbation." After writing *The New Guide to Rational Living*, he concluded that these ten ideas just include three main ideas. The three types of "musts" invented by humans who use them to torment themselves without mercy include "I MUST do well ... ", "You MUST treat me fairly ... " and "The universe MUST make things easy for me ...."

In the midst of emotional discord, ask yourself what you are demanding. Change your "musterbation" to "I would prefer ... " This can improve your motivation to work for what you want without undue emotional turmoil.

A relatively easy technique for change is to listen for all-or-nothing words in what you say and think. These includes words such as "all," "every," "any" "nothing", "everything," "always," and others which imply including a whole universe. Changing the universal word to something less broad can be a powerful way to elevate your mood.

Add to that changing the requirement of "must" to a mere want. For example, if you have been thinking, "I must have the love and approval of all people that are important to me," change the "must" and the "all." You can be a lot happier thinking, "I do *prefer* to have the love and approval of *most* of the people that are important to me."

Here are some examples. Use the ones most applicable to your unique situation. The repetition of intentional substitution of one of these sentences can begin to create the conditioned response of greater happiness. This is the outcome associated with reduced chemistry of stress and, therefore, improved brain fitness.

1. Everyone will hate me for being slow.	1. They appreciate who I am even when I am slow.
2. I'm a loser because I didn't answer the question.	2. A question is an invitation to answer, not a requirement. I didn't have the answer.
3. Those terrible people didn't even give me a clue!	3. They were probably busy thinking through the problem themselves.
4. This is such a catastrophe that I'll never be invited again.	4. This was frustrating because I wasn't prepared. I'll get it right the next time.
5. They have to treat me better.	5. I am choosing to feel only sad. I am encouraged because I will learn.
6. I am so frightened for my future that I'm losing sleep over this danger.	6. By changing my thoughts to feel less fear I improve my chances of doing better.
7. I'm just going to hide until the storm passes.	7. I have the courage to face my worst fears and do it anyway.
8. I was taught to stay out of trouble.	8. I can be cautious and still take action that will lead to mastery.
9. It's absolutely horrible to lose my job at this point in my life. I'll never recover.	9. Even though this in inconvenient timing, I see this job loss as an opportunity to explore different career options.
10. It will be good to settle into my rocking chair and just enjoy watching the world rushing by.	10. It will be delicious to have time to be more creative, to write those books that have been nestled in the attic of my mind.

Burns not only describes more thoughts that are troublesome, he also offers "50 Ways to Untwist Your Thinking." He has a fine appreciation for individual differences and a great respect for how much courage it takes to confront fears and learn from failures. His focus on frequent measures of progress adds power to your efforts. For much greater detail on his contributions to emotional healing, use ideas from several of his books and articles listed below.

He begins with the use of a Daily Mood Log. Identify the upsetting event on which you want to work. Make a list of the emotions you felt when this happened such as sad, anxious, guilty, inferior or lonely. Rate each one of them on the strength of the emotion from zero to 100%. Find the negative thoughts you were thinking related to those emotions. Choose one of those negative thoughts to work on. Rate how strongly you believed that thought–again, from zero to 100%.

> "Niceness is the cause of all anxiety."
> "When do I want you to get better? Today!"
> In role playing, "I'm that little voice inside you that
> makes sure you maintain that certain level of misery throughout your life."
> David Burns, MD, author of *Feeling Good,* in *Scared Stiff* Workshop November 2006

At this point the more interesting work begins. Be the detective that figures out how you have been distorting your thinking. From the works of Burns, decide which one or more of these you were doing?

1. **All-or-Nothing Thinking.** Are you forcing things into black-and-white categories?
2. **Overgeneralization.** Are you seeing one bad event as *always* happening?
3. **Mental Filter.** Do you focus on the negatives while ignoring the positives?
4. **Discounting the Positive.** Do you refuse to enjoy your positive qualities? In one of my workshops people took turns being flooded with compliments. The rule was that they could only listen and agree with each compliment as it was spoken. No denial of the positive was permitted. A woman told one of the men, "I really like your hands. They are strong." "They were on sale," was his quick response. Did he break the rule? Comedic relief can be a tension buster.
5. **Jumping to Conclusions.** Have you looked at enough facts? Or are you **Mind-Reading** in assuming people react badly to you? Or **Fortune-Telling** in predicting a bad outcome?
6. **Magnification and Minimization.** Are you making too much or too little out of things?
7. **Emotional Reasoning.** Is it your logic that "I **feel** like an idiot; therefore, I **am** one?"
8. **Should Statements.** Do you believe that you should, shouldn't, must, ought to or have to?
9. **Labeling.** Instead of regretting an error do you call yourself a jerk, loser or knucklehead?
10. **Blame.** Do you find fault with yourself and others or solve the problem?

Some people prefer to be home alone with their distortions while they dispute, challenge, change and become comfortable with the healthier perspective. That's OK! As long as you are empathic, tender, efficient and effective in converting a self-sabotaging thought (SST) to a self-empowering thought (SET), congratulate yourself. You could be on your way to being SET for a healthier and happier life.

Up to this point you have already used three of the basic techniques taught by Burns: 1) *Empathy.* You have listened to yourself without judgment or advice. 2) *Agenda Setting.* You have chosen one SST to focus your efforts on. 3) *Identify the Distortions.* Using the checklist on the previous page you have identified the errors in your thinking. Finding the distortions is factual and without blame.

Now take a fourth step. Turn your negative SST into a positive SET. Empower yourself with a positive thought which is 100% true AND that disproves the negative parts of what you were saying to yourself. That's the *Straightforward Technique.* It often works.

In my clinical experience the fifth technique proposed by Burns usually worked better than being straightforward with your self. The *Double Standard Technique* is asking yourself how you would talk to your best friend. Very often we are our own worst enemy. We think thoughts about ourselves that we would never say to anyone else. We want our best friends to thrive. Yet to the one person we spend twenty-four/seven with we say the worst things! Learning to talk to yourself as you would to your best friends might be your most powerful and positive form of achieving enduring happiness.

> "I am forever impressed with the extent to which we march to the beat of the historical drummer as if its worldview were worthy of note."
> Dr. Joyce

Remember: it is never too early and never too late to change to healthier thinking and behaving. Pick one little thought at a time. Work with it lovingly until it nourishes your evolution.

Seligman teaches us a great deal about "flexible optimism." The style of explaining outcomes is related to your mood. Pessimism predicts feeling depressed, being dejected and staying passive rather than taking action to improve your situation. His years of research found differences between being pessimistic versus optimistic.

Working with dogs Seligman discovered "immunization" against learned helplessness that leads to low self-esteem, a sense of failure and becoming passive. The earlier in life mastery over helplessness occurred, the more effective it was. Their research showed that dogs who learned that their responses would make a difference were immunized all their lives against learned helplessness. When their own activity worked, their "cure was one hundred percent reliable and permanent." Some animals would not give up no matter what. Having some control over your situation is invaluable.

Do you see an outcome as permanent and pervasive? Or do believe it is temporary and relate it to some specifics of the situation? The pessimistic point of view is that you "always fail." The optimistic point of view is that you failed this one test because you had gotten too little sleep and had not studied enough. Pessimism robs you of your power. Optimism helps you identify how to improve on the next go around. The self can change itself. You can change you. You can learn optimism.

When you develop a conditioned response to explain outcomes optimistically, your change to greater health and happiness can be permanent. Cognitive Behavioral Therapy works because it celebrates the power of you, the only person to ever spend twenty-four hours of every day with you. It teaches you tools that you can use in the interest of enhancing who you are.

Does "permanent" mean you will never again think pessimistic thoughts? NO!

I teach my clients that you need to think those pessimistic thoughts occasionally. It's your best research in you. It is critical to maintaining optimism and happiness. It gives you repeated measures of what you used to do to maintain that certain level of misery. Your repeated measures tell you how far you've come! They tell you how positive and powerful your changes to healthier thinking are. The contrast in misery versus happiness reflected in these repeated measures makes happiness self-maintaining because it's FUN!

Under stress people regress. Each time you regress to the pessimistic thoughts you have another opportunity to study what you are thinking. You get another chance to do the costs-benefits analysis so you strengthen your motivation to be optimistic while also having increased compassion for how and why you learned pessimism. It fosters agape for people around you as they go through their struggles.

It's just plain imperative to resort back to old behaviors on rare occasions for the compassionate research and development of your evolving self. Sometimes you will wish you had done so while you were home alone. That way the only repair work necessary is with your self. Other times you'll have the pleasure of sharing new found wisdom about the value of optimism with witnesses to your brief regression in the interest of your personal research and growth.

Measuring Goals

On a daily basis do the short form of the SUFI Report™. Rate the negative feelings zero to minus 10 on how intense each painful emotion is.

Subjective Units of Feelings Index (SUFI Report™)

-10   0   +10

Label the negative emotions. _____, _____, _____, _____

How strong is each of these negative emotions? ____, ____, ____, ____

Identify the self-sabotaging thoughts (SST) behind the negative feelings and how strongly you believe them.

1. _____

2. _____

3. _____

4. _____

5. _____

6. _____

7. _____

Choose one SST thought to dispute. Just one little thought at a time. Change it to the positive self-empowering thought (SET). Use the measures taught by Burns and rate these thoughts before and after you change them. How strongly do you believe the SST? How strongly do you believe the SET?

Remember, to be effective, the self-empowering thought must be positive AND it must prove the self-sabotaging thought is false.

SST _____	%	SET _____	%
_____		_____	
_____		_____	
_____		_____	
_____		_____	
_____		_____	

This is a good time to re-do the short form of the SUFI Report™. Rate the negative feelings zero to minus 10 on how intense that painful emotion is **after** you have a SET for change.

Subjective Units of Feelings Index (SUFI Report™)
-10　　　　　　　　　　　　　0　　　　　　　　　　　　　+10

Sometimes people feel some fear or anxiety just at the thought of making change. Other times you might find it difficult to do all the detective work on your own. When the time is right, give yourself the gift of psychotherapy with a Cognitive Behavioral Therapist who can facilitate your progress. It takes courage to do this on your own. It just takes a different kind of courage to get professional help. When the changes you made in your self-sabotaging thoughts give you a more positive score on the SUFI Report™, remember to celebrate. That can reinforce your progress.

Summary

Thought is simply learned behavior. What you think now must have had value when you first learned to think that way. You thought it because it worked out the way you wanted it to … or thought you wanted it to.

Times change. You change with the times. You want different things across your life.

The most powerful way of creating these changes is through changing our thoughts. The tools are pretty straightforward. Keep a daily record of your emotions. Figure out what you were thinking with those emotions.

Reinforce the thoughts that resulted in happiness. That's how you form long term potentiation (LTP), i.e., new habits; new default options.

Challenge the self-sabotaging thoughts (SST) and replace them with self-empowering thoughts (SET) so you are SET for improving mental, intellectual, emotional, physical, social and career health. Afford yourself the same gentle compassion you do your other best friends.

Regularly celebrate your own progress. That helps maintain it.

Will you master it over night? Sometimes that happens. Seligman and his researchers did teach old dogs new tricks. Once dogs learned that their behavior could effect the outcome, they were "immunized" against helplessness. That is an example of one trial learning. Mastery on one occasion led to the dogs' not giving up again.

Should you count on one trial learning for yourself? You could aim for it and remember: the real power of developing a conditioned response, even in thoughts is repetition. So, plan to repeat, refine and reinforce each bit of your progress along the way.

Most often we learn something and then learn it again. There is no benefit in being discouraged. It's usually more compassionate and effective to remember that making mastery permanent requires repetition, refinement and reinforcement. Give yourself the gift of psychotherapy when change doesn't come easily. Celebrate small movement in the healthier direction.

It's worth remembering: older adults living in the community were more satisfied with their lives when they had hope, were active citizens in their community and were in loving relationships. Reducing depression, anxiety and other negative emotions to the point that you feel good can often be managed by changing what you think.

Using Cognitive Behavioral techniques to change your thoughts is at least as effective as prescribed antidepressants. That could be a compelling argument to avoid the side effects prescribed drugs have. Equally important is the finding that the positive effects of Cognitive Behavioral Therapy last longer with less relapse.

> "In essence, science and spirituality,
> though differing in their approaches,
> share the same end,
> which is the betterment of humanity."
>
> His Holiness the Dalai Lama
> in *The Universe in a Single Atom*

David Burns, MD
Psychiatrist
Adjunct Clinical Professor at Stanford University School of Medicine
Author of *Feeling Good*, the #1 book on depression.

I did several years of research in biological psychiatry. That's the idea that emotional problems like depression and anxiety result from a chemical imbalance in the brain and that you can cure these disorders by finding just the right pill. I was quite enthusiastic about that approach except for two problems. Number 1, in my research as well as my review of the world literature, I couldn't find any evidence that depression or anxiety resulted from a chemical imbalance in the brain. In addition, I was treating large numbers of patients with buckets full of pills and large numbers of them just were not recovering and getting back their joy and self-esteem. So I was looking around for a different approach or something to supplement the medications because I wanted my patients to recover, to get out of the trap of misery and self-hatred and beating up on themselves and being helpless. Then I heard about a relatively new approach.

Cognitive Therapy is the idea that our thoughts create our moods. When you're upset, you're thinking about things in a very negative manner. People could be trained to change the way they think. It sounded a little bit too slick. I decided to try them with a number of my patients just to satisfy myself that these methods wouldn't work, and lo and behold, people who had been depressed or anxious and unsuccessfully treated for years and sometimes for decades, suddenly began to turn the corner on their problems and get out of the trap of depression and anxiety! They loved these techniques and asked for more. I gave up a full-time academic career at the medical school to go into private practice for about 20 years. Now I'm teaching, doing workshops, researching and writing.

My book, *Feeling Good,* has sold well over four million in the U.S. It's been translated into large numbers of different languages and it's been published in many, many countries around the world. That was one of the first things I did when I went into clinical practice. I was excited about what I was seeing but there was a lot to explain to patients about all the cognitive distortions and how to turn these negative thinking patterns around. The book was originally a series of handouts I was creating for my patients.

Ideal Aging™ is not even a concept I think about. I just like to keep a lot of irons in the fire, be learning new things and be doing a lot of things. Sometimes I feel like I'm about 16 years old because every day is bringing new projects, new ideas and new sources of excitement. The only difference was, when I was 16, I had just as many ideas but nobody took me seriously. Now I shoot something out there that somebody thinks is really important and I get entangled in all kinds of projects. One of the rules I give myself is, if nine-tenths of the things I try fail and one-tenth turn out, that's a pretty good batting average. I'm not afraid to try lots of new things all the time.

I just enjoy learning. Now we're getting into very high-speed techniques and are often seeing patients recover in just one or two therapy sessions. One of the things I love about Cognitive Therapy is I have a kind of Buddhist perspective that on some level you can imagine we're all one. This is certainly true in the therapy session because when a patient suddenly goes from misery to joy before your very eyes, it makes the therapist feel as excited as it does the patient. Then if you have a session that isn't going well, you feel that as well. I love doing workshops. Every workshop is an opportunity for magic. Sometimes we all get criticized and attacked. Sometimes we make the mistake of getting defensive. One of the greatest things for me to learn is to find truth in what the person is saying and treating the person who seems to be attacking you with respect. When an audience sees you doing that, they say this is a safe place. The workshop leader will not hurt me. I can be free and open and exchange ideas.

Forest Scogin has done many outcome studies on my book *Feeling Good*. He asked: if we had to do the cheapest treatment for depression, what would it be? At the time he started his research, he could buy copies of *Feeling Good* from the publisher in batches of 100 or more for $2.40 each. They did a controlled outcome study giving the book to 60 or 80 randomly assigned depressed people. The comparison group was just on the waiting list for therapy while the experimental group on the waiting list received a copy of *Feeling Good*. Then they studied their depression levels once a week, but they had no treatment of any kind. What they discovered was in that four weeks, two-thirds of the people to whom they gave the *Feeling Good* book recovered and needed no further treatment. Patients that didn't get a copy of the book did not recover. They replicated that. They thought, maybe it's a placebo effect, so they did another study and gave half of the subjects Viktor Frankl's book *Man's Search For Meaning*. Two-thirds of the people receiving *Feeling Good* recovered but the patients who got the Viktor Frankl book did not. They published six or eight of these studies in the *Journal of Consulting and Clinical Psychology*. The researchers have also done long-term follow-up studies on these patients and reported that those who had read *Feeling Good* didn't relapse or ever need treatment. So if my dream came true, I could create an interactive version of the book that would be on the Internet. It would know who you are. It would be more effective than the book *Feeling Good*. It would test you and actually treat you. I think something like that could be just tremendous because so many people can't afford therapy or they go and get pills, pills, pills, or they get therapists who are not trained in these newer techniques.

I'm kind of an anti-advice person. But I think that one of the greatest robbers of joy and productivity is depression. Very few of us are immune from falling into periods of despair and self-doubt. I've experienced this myself and I think nearly all human beings have anxiety or insecurities or feelings about not being good enough and asking themselves what does my life amount to, what's special about me, what did I ever contribute? That
kind of inner dialogue can rob all of us of joy. I think I would want people to know, particularly people who are feeling worthless and hopeless, that there is real hope

not only for improvement but for defeating those kinds of feelings entirely and getting back to feelings of joy and self-esteem. I think when you're involved with joy and positive self esteem, then you don't care so much about aging or anything else. You're just too busy having fun and feeling grateful for life and all the wonderful opportunities that we have.

I think our strengths and weaknesses are often the same thing. The very thing that gives us power and strengthens us is our own down-coming, too. They just kind of get out of hand.

I think as I get older I'm learning the power of humility and compassion. When I feel the most alive, when I'm thinking about somebody perhaps that I've treated and how the patient was suffering and how he was able to turn his life around. I find those things moving and tears come to my eyes. I don't think all tears involve depression. I think that when we have the sense of real compassion for the suffering of other people, compassionately feel at a deep level, that's when real miracles, some of the most magical aspects of life, can occur. That's not only true if you're a therapist, but life in general. I just see that there's a dark side to human nature and I look at how most of the world's at war and attempts on killing, self-promotion and exploitation of others and always under the name of some kind of political or religious principle to disguise it as something good. When I'm doing a workshop, I think when I can project warmth and compassion and humility is when people respond the most. We're all kind of the same. We're all kind of flawed. Once you accept that, that's when really phenomenal things can occur.

Excerpts from a phone conversation with
a man who is a living example of joy and spreading cheer on January 24, 2007.

SET STRATEGIC GOALS

"When it is obvious that the goals cannot be reached, don't adjust the goals, adjust the action steps."
Confucius

Goals

- Create an awareness of always being in control… because that enhances brain chemistry that strengthens emotional health and your ability to cope with stress

- Explore what your next chapter might be … because novelty fosters building better brains

- Measure change … because Ideal Aging™ includes the optimistic anticipation of even greater and more exciting things ahead

Ample science exists in this realm. One interesting cycle: the more positive your attitude, the more likely it is that you will achieve your goals. By the same token, the more goals you achieve, the greater your probability of happiness in your Ideal Aging™. In either case, your brain fitness can be enhanced by the happiness as well as the challenge of achieving new goals.

Perhaps the master goal setter and achiever is my great friend, John Goddard. He created a "Life List" as a teenager that included 127 goals. His book, *The Survivor: 24 Spine-Chilling Adventures on the Edge of Death*, captures thrilling accounts of the completion of several of these goals. What an exhilarating read his book is! I can relate to his living with the headhunters of Borneo as I had that experience during my Peace Corps days. The rest go beyond anything I had imagined. He led the first expedition down the world's longest river, the 4,200-mile-long Nile. The 2,700-mile-long Congo River in Africa was another goal and he was the first human to explore its entire length.

John Goddard
Explorer Extraordinaire

Volmer Jensen was one of my heroes from the time when I was twelve. He was my hang gliding instructor when he was 76. Because of his youthfulness, his wit, his energy, his interest in everything, his zest … he was a magnet for younger people! They loved to hang out with him. He was in better shape than half the people half his age. And he was always an example of the ridiculousness of categorizing people according to their decade of life.

"In our family we don't keep track of aging. We don't think about our age. We are just so intent on fulfilling our dreams and doing goals that it just is not a factor in our lives. I was 42 yesterday. Today I'm a little tired, like 45.

Age is only important in terms of wine and cheese.

Youthful attitude is paramount—your zest and enthusiasm and having that optimistic anticipation of even greater things. I'm asked, 'How many goals have you done now?' Generally, I don't keep track of them. I accomplish them and proceed to something else.

Just focus on goal setting and getting more life in life.

Since I'm associated with unusual goals and doing them with a confident, no-holds-barred attitude in which I blast away obstacles and any self imposed limitations, I just write down a goal knowing that I can do it. As I write the goal I visualize actually doing it so I program my brain for success. Devoting time, identifying resources, raising funds and creating opportunities enable you to successfully achieve each goal. You make that possible on your own initiative. Then you do the goal. You demonstrate a real commitment to them and assure yourself of success when you write down each of your goals, short term and long. As a consequence, you elevate yourself to a higher level of awareness, interest in and enjoyment of everything around you.

During one expedition I was able to achieve thirty goals in three months … simply because I had listed them on paper and had them vividly established in my mind. Then I worked out each one, one after another. That's precisely what it takes. Anyone can do that sort of thing.

When you write down goals you have a genuine commitment to transform your hopes, dreams and ambitions from abstractions to reality.

Devoting time, raising funds, creating opportunities and, *importantly*, establishing deadlines have been some of the most essential steps for me to achieve more than 500 challenging goals out of a total list of 600.

Write them down. You would accomplish so much more. We all need continual reminders with documentation and a little pressure of deadlines."

Personal chat with a kindred spirit, John Goddard, on February 14, 2007

"Savor each day!" says one of the world's most famous explorers. His focus has been cultural anthropology. "Believe that there is *always* something even better ahead." Set a timeline on each goal as your write it down. These little reminders form the gentle pressures that add up to your adding more life to your life. That's a model of Ideal Aging™ that's a joy to endorse. It places the factor of age where it is most fitting—on wine and cheese.

You can look back on those written goals and say, "I did what I said I would because I knew I could." You could feel deep satisfaction in measured and monitored accomplishments. You could enjoy being a good model to youth and others. These would be suitable rewards for good solid values, achievement, planning, work ethics, etc.

You can share written goals with others who will support you. Knowing that they'll be interested in your progress can fuel your motivation. People who know of your goals could also aid you in being accountable. If you are "as good as your word," you will keep your contract for progress. My brother, Charles Shaffer, came home from the US Navy for a brief visit when I was in my adolescence. When he learned that I would not go on to school beyond high school because of lack of funds, he said, "Tell me how much you need for the three years and I will send it." That was a tipping point. I didn't make it on my own.

Part of the fun of examining goals with people you love and trust is in capturing the added value of a master minding group. Martin Seligman provides an excellent example in the Positive Psychology Network. Because "creative thinking and scientific breakthrough" were high priorities, his group meets "each January for a week in Akumal, a modestly priced vacation town in the Yucatan." Without much preset agenda, they meet morning and evening for discussions, have ample time with family and spend afternoons in small groups writing or chatting about specific topics. From their efforts has come stellar and pivotal research which is the focus in the chapter on **Enduring Happiness**.

To Do lists. A few days ago I held an Ideal Aging™ forum in a retirement center. A refined 80-something years young woman lamented that she felt so overwhelmed by a To Do list because it had so many things written on it.

Another elegant 80-something years young woman nearly leapt out of her seat protesting. "No! No! Don't write your To Do list that way! Only put one or two things on it, three at the most!" She gave me permission to tell her process here without giving away any identifying data: "When I'm really down in the dumps, I write one to three items on a list in the morning when I get up. In the evening I cross them all off. It really lifts my spirits to see that I got them done."

Others have found it helpful to have a long To Do list with priority items numbered or highlighted in some way. Another respected mentor takes particular pleasure in crumpling a finished list and throwing it in the waste basket. I put mine in a file in a filing cabinet in case I want to review them later.

Appointments. There may be more uses for an appointment calendar than may meet the eye at first glance. They're worth exploring.

Social appointments are probably the first to come to mind. Are you the kind of social butterfly who needs a calendar just to keep track of all your friendly encounters? Or the one who needs an appointment in the future to soften the loneliness of today? Or have you lived your life so tightly scheduled that you have thrown away all calendars with relief?

The **Create Conditioned Responses** chapter teaches you how to use a conditioned relaxation response to regain control in tense moments. That's an invaluable skill. However, sometimes the gravity of a situation is so difficult to rise above that even a highly effective use of conditioned relaxation will seem to have brief holding power. As you repetitively cue yourself back to the conditioned relaxation you could begin to feel like you are on an emotional seesaw bouncing between worry and being relaxed.

I've found it clinically useful in those times to do several things. First, be grateful for the conditioned relaxation response for its power in decreasing stress and improving your immune response. Second, set an appointment to worry at the time when it is most likely to be useful. See the Science behind your plan section below for a fascinating study on worrying. Third, every time the muscular tension builds, try to see some value in it—as an isometric exercise, for example. Fourth, also try to see some value in the personal research you get in measuring how effectively you are using your new awareness and skills.

Admittedly, steps three and four are aimed at countering any tendency you may have had to put yourself down. Do you find it amazing how quickly most people resort to that? "I've just spent weeks getting a conditioned relaxation response and I've already lost it!"

No. Tragedy happens. Related emotions have their use and value.

Don't deny or relinquish your emotions in response. They are real. Change any distorted thinking as described in the chapter on **Untwist Twisted Places**. Becoming an expert in many skills can enhance Ideal Aging™ when tragedy leaves it mark.

Make expanding your expertise your goal. Remain open to a broad range of emotions while creating enduring health and happiness. Make negative emotions evanescent by releasing them as soon as you capture their message. And schedule as much positive stuff as possible.

Science behind your plan

Studies have clearly shown that individuals who believed they are in control, even when they were wrong about that, fared better than people who knew there was nothing they controlled about a situation. Their performance and their measures of stress were better than the group that recognized or believed that they had no control.

Simply measuring a behavior changes it. There seems to be a natural goal to rise above one's own personal best.

Adding a master mind to your goal setting could be valuable. Napoleon Hill spoke uniquely of a "Master Mind" which he defined as: "Coordination of knowledge and effort, in a spirit of harmony, between two or more people, for the attainment of a definite purpose." He elaborated on the "psychic phase of the Master Mind principle."

> "No two minds ever come together without, thereby, creating a third, invisible, intangible force which may be likened to a third mind."
> Napoleon Hill in *Think and Grow Rich*.

His thesis was based on his lifetime of research on over 500 wealthy men to discover the secrets of their success. It shares an interesting link with new social neuroscience as discussed in the **Connect** chapter. Goleman described our link between two brains as a brain-to-brain two-lane super-high-speed highway in which information is exchanged between people in a feedback loop. This data sharing goes through skin and skull barriers in Goleman's theory.

Hill called the work of Mahatma Gandhi a miracle because Gandhi used no force when he induced "over two hundred million people to coordinate, with mind and body, in a spirit of harmony, for a definite purpose." That's a sound argument.

Is progressive relaxation always indicated, useful and harmless? There was one fascinating study I read many years ago. Since I cannot find the reference now, I wouldn't refer to it if it didn't seem pertinent.

A group of patients was taught to use progressive relaxation during the days prior to surgery. Their post-operative course was worse than others who did not use this technique. The researchers thought this finding suggested that the relaxation had interfered with the process of brief worry. Patients not so relaxed may have mulled over the "What if … " questions and come up with their own "In that case … " unique solutions. This fits nicely with my clinical bias that all human emotions have their value. Worry visited briefly can yield both unique solutions as well as a sense of being in control.

How to do it

Goals. Whether you write them or speak them, share them with people you love and trust. That way you can benefit from some support, accountability and sense of being in control. Be specific: I will read. Make it measurable: I will read twenty pages. Be sure it's attainable: Have a book. Keep it realistic: A book in Mandarin characters won't hack it if you only read English. Time limits are essential: I will read 20 pages of Thoreau's *Walden Pond* before noon today.

Goddard suggests creating detailed mental images of each goal along with continual determination to complete each one. Ideally, you will have a master mind team. Based on the research of Hill, Seligman, and Goleman, choose to stay surrounded by positive people who will broaden and deepen your vision and purpose. These positive people could improve your immune response as well as your goal setting.

Appointments. If you are facing surgery soon, you might want to set an appointment to worry during the hour prior to the pre-operative visit. That could increase your list of questions to ask of your healthcare provider. It could also be helpful to set an appointment to worry for five minutes with a friend prior to that visit for social support and expanding your list of questions. Until these appointment times come up, keep a written list of questions as they occur to you while reminding yourself that it's not timely to worry. Between worry appointments your focus is on those skills which improve your immune response.

Socially? Celebrate randomly as well as by appointment.

For your master mind team it could be lovely to replicate the Seligman model of meeting in Akumel with families and informal agendas. Many of us will make do with less. Between meetings, even twenty minutes weekly by phone with my brilliant friend in the East have been eye-opening and have brought astonishing value. Episodic group teleconferences enlarge on what each one contributes.

To Do list. My elegant 80-something years young friend said it best. Keep your list small enough to cross off completed tasks at the end of the day. You deserve success today. Some people share my preference for long To Do lists. I enjoy the whimsy of multiple choice with never a dull moment. It's satisfying to cross off more items. It's even better to for me to prioritize and complete big stuff first.

Measuring Goals

This is a good place to use the BARE BONERS process.

Begin
A
Realistic
Effort.

Baseline measures come first.
Organize your options.
Now take action with a specified time line.
Evaluate your progress.
Remember, **R**einforce, **R**eward.
Start over with episodic measures.

Given your baseline today, what do you want to do? When do you want to accomplish it? With whom do you want to share the journey and celebrations of progress?

Let me clarify why all of these questions are slanted toward the positive. From the initial study by Hill in 1938 to the present advances in social neuroscience the findings have had a similar ring. Don't ignore or deny the negatives. There will be extensive work, struggles and even tragedy. That only strengthens the science-based recommendation to focus on the positives for the health of it. What Hill observed in his years of observations of 500 successful wealthy men can now be addressed differently with advances in neuroscience. Goleman brings clarity to these new research findings in *Social Intelligence*. His argument in favor of positive psychology and surrounding yourself with positive thinkers is clear, cogent and convincing.

Remember in setting goals to Begin A Realistic Effort. That means make each goal specific, measurable, achievable, realistic and time-lined.

Goals	Details	Timing
Health		
Personal		
Social		
Spiritual		
Educational		
Financial		

John Goddard enjoyed a few decades of accomplishing huge goals. That is both comforting and inspiring. Let your list evolve. Set realistic timelines. You could have a great deal to look forward to. This can add another kind of nutritional spice to your Ideal Aging™ dance of life.

I have a ton of respect for a To Do list. Mine is an ACe list to separate things into three categories: Actions, Calls and electronic tasks. It covers a week or more. I type in red the items that are time pressured and bold those which must get priority.

ACe list for Week of ___/___/___

Actions	Calls	electronic
Jury Duty	**Producer re taping—Lisa**	e-mail DOB greetings
Bio to Ellen @ UW	**Alberto, Selena re dances**	RobertAllen.com
TY—John & Peggy	Janice Katz re writing	MarkVictorHansen.com
arrange **Ideal Aging™ Summit 4th week in July**	Rotary	JohnChilders.com
movie: The Illusionist (recommendation of Dr. Burns)	Wes & Joyce Len & Stell Diane Sumter	GrandParentsRock.com GoodStoryADay.com
O2K potluck and pedal		www.PlantATreeUSA.com
Pick up and return library books	**Jose Espana**	www.Credit-Millionaire.com
		www.JohnGoddard.info
		www.FeelingGood.com
		AuthenticHappiness.com
		Robert Sapolsky
		www.YoungerNextYear.com
		Peggy McGee-Copy editor
		FTP **Ideal Aging™** **ID Theft Paper**
		www.DrTanyaHeals.com

Appointments are probably best handled electronically. If the BARE BONERS, ACe list and Goals information shows more work than play, consider adding appointments that address your goals. Stress is reduced with a sufficient sense of control, novelty and happiness to keep your brain fit. Setting regular appointments for master mind calls with positive, supportive people could also add richness for vigorous longevity in Ideal Aging™.

The area where I live is theatre rich. And the bus system is good. That makes it convenient to arrange a season series to share with local loved ones.

Summary

Ideal Aging™ can be a work in progress. Goals, appointments and To Do lists can provide information to measure progress as well as to celebrate accomplishments. If you keep yourself surrounded by a Master Mind of positive people, the benefits can also include a boost to your immune system, less stress, support in achieving your goals, shared celebrations, and novelty. Our brains crave novelty. The chapter **Smarter This Year** describes how novelty can stimulate your brain to become a "self fertilizing garden." That could be a good thing on all measures.

CELEBRATE RANDOMLY

"There are some outcomes in life that are truly tragic."
Personal communication in 1978 of Albert Ellis, PhD, a giant in the realm of
Cognitive Behavioral Therapy

"You deserve to celebrate today … at Your Discretion!"
Dr. Joyce

Had I mentioned the Great Depression that came over me when my grandma died? Some said I was her favorite of about twenty grandkids. That is one of those family myths where Truth is unimportant. What matters is that she was a gentle, brilliant pillar in my life.

She had an unspoken rule. I would say, "Grandma?" just softly while she sat gently moving her rocking chair back and forth, reading the Grit – an ancient newspaper on that distant farm. Then I knew to wait silently and study that bun of white hair nestled neatly near the base of the back of her studious and elegant head. When she came to a logical place in the text for a break, she'd see to my tender loving care.

How can I tell you how much I loved that woman? My little life was shattered by her death! I responded by eating everything in sight. I am sorry I confessed to that. It would be against the purpose of this workbook for anyone to model after me in that behavior. Obese. That's what I was for years! It didn't bring my Grandma back.

I'm tempted to defend myself by saying gluttony was my first realization of the healing power of random celebration. Nah! It was my first proof that healthy random celebration would have been a better way to balance the pain of her loss. It would have enhanced my Ideal Aging™ earlier if I had celebrated daily how gifted I still am to have had so much love and protection under her watchful eye.

Since this chapter is primarily based on clinical and personal experience with no science cited, it will be just long enough to make the point. A couple of decades of service in healthcare on top of enough other trauma to fill a few bookshelves can alter one's perspective. My bias is evident.

If solid research in peer review journals showing real benefit from learning every new dance step is your requirement, I understand. I initially refused to read *Anatomy of an Illness* by Cousins. Feel free to honor that part of yourself and skip this chapter if the scientist within demands that. Otherwise, come along and see if it might be useful to you to create a random celebration under the right circumstances.

Goals

- After severe trauma when every practical thing that can be done has been done, find a reason to celebrate and tell everybody in passing ... because many people will be positive. In tragedy, you need that.

- Balance minor difficulties with something positive ... because this can promote optimal growth:

    (minor stress –> rest and Eat Smart Deliciously –> repair) ∞

- In the quiet of being alone celebrate ... because it gives your eardrums a rest.

- Mingle in a crowd to celebrate sounds of human communion ... because their happy emotions are contagious.

- Celebrate being able to read and having the resources to set your unique plan for Ideal Aging™ ... because this reinforces your strengths.

- If it's fitting for you, celebrate having two kidneys ... because a wonderfully talented friend of mine gave one of hers to her ailing husband that he, too, might live.

Celebrations for Ideal Aging™

A brief PubMed search only yielded articles describing specific events. If you find any science describing the benefits of celebration and wish to have them reviewed, please send them to **DrJoyce@StressPower.com**. That would be seriously celebrated. Meanwhile, comments and examples will have to come from the media.

The movie "It's a Beautiful Life" is a prime example. Roberto Benigni brought us a poignant portrayal of life in a Nazi concentration camp. Most of us cannot even fathom the level of trauma in that experience. Yet Benigni didn't have that as his focus. How many quiet, spontaneous, instantaneous, and powerful ways did he manage to celebrate life, love and laughter right up to the moment of the final shot?

We can learn from that.

If all you do is smile brightly at everyone you pass while saying: "It's a Beautiful Life," you might purchase a lot. For example, most folks will at least nod. Some will smile. There may be an occasional chuckle. A few may reward you with a grin (Positive Reinforcement, yes?). It's probably worth your having another sentence ready for those rare folks who stop to chat on the topic. Make the sentence short and focused on celebration to maintain the joy. For example, "I am so grateful to be alive in the age of technology. Just look at how many people walking by on this street are calling home!"

It's been helpful to me to have some friends who just don't understand intense emotions. I've especially appreciated those friends who also had the compassion to see the bigger picture. To quote one wise woman when confronted about her lack of empathy in underestimating how much pain another would express: "You're right. I haven't been challenged."

Hopefully less-challenged people can recognize the role they play in being models of health. If you are fortunate to be one of those, celebrate that you normalize the picture for victims of trauma. Celebrate that you can give the gift of silent, active listening to the pain of another. Celebrate that you can visit another's pain briefly and follow them into celebration as soon as they are ready to quiet the storm.

In fairness, there are two perspectives here. I wouldn't wish on anyone the experiences that would give you a deeper personal measure of emotions that can be part of catastrophic events. Also, my hat is off to those I've known who have taken comfort in knowing that "God has a plan" even in the midst of tragedy which has left others devastated. In my years in healthcare I've witnessed both. TV news portrays both.

Note of caution: This is not meant to down play genuine feelings in response to serious trauma. Read the quote at the beginning of this chapter by Albert Ellis, a giant in the field of reducing emotional pain by disputing distorted thoughts: "There are some outcomes in life that are truly tragedies."

Albert Ellis is considered by many people to be the grandfather of Cognitive Behavioral Therapy. The title of one of his books is *How to Stubbornly Refuse to Make Yourself Miserable about Anything. Yes, Anything!*

Yet Albert Ellis knew compassion as well as he knew that reality can be harsh. So that's the caveat: compassion first in the face of tragedy. And then respect the unique needs of the victim of tragedy whether that is you or someone else.

It was a real chin-dropper for me in a distant history when my dear friend, Rich Levine, softly said: "Joyceeee, I think you should spend all day Saturday wallowing in self-pity."

He actually meant it.

That was early enough in a dismal week for me to give it serious consideration. I tried it. It worked … for an hour or less. After the depths of that, it just came naturally for me to appreciate the blue sky, the freedom to enjoy a rocking chair, the long list of loving people I could call, etc. I didn't get up and dance immediately although being aerobic would have been smart. I just enjoyed the benefit of compassion and acceptance after the freedom to grieve deeply without time constraints. That was ancient history. With the benefits of new science, I definitely add aerobic exercise to the cure now.

Am I recommending wallowing in anything? No. I only provide this as an example of compassion first. If it's not convenient to express your emotions immediately, make an appointment to linger with emotions that are real in the face of tragedy. Then decide when you are ready to add aerobic exercise and ready to celebrate. I believe it does the body good to balance the slate.

How many instant celebrations can you make happen today?

1. _____

2. _____

3. _____

4. _____

5. _____

6. _____

7. _____

Don't assume you have to stop because the numbers have run out. If this page isn't long enough, make multiple copies. One of my favorites was taking my small son to a museum or to the zoo. They were free entertainment. Free usually wins before a lot of other options.

Summary

Research shows the healing influence of positive emotions. Add some by intent. Tragedy happens. After solving every conceivable problem and using every known remedy, have compassion first. Then be aerobic. Celebrate randomly. For free whenever possible. It's a light step in the choreography of your dance of life for Ideal Aging™.

PART C. THE LAST SUMMARY

"I've had so much fun, I think I'll stick around another year."
By Sister Esther on her 105th birthday as quoted in
Aging with Grace by David Snowdon, PhD

Strong ... Confident ... Beautiful ... Empowered ... Wise ... Well ... That's who you are and who you want to continue to be. Ideal Aging™ that keeps your brain fit could be your best investment for vigorous longevity.

If you don't know where you started it will be decidedly more difficult to celebrate your progress. The goal of the BARE BONERS process is to maximize growth. Begin A Realistic Effort: Baseline measures help you define your Options. Now do it. Evaluate again. Reinforce, Refine and Reward steps in the direction you've chosen. Start over for continued growth. That's the essence of BARE BONERS.

Fortunately, there are many more opportunities for healthy growth throughout human life than had ever been appreciated until recent years. We had always been taught that our brain cells at birth were the most we would ever have. It was supposed to be declining numbers thereafter. After about age thirty it was all downhill, they taught. "Use them or lose them" was particularly threatening in terms of our number of brain cells and how well they would work on our behalf. Part of the gift of being alive in the Information Age is appreciating a greater optimism for our future.

In 1998 Fred Gage proved a different story. On autopsy of humans between the ages of fifty-five and seventy he found evidence of neurogenesis, the birth of new brain cells. Years prior Marian Diamond had found this in rats of various ages. Both Gage and Diamond suggested that neurogenesis was possible at any age.

A tsunami of subsequent research has focused on neuroplasticity, the capacity of the brain to change in complexity of architecture and function. Much of what we know comes from animal research. Running rats increased neurogenesis. With tender handling to deprive them of one night of sleep, they had increased neurogenesis on day 0. There was an increased rate of survival of these new brain cells fifteen and even thirty days later.

A landmark study published in 2007 also found a way to increase the number of new neurons created in humans. Fred Gage and colleagues reported exercise-induced neurogenesis in the dentate gyrus of the human hippocampus. That's the part of the brain involved in memory and learning. It is implicated in cognitive losses associated with aging.

It actually is true that, if you don't use it, you lose it. It is equally true that behavioral interventions that strengthen complex and novel learning can influence your brain to grow and function better with time. What a delicious gift to realize that you can be **Smarter This Year**. Sensory, behavioral, cognitive, memory and emotional improvements in function can be significant. Advances in neuroscience show structural and functional brain changes as a result of these behavioral programs. These changes can persist.

Diamond had clarified some of this in rats. Those with the most toys did win. Their neurons had more complex branching of the dendrites and more spines on the dendrites in comparison to the rats in a nearby cage that could only observe but not play. Her research demonstrated positive brain plasticity with an enriched environment which included active new learning.

Merzenich and colleagues work with humans. They believe that a brain-plasticity-based program could be beneficial for all aging adults. With this intervention age-related cognitive decline can be slowed, arrested and even reversed with appropriate behavioral training. Memory improvements in their subjects lasted for three months with no further contact after the initial testing.

Our brains crave novelty. New and complex learning builds cognitive reserve for a richer lifespan. Conditioned responses are like auto-responders. They carry the mundane until you choose to rewrite them. Since positive interactions can actually boost your immune response and influence your brain architecture, Goleman suggests connecting with positive people. That suggests a whole new aspect to social responsibility.

If knowing how much you can influence your Ideal Aging™ helps you sleep better, that is all good. Sleep, laughter and enduring happiness are important components of healthy growth. **Exercise Right, Eat Smart Deliciously** and you can earn vigorous longevity with energy.

Neurobics is becoming a household word. This is a new science of brain exercises that can help maintain memory and increase brain fitness. Combining many senses in complex novel learning can increase your brains production of neurotrophins. These molecules nourish the brain cells that secrete them, their neighboring brain cells and the synapses between them. That led Katz and Rubin to state: *"To think that a good sexual encounter also helps keep the brain alive is almost too good to be true. But it is; more than most 'routine activities,' sex uses every one of our senses and, of course, engages our emotional brain circuits as well."*

Another rich dance of life is having the resources to enjoy civic participation. That can contribute to your Ideal Aging™ through keeping your brain fit. That makes a major point of this book worth restating: No one can read the whole library. That's why I have repeated the invitation to email brief questions, corrections or additions to what you have found here. Please send this information to **DrJoyce@StressPower.com**.

There's another point worth restating:

It's never too early
and never too late
to improve your body and brain
fitness
... for Ideal Aging™ ...
because you simply want more out of
life.

PART D. REFERENCES AND OTHER RESOURCES

Ader, Robert. *Psychoneuroimmunology,* 2nd Ed. San Francisco: Academic Press, 1991.

Amundson, Marion, Cheryl Hart, and Thomas Holmes. *The Schedule of Recent Experience (SRE).* 1981.

Anderson, R. M., and Richard Weindruch. Metabolic "Reprogramming in Dietary Restriction." *Interdisciplinary Topics in Gerontology.* (2006): 35:18-38.

Antonuccio, D. L., W. G. Danton, G.Y. DeNelsky, R. Greenberg, and J. S. Gordon. "Raising Questions about Antidepressants." *Psychotherapy and Psychosomatics* (1999) 68: 3-14.

Avery D. "The Proper Use of Light Therapy." *Direction in Psychiatry* (1999): 19(24): 379-398.

Beck, Aaron T. *Cognitive Therapy and the Emotional Disorders.* New York: New American Library, 1976.

Beck, Aaron T. "How an Anomalous Finding Led to a New System of Psychotherapy." *Nature Medicine* (2006, Oct): 12(10):1139-41.

Becker, Wesley C. *Parents Are Teachers.* Champaign IL: Research Press, 1971.

Begley, Sharon. *Train Your Mind Change Your Brain: How a New Science Reveals Our Extraordinary Potential to Transform Ourselves.* New York: Ballantine Books, 2007.

Bengmark, Stig. "Curcumin, an Atoxic Antioxidant and Natural NFkappaB, Cyclooxygenase-2, Lipooxygenase, and Inducible Nitric Oxide Synthase Inhibitor: A Shield Against Acute and Chronic Diseases." *Journal of Parenteral and Enteral Nutrition* (2006): 30(1):45-51.

Benson, Herbert. *The Relaxation Response.* New York: Quill, 2001.

Berk, Lee, D. L. Felten, S. A. Tan, B. B. Bittman, and J. Westengard. Modulation of Nneuroimmune Parameters During the Eustress of Humor-Associated Mirthful Laughter." *Alternative Therapies in Health and Medicine.* 2001, 9(2):62-76.

Berk, Lee, S. A. Tan, W. F. Fry, B. J. Napier, J. W. Lee, R. W. Hubbard, J. E. Lewis, and W. C. Eby. "Neuroendocrine and Stress Hormone Changes During Mirthful Laughter. *American Journal of the Medical Sciences.*" (1989): 298(6):390-396.

Bernstein, Adam M., Bradley J. Willcox, Hitoshi Tamaki, Nobuyoshi Kunishima, Makoto Suzuki, D. Craig Willcox, Ji-Suk Kristen Yoo, and Thomas T. Perls. "First Autopsy Study of an Okinawan Centenarian: Absence of Many Age-Related Diseases." *Journal of Gerontology* (2004): 59A(11): 1195-1199.

Bischoff-Ferrari, Heike, Edward Giovannucci, Walter Willett, Thomas Dietrich, and Bess Dawson Hughes. "Estimation of Optimal Serum Concentrations of 25-Hydroxyvitamin D for Multiple Health O"utcomes." *American Journal of Clinical Nutrition* (2006): 84(1):18-28

Blake, David, Marc Heiser, Matthew Caywood, and Michael Merzenich. "Experience-Dependent Adult Cortical Plasticity Requires Cognitive Association Between Sensation and Reward." *Neuron* (2006 Oct 19): 52(2):371-81.

Buchowski, M. S., K. M. Majchrzak, K. Blomquist, K. Y. Chen, D. W. Byrne, and J.A. Bachorowski ."Energy Expenditure of Genuine Laughter." *International Journal of Obesity*. (2006): Epub, pages 1-7.

Buckley, Cara. Man is Rescued by Stranger on Subway Tracks. New York Times, January 3, 2007.

Buell, Stephen, and Paul Coleman. "Quantitative Evidence for Selective Dendritic Growth in Normal Human Aging but Not in Senile Dementia." *Brain Research* (1981); 214(1): 23-41.

Burns, David D. *Feeling Good: The New Mood Therapy.* New York: Avon, 1992.

Burns, David D. *The Feeling Good Handbook.* New York: Plume, 1999.

Burns, David D. *Ten Days to Self-Esteem.* New York: Quill, 1993.

Burns, David D. *Ten Days to Self-Esteem – The Leader's Manual.* New York: Quill, 1993.

Burns, David D. *Therapist's Toolkit.* Los Altos: author, 2006.

Buysse, D. J. "Diagnosis and Assessment of Sleep and Circadian Rhythm Disorders." *Journal of Psychiatric Practice* 2005;11(2): 102-115.

Cousins, Norman. *Anatomy of an Illness as Perceived by the Patient: Reflections on Healing and Regeneration.* New York: Norton, 1979.

Cross, M. A. I.T. "Laughter Makes Good Medicine." *Health Data Management* (2006), 14,9 ProQuest Computing, page 64.

Crowley, Chris, and Henry S. Lodge. *Younger Next Year: A Guide to Living Like 50 until You're 80 and Beyond.* New York: Workman Publishing, 2004.

Crowley, Chris, and Henry S. Lodge. *Younger Next Year for Women: Live Like You're 50*

— *Strong, Fit, Sexy - Until You're 80 and Beyond.* New York: Workman Publishing, 2005.

Cueva, M., R. Kuhnley, A. Lanier, and M. Dignan. "Healing Hearts; Laughter and Learning." *Journal of Cancer Education* (2006): Summer, 21:104-107.

Davidson, Richard. In *Time*, January 27, 2005.

Davidson, Richard, Jon Kabat-Zinn, Jessica Schumacher, Melissa Rosenkranz, Daniel Muller, Saki Santorelli, Ferris Urbanowski, Anne Harrington, Katherine Bonus, and John Sheridan. "Alterations in Brain and Immune Function Produced by Mindfulness Meditation." *Psychosomatic Medicine* (2003 Jul-Aug):65(4):564-70.

Dawson-Hughes, Bess. "Invest in Your Bones." *International Osteoporosis Foundation-Outreach and Education.* August, 2006.

Diamond, Marian Cleeves. *Enriching Heredity: The Impact of the Environment on the Anatomy of the Brain.* New York: The Free Press, 1988.

Diamond, Marian, and Janet Hopson. *Magic Trees of the Mind: How to Nurture Your Child's Intelligence, Creativity, and Healthy Emotions from Birth Through Adolescence.* New York: Plume, 1998.

Diamond, Marian, Arnold Scheibel, Greer Murphy Jr. ,and Thomas Harvey. "On the Brain of a Scientist: Albert Einstein." *Experimental Neurology* (1985): 88(1):198-204.

Dryden, Gordon, and Jeannette Vos. *The Learning Revolution.* Auckland, New Zealand: The Learning Web. **TheLearningWeb.net**, 1999.

Ebrahim, S., M. May, Y. Ben Shlomo, P. McCarron, S. Frankel, J. Yarnell, and G. Davey Smith. "Sexual Intercourse and Risk of Ischaemic Stroke and Coronary Heart Disease: The Caerphilly Study." *Journal of Epidemiology and Community Health* (2002): 56(2):99-102.

Ephron, Nora. *I Feel Bad About My Neck.* New York: Knopf, 2006.

Ellis, Albert. "Why I (Really) Became a Therapist." *Journal of Clinical Psychology* (2005): 61(8): 945-948.

Ellis, Albert. "The Impossibility of Achieving Consistently Good Mental Health." *American Psychologist* (1987): 42, **No.** 4: 364-375.

Ellis, Albert, and Robert Harper. *A New Guide to Rational Living.* Englewood Cliffs NJ: Prentice-Hall, 1975.

Eriksson, Peter, Ekaterina Perfilieva, Thomas Bj☐rk-Eriksson, Ann-Marie Alborn, Claes Nordborg, Daniel Peterson, and Fred Gage. "Neurogenesis in the Adult Human Hippocampus." *Nature America, Inc.* **Medicine.Nature.com**, 1998.

Gage, Fred. "Neurogenesis in the Adult Brain." *The Journal of Neuroscience* (2002): 22(3): 612-613.

Goddard, John. *The Survivor: 24 Spine-Chilling Adventures on the Edge of Death.* Deerfield Beach, FL: Health Communications, 2001.

Goleman, Daniel. *Social Intelligence: The New Science of Human Relationships.* New York: Bantam, 2006

Goleman, Daniel. Healing Emotions: Conversations with the DALAI LAMA on Mindfulness, Emotions and Health. Boston: Shambala, 2003.

Gordon, Thomas. *P.E.T. Parent Effectiveness Training.* New York: New American Library, 1975.

Gore, Al. *An Inconvenient Truth: The Planetary Emergency of Global Warming and What We Can Do about It.* Emmaus PA: Rodale, 2006.

Gortner, E. M., S. S. Rude, and James W. Pennebaker. "Benefits of Expressive Writing in Lowering Rumination and Depressive Symptoms." *Behavior Therapy* (2006 Sep): 37(3):292-303. Epub 2006 May 30.

Guzman-Marin, R., and D .McGinty. "Sleep Deprivation Suppresses Adult Neurogenesis: Clues to the Role of Sleep in Brain Plasticity." *Sleep and Biological Rhythms* (2006): 4: 27-34.

Haake, P., T. Krueger, M. Goebel, K. Heberling, U. Hartmann, and M. Schedlowski. "Effects of Sexual Arousal on Lymphocyte Subset Circulation and Cytokine Production in Man." *Neuroimmunomodulation* (2004):11(5):293-8.

Halton, Thomas, Walter Willett, Simin Liu, JoAnn Manson, Christine Albert, Kathryn Rexrode, and Frank Hu. "Low-Carbohydrate-Diet Score and the Risk of Coronary Heart Disease in Women." *New England Journal of Medicine.* 2006, 355(19): 1991-2002.

Harker, LeeAnne, and Dacher Keltner. "Expressions of Positive Emotion in Women's College Yearbook Pictures and Their Relationship to Personality and Life Outcomes across Adulthood." *Journal of Personality and Social Psychology* (2001 Jan): 80(1):112-24.

Hasler, Gregor, Daniel J. Buysse, Richard Klaghofer, Alex Gamma, Vladeta Ajdacic, D. Eich, Wulf Rossler, and Jules Angst. "The Association between Short Sleep Duration and Obesity in Young Adults: A 13-Year Prospective Study." *Sleep* (2004, Jun 15): 27(4):661-6.

Hayashi, K., T. Hayashi, S. Iwanaga, K. Kawai, H. Ishii, S. Shoji, and K. Murakami. "Laughter Lowered the Increase in Postprandial Blood Glucose." *Diabetes Care* (2003) 26(5):1651-1652.

Heinonen A., P. Kannus, H. Sievanen, P. Oja, M. Pasanen, M. Rinne, K. Uusi-Rasi, and I. Vuori. "Randomised Controlled Trial of Effect of Hi-impact Exercise on Selected Risk Factors for Osteoporotic Fractures." *Lancet* (1996): 348:1343-1347.

Heinrich, Liesl, and Eleonora Gullone. "The Clinical Significance of Loneliness: A Literature Review. "*Clinical Psychology Review* (2006): 26: 695-718.

Hill, Napoleon. *Think and Grow Rich.* New York: Fawcett Crest, 1983.

Howard, Pierce. *The Owner's Manual for the Brain: Everyday Applications from Mind-Brain Research, 3rd Ed.* Austin: Bard Press, 2006.

Isaacowitz, Derek, George Vaillant, and Martin Seligman. "Strengths and Satisfaction across the Adult Lifespan." *International Journal of Aging and Human Development* (2003): 57(2): 181-201.

Isen, A. M., K. A. Daubman, and G. .P Nowicki. "Positive Affect Facilitates Creative Problem Solving." *Journal of Personality and Social Psychology* (1987): 52(6):1122-31.

Jacob, Gregg, Edward Pace-Schott, Robert Stickgold, and Michael Otto. "Cognitive Behavior Therapy and Parmacotherapy for Insomnia: A Randomized Controlled Trial and Direct Comparison." *Archives of Internal Medicine* (2004 Sep 27):164(17):1888-96.

Jacobson, Edmund. *Progressive relaxation.* Chicago: University of Chicago Press, 1938.

Jakubowski, Patricia, and Lange, A. J. *The Assertive Option: Your Rights and Responsibilities.* Champaign, Illinois: Research Press, 1978.

Katz, Lawrence, and Manning Rubin. *Keep Your Brain Alive: 83 Neurobic Exercises to Help Prevent Memory Loss and Increase Mental Fitness.* New York: Workman, 1999.

Laumann, Edward, Anthony Paik, Dale Glasser, Jeong-Han Kang, Tianfu Wang, Bernard Levinson, Edson Moreira Jr.., Alfredo Nicolosi, and Clive Gingell. "A Cross-national Study of Subjective Sexual Well-being among Older Women and Men: Findings from the Global Study of Sexual Attitudes and Behaviors." *Archives of Sexual Behavior.* (2006, Apr): 35(2):145-61. Epub 2006 Apr 26.

Lindau, Stacy, Edward Laumann, Wendy Levinson, and Linda Waite. "Synthesis of Scientific Disciplines in Pursuit of Health: the Interactive Biopsychosocial Model." *Perspectives in Biology and Medicine* (2003 Summer): 46(3 Suppl):S74-86.

Leger, Damien, Marie Massuel, and Arnaud Metlaine. SISYPHE Study Group. "Professional Correlates of Insomnia." *Sleep* (2006): 29(2): 171-178.

Leuner, Benedetta, Elizabeth Gould, and Tracey Shors. "Is There a Link Between Adult Neurogenesis and Learning?" *Hippocampus.* (2006): 16(3):216-24.

Li, L., F. S. Braiteh, and R. Kurzrock. "Liposome-encapsulated Curcumin: in Vitro and in Vivo Effects on Proliferation, Apoptosis, Signaling, and Angiogenesis." *Cancer* (2005): 104(6):1322-31

Lipton, Bruce. "The Role of the Mind in the New Biology," an essay, 2006.

Lucock, Mark. "Is Folic Acid the Ultimate Functional Food Component for Disease Prevention?" *British Medical Journal* (2004): 328:211-214.

Lyubomirsky, Sonja, Laura King, and Ed Diener. "The Benefits of Positive Affect: Does Happiness Lead to Success?" *Psychological Bulletin.* (2005): 131(6); 803-855.

Lynch, James. *The Broken Heart: The Medical consequences of Loneliness.* New York: Basic Books, 1977.

Maffetone, Philip. *The Maffetone Method: The Holistic, Low-Stress, No-Pain Way to Exceptional Fitness.* New York: Ragged Mountain Press/McGraw-Hill, 2000.

Mahncke, Henry, Amy Bronstone, and Michael Merzenich, "Brain Plasticity and Functional Losses in the Aged: Scientific Bases for a Novel Intervention." *Progress in Brain Research.* 2006, 157:81-109.

Mahncke, Henry, Bonnie Connor, Jed Appelman, Omar Ahsanuddin, Joseph Hardy, Nicholas Joyce, Tania Boniske, Sharona Atkins, and Michael Merzenich. "Memory Enhancement in Healthy Older Adults Using a Brain Plasticity-based Training Program: A Randomized, Controlled Study." *Proceedings of the National Academy of Science USA* (2006): 103(33):12523-8. Epub 2006 Aug 3.

Mang, B., M. Wolters, B. Schmitt, K. Kelb, R. Lichtinghagen, D. Stichtenoth, and A Hahn. "Effects of a Cinnamon Extract on Plasma Glucose, HbA, and Serum Lipids in Diabetes Mellitus type 2." *European Journal of Clinical Investigation.* (2006): 36(5):340-4.

Markham, Julie, and William Greenough. "Experience-driven Brain Plasticity: Beyond the Synapse." *Neuron Glia Biology* (2004): 1(4): 351-363.

McAllister, A. Kimberley. "Neurotrophins and Neuronal Differentiation in the Central Nervous System." *Cellular and Molecular Life Sciences* (2001): 58(8):1054-60. Annual Review of Neuroscience. 22: 295-318.

McAllister, A. Kimberley, Lawrence Katz, and Donald Lo. Neurotrophins and Synaptic Plasticity. *Annual Review of Neuroscience.* (1999): 22:295-318.

McEwen, Bruce. *The End of Stress as We Know It.* Washington, DC: Joseph Henry Press, 2002.

Mittleman, Stu. *Slow Burn: Burn Fat Faster by Exercising Slower.* New York: Harper Collins,

2000.

Pandi-Perumal, S. R., N. Zisapel, V. Srinivasan, and D. P. Cardinali. "Review: Melatonin and Sleep in Aging Population." *Experimental Gerontology*. (2005); 40:911-925.

Park, Yon, Jing Wen, Seungmin Bang, Seung Park, and Si Song. "[6]-Gingerol Induces Cell Cycle Arrest and Cell Death of Mutant p53-expressing Pancreatic Cancer Cells." *Yonsei Medical Journal* (2006): 47(5):688-97.

Pavlov, Ivan. "The Nobel Prize in Physiology or Medicine 1904." From *Nobel Lectures, Physiology or Medicine 1901-1921.* Amsterdam: Elsevier Publishing.

Pereira, Ana C., Dan E. Huddleston, Adam M. Brickman, Alexander A Sosunov, Rene Hen, Guy M. McKhann, Richard Sloan, Fred H. Gage, Truman R. Brown, and Scott A. Small. "An in Vivo Correlate of Exercise-Induced Neurogenesis in the Adult Dentate Gyrus." *Proceedings of the National Academy of Sciences of the United States of America, (2007);104(13):5638-5643.*

Pritikin, Nathan. *The Pritikin Promise.* New York: Simon & Schuster, 1983.

Ohayon, Maurice. "Prevalence and Correlates of Nonrestorative Sleep Complaints." *Archives of Internal Medicine* (2005): 165: 35-41.

Paul Zane Pilzer. *God Wants You to Be Rich: How and Why Everyone Can Enjoy Material and Spiritual Wealth in Our Abundant World.* New York: Fireside, 1997.

Rechtschaffen, Allan, and Bernard Bergmann. "Sleep Deprivation in the Rat: An Update of the 1989 Paper." *Sleep* (2002): 25: 18-24.

Ratey, John. *A User's Guide to the Brain.* New York: Pantheon, 2001.

Rowe, John W., and Robert L. Kahn. *Successful Aging.* New York: Dell Publishing, 1998.

Sapolsky, Robert M. *Why Zebras Don't Get Ulcers: The Acclaimed Guide to Stress, Stress-Related Diseases, and Coping, 3rd Edition.* New York: Henry Holt, 2004.

Segal, Daniel. "Relationships of Assertiveness, Depression, and Social Support among Older Nursing Home Residents." *Behavior Modification* (2005): 29(4):689-95.

Seligman, Martin E. P. *Authentic Happiness: Using the New Positive Psychology to Realize Your Potential for Lasting Fulfillment.* New York: Free Press, 2002.

Seligman, Martin E. P. *Learned Optimism: How to Change Your Mind and Your Life.* New York: Pocket Books, 1998.

Seligman Martin E. P., P. Schulman, and A. M. Tryon. "Group Prevention of Depression and

Anxiety Symptoms." *Behaviour Research and Therapy.* Epub ahead of print, 27 Oct 2006.

Shaffer, Joyce. *Secrets Inside Bones, Brains and Beauty®.* Bellevue, WA: Osteoporosis Updates, 2005.

Shaffer, Joyce. *Stress Power with Relaxation Conditioning and Visualizing Your Inner Guide.* Ideal Press: Bellevue, WA 2005.

Sheline Yvette, Milan Sanghavi, Mark Mintun, and Mokhtar Gado. "Depression but Not Age Predicts Hippocampal Volume Loss in Medically Healthy Women with Recurrent Depression." *Journal of Neuroscience* (1999): 19: 5034-43.

Shimizu, Takashi, Shinya Kubota, Norio Mishima, and Shoji Nagata. "Relationship between Self-esteem and Assertiveness Training among Japanese Hospital Nurses." *Journal of Occupational Health* (2004): 46(4):296-8.

Snowdon, David. *Aging with Grace: What the Nun Study Teaches Us about Leading Longer, Healthier and More Meaningful Lives.* New York: Bantam Books, 2001.

Spiegel, Karine, Rachel Leproult, Mirielle L'Hermite-Baleriaux, Georges Copinschi, Plamen Penev, and Eve Van Cauter. "Leptin Levels are Dependent on Sleep Duration: Relationships with Sympathovagal Balance, Carbohydrate Regulation, Cortisol and Thyrotropin." *The Journal of Clinical Endocrinology and Metabolism* (2004): 89(11): 5762-5771.

Spiegel, Karine, Esra Tasali, Plamen Penev, and Eve Van Cauter. "Brief Communication: Sleep Curtailment in Healthy Young Men Is Associated with Decreased Leptin levels, Elevated Ghrelin Levels and Increased Hunger and Appetite." *Annals of Internal Medicine* (2004, Dec 7):141(11):846-50.

Stickgold, Robert. "Sleep-dependent Memory Consolidation." *Nature* (2005); 437(7063):1272-8

Tannen, Deborah. *You Just Don't Understand: Women and Men in Conversation.* New York: William Morrow and Company,1990.

Thoreau, Henry David. *Walden.* New York: Houghton Mifflin, 1996.

Vaillant, George. *Aging Well.* New York: Little, Brown, 2002.

Vermetten, Eric, Meena Vythilingam, Steven Southwick, Dennis Charney, and J. Douglas Bremner. "Long-term Treatment with Paroxetine Increases Verbal Declarative Memory and Hippocampal Volume in Post-traumatic Stress Disorder." *Biological Psychiatry* (2003): 54: 693-702.

Vinson, J., J. Proch, P. Bose, S. Muchler, P. Taffera, D. Shuta, N. Samman, and G. Agbor. "Chocolate Is a Powerful ex Vivo and in Vivo Antioxidant, an Antiatherosclerotic Agent in an Animal Model, and a Significant Contributor to antioxidants in the European and American

Diets." *Journal of Agricultural and Food Chemistry* (2006): 54(21):8071-6.

Xiaofu Wang, Qingding Wang, Kirk Ives, and B, Mark Evers. "Curcumin Inhibits Neurotensin-mediated Interleukin-8 Production and Migration of HCT116 Human Colon Cancer Cells." *Clinical Cancer Research* (2006): 15;12(18):5346-55.

Wagner Ullrich, Steffen Gais, Hilde Halder, Rolf Veriger, and Jon Born. "Sleep Inspires Insight." *Nature* (2004): 427: 352-355.

Watson, Karli, Benjamin Matthews, and John Allman. "Brain Activation during Sight Gags and Language-Dependent Humor." *Cerebral Cortex* (2006):[Epub ahead of print].

Wei Zheng, and Shlow Wang. "Antioxidant Activity and Phenolic Compounds in Selected Herbs." *Journal of Agricultural and Food Chemistry* (2001): 49:5165-5170.

Weindruch, Richard, and R. Sohal. "Caloric Intake and Aging." *New England Journal of Medicine* (1997): 337(14): 986-994.

Weil, Andrew. *Richard Davidson: East Meets West in His Laboratory.* TIME Magazine, 30 April 2006.

Weisel, Elie. *Night.* New York: Bantam Books, 1986.

Whipple, Beverly, G. Ogden, Barry Komisaruk. "Physiological Correlates of Imagery-induced Orgasm in Women." *Archives of Sexual Behavior* (1992 Apr): 21(2):121-33.

Willcox, Bradley J., D. Craig Willcox, Qimei He, J. David Curb, and Makoto Suzuki. "Siblings of Okinawan Centenarians Share Lifelong Mortality Advantages." *Journal of Gerontology* (2006): 61A(4): 345-354.

Willcox, Bradley J., D. Craig Willcox, and Makoto Suzuki. *The Okinawa Program: How the World's Longest-Lived People Achieve Everlasting Health—And How You Can, Too.* New York: Clarkson Potter, 2001.

Willcox, D. Craig, Bradley J. Willcox, Hodemi Todoriki, J. David Curb, and Makoto Suzuki. "Caloric Restriction and Human Longevity: What Can We Learn from the Okinawans?" *Biogerontology* (2006): 7:173-177

World Health Organization. *1995 World Health Statistics Annual.* Geneva, 1996.

Vaillant, George. *Aging Well.* New York: Little, Brown, 2002.

AuthenticHappiness.com for questionnaires on signature strengths and various emotions.

BonesBrainsAndBeauty.com to download a free color poster on nutrition and exercise for optimal bone health.

CooperInst.org for information on fitness.

FeelingGood.com for David Burns, MD on Cognitive Behavioral Techniques

healthierus.gov/dietaryguidelines/ for the Dietary Guidelines released by the US Departments of Health and Human Services and Agriculture

MyPyramid.gov to personalize your Food Guide Pyramid for optimal health

nal.usda.gov/fnic, the Food and Nutrition Information Center for extensive information on nutrition.

nap.edu for Dietary Reference Intakes (DRI).

http://okicent.org/index.html for information on the study began in 1976 on centenarians and other elderly people in Okinawa with what may be the world's longest health expectancy.

ods.od.nih.gov/factsheets/calcium.asp for Dietary Supplement Fact Sheet by National Institutes of Health (NIH) on Calcium last updated 9/23/2005

ods.od.nih.gov/factsheets/vitaminD.asp for Dietary Supplement Fact Sheet by NIH on Vitamin D last updated 8/5/2005

ods.od.nih.gov/factsheets/magnesium.asp for Dietary Supplement Fact Sheet by NIH on Magnesium last updated 8/5/2005

StressPower.com to learn how to go from Misery to Mellow in Miliseconds.

TheLearningWeb.net for information about the Learning Revolution by Gordon Dryden and Jeannette Vos.

YoungerNextYear.com for more insights from Chris Crowley and Henry Lodge.

who.int/topics/ageing/en/ for World Health Organization information on ageing.

If you want more information about building a healthful diet, refer to the *Dietary Guidelines for Americans* (http://www.usda.gov/cnpp/DietGd.pdf) and the US Department of Agriculture's Food Guide Pyramid (http://www.nal.usda.gov/fnic/Fpyr/pyramid.html).

> Nothing in the world can take the place of persistence. Talent will not; nothing is more common than unsuccessful men with talent. Genius will not; the world is full of educated derelicts. Persistence and determination alone are omnipotent. The slogan "press on" has solved and always will solve the problems of the human race.
> Calvin Coolidge

ABOUT THE AUTHOR:

Joyce Shaffer, PhD, is a Psychologist, Nurse, Speaker, Bicyclist and Author.

Dr. Joyce is uniquely qualified to write and teach about *Ideal Aging*™. She received a Doctorate in Psychology from Hofstra University in 1978. In 1961 she graduated from Thomas Jefferson University and is licensed as a registered nurse. She also earned diplomate status with the American Board of Professional Psychology. Currently she is a Clinical Assistant Professor at the University of Washington.

Since 1982 she has served as an expert for the University of Washington mental health court (and other court systems) on psychiatric & medical matters. This has kept her at the cutting edge of science. Dr. Joyce excels at bringing hard scientific data alive so you enjoy its benefits.

She has more than 40 years of experience in healthcare. Her online **Osteoporosis Updates Newsletter** has been requested by an average of 67 people every day. She has academic and nonacademic publications. Her book on osteoporosis, **Secrets inside Bones, Brains & Beauty**™, resulted in an offer for her to host a segment for TV.

Averaging 80 miles a day bicycling with the Odyssey 2000 trek into and out of 45 countries on 6 continents during the entire year 2000 is evidence of her fitness.

Plant a Tree USA™
BOOKS — PLANTINGS — TREES — PAPER

Trees are used to make paper.
Paper is used to make books.
To offset the number of trees which have been chopped down,
Please PLANT A TREE so our planet will have more trees!

Purchase a tree, in honor of a loved one or a special event.

Make a difference immediately healing Mother Earth!

Click: www.PlantATreeUSA.com

Enter promo code: IdealAging

READER/CUSTOMER CARE SURVEY

We care about your opinions! Please take a moment to fill out our online Reader Survey at www.IdealAging.com/survey.html. As a "THANK YOU," you will receive a VALUABLE INSTANT COUPON towards future book purchases as well as SPECIAL GIFTS available only online! Or, you may mail this card back to us and we will send you a copy of our exciting catalog with your valuable coupon inside.

PLEASE PRINT:

_____
FIRST NAME   MI.   LAST NAME

_____
ADDRESS   CITY

_____
STATE   ZIP   EMAIL

GENDER
☐ M   ☐ F

AGE
☐ 8 OR YOUNGER   ☐ 12+
☐ 13-19   ☐ 20-39
☐ 40-59   ☐ 60+

DID YOU RECIEVE THIS BOOK AS A GIFT?
☐ Y   ☐ N

ANNUAL HOUSHOLD INCOME
☐ UNDER $25,000
☐ $25,000 - $34,999
☐ $35,000 - $49,999
☐ $50,000 - $74,999
☐ OVER $75,000

WHAT ARE THE AGES OF CHILDEREN LIVING IN YOUR HOUSE?
☐ 0-14   ☐ 15+

MARITAL STATUS
☐ SINGLE
☐ MARRIED
☐ DIVORCED
☐ WIDOWED
☐ COMMITTED RELATIONSHIP

HOW DID YOU FIND OUT ABOUT THIS BOOK?
☐ RECOMMENDATION
☐ STORE DISPLAY
☐ ONLINE
☐ CATALOG
☐ INTERVIEW/REVIEW/EVENT

WHERE DO YOU USUALLY BUY BOKS?
☐ BOOKSTORE
☐ ONLINE
☐ BOOK CLUB/MAIL ORDER
☐ PRICE CLUB (SAM'S CLUB, COSTCO, ETC)
☐ RETAIL STORE

WHAT SUBJECT DO YOU ENJOY READING ABOUT MOST?
☐ HOW TO KEEP YOUR BRAIN FIT
☐ PHYSICAL HEALTH/NUTRITION
☐ ENDURING HAPPINESS
☐ SOCIAL INTELLIGENCE
☐ WOMEN'S ISSUES
☐ IDEAL AGING™
☐ BICYCLING

WHAT ATTRACTS YOU MOST TO A BOOK?
☐ TITLE
☐ COVER DESIGN
☐ AUTHOR
☐ CONTENT

Comments: _____

Ideal Aging™
PO Box 765
Bellevue WA 98009-0765

Do you have your own Ideal Aging™ story that you would like to send us?
Please submit at: www.IdealAging.com